New Agendas in the Study of the Policy Process

Edited by
Michael Hill
University of Newcastle upon Tyne

HARVESTER WHEATSHEAF

New York London Toronto Sydney Tokyo Singapore

First published 1993 by
Harvester Wheatsheaf
Campus 400, Maylands Avenue
Hemel Hempstead
Hertfordshire, HP2 7EZ
A division of
Simon & Schuster International Group

Typeset in 10pt Times
by The Midlands Book Typesetting Company

Printed and bound in Great Britain by
Biddles Ltd, Guildford and King's Lynn

British Library Cataloguing in Publication Data

A catalogue record for this book is available from the British Library.

ISBN 0–7450–1291–4 (hbk)
ISBN 0–7450–1292–2 (pbk)

2 3 4 5 97 96 95 94

Contents

Acknowledgements

The origins of this book lay in a seminar at the George Hotel in Northumberland in July 1991. We are grateful to Dorothy McLouglin for her help in organising that event and to the staff of the hotel who made us very comfortable on that occasion. Those of us who enjoyed the conference are grateful to two authors who joined us subsequently, without having participated in our pleasant occasion, Geoff Fimister and Mai-Brith Schartau. We were very fortunate that Clare Grist of Harvester Wheatsheaf took an interest in the enterprise from the outset, helped us to shape our work into a book and ensured its publication. We owe particular gratitude to her.

Notes on contributors

Bjorn Beckman is Reader (Associate professor) in Political Science, University of Lund, Sweden. He wrote his PhD-thesis on regional development planning and regional administration in 1977 and has studied the changes in regional development policy in the 1980s and 1990s. During 1992–1996 he is responsible for the sub-program 'The power of the local administration' in the Swedish Research program on 'Local democracy in change'.

Pieter Degeling is Senior Lecturer in Health Services Management at the University of New South Wales and Deputy Director of its Centre for Hospital and Information Systems Research. His current research interests cover organisation theory, health policy and hospital administration.

Geoff Fimister is Principal Welfare Rights Officer in Newcastle City Council. He is a welfare rights adviser to the Association of Metropolitan Authorities, working in the fields of housing, social services and local government taxation. He is author of *Welfare Rights Work in Social Services* and of various reports and articles on welfare rights and social security issues.

Rob Flynn is Senior Lecturer in Sociology at the University of Salford. He has researched and published widely in urban and political sociology, social policy and policy analysis of health services. He is author of *Structures of Control in Health Management* (Routledge, 1992).

Erica Haimes is a lecturer in the Department of Social Policy, University of Newcastle upon Tyne. Her current research covers the policy context of the new reproductive technologies, plus more general issues in the study of health care, the state and the family.

Kenneth Hanf received his university training in the United States and presently teaches in the joint program of Public Administration of the Erasmus University of Rotterdam and the University of Leiden. Before coming to the Netherlands, he worked as a Research Fellow at the Science Center in Berlin. His research is focused on questions of multi-actor and multi-level implementation of environmental policy at both the national and international levels.

Michael Hill is Professor of Social Policy at the University of Newcastle upon Tyne. He is author of numerous books on social policy and on the study of the policy process including *The Policy Process in the Modern Capitalist State* (with Chris Ham), *Understanding Social Policy* and *The Welfare State in Britain*.

Peter L Hupe worked for several years in the Dutch civil service as a policy adviser. Since 1986 he has been teaching Public Administration at Erasmus University in Rotterdam and the University of Leiden. He has published numerous articles on issues of the welfare state, institutional analysis and policy implementation, in particular in the field of social and economic policy.

Jaqi Nixon is Head of Department of Health and Social Studies at Bradford and Ilkley Community College. Her previous publications have been concerned with the implementation of race relations policy and the role of Parliamentary Select Committees in policy-making.

Mai Brith Schartau is a PhD candidate in the Department of Political Science at the University of Lund in Sweden. Her PhD is titled 'The Public Sector Middle Manager: The puppet who pulls the strings?' It will be submitted early in 1993.

CHAPTER 1

Introduction

Michael Hill

In the study of the policy process we may distinguish two sources of development in ideas. One of these is the product of academic work, of writing, teaching and thinking and of the interchange between intellectuals, drawing upon data from research and from the observations of participants in the policy process. The other is the product of developments in the policy process, of new techniques in public administration and of new devices used to try to solve policy and implementation problems. In a field of study like this it is difficult to disentangle those advances which arise from the first and those which are provoked or made necessary by the second. It is probably the case that revisions in thinking about policy analysis have been rather more forced upon analysts by real-world changes than emergent from deeper thinking about the policy process.

We may, however, identify a number of areas of debate and controversy in the study of public policy where developments have occurred, or where (in our view) new thinking is necessary. In each of these areas case-study work illuminates interesting developments. The areas to be given particular attention in this book are as follows:

- The debate about 'top-down' and 'bottom-up' approaches to the study of implementation.
- The examination of the role of professionals in the policy process, including their relationships to managers.
- The development of some of the ideas about street-level

bureaucrats and discretion by contextualising these further, acknowledging the extent to which relationships create situations in which 'co-production' of policy outputs may occur, and exploring related 'accountability' issues.
- The concern about whether 'public-sector' decision and management processes can be seen as distinctively different from private-sector ones.
- The debate about the extent to which policy decision processes can be described as rational or incremental.

In addition, lying behind these more detailed questions are two more general ones: first, about the nature of power within the state; and second, about the relationship between descriptive work and prescription in policy analysis. The first of these is not explored further here, but it is important to bear it in mind when considering more detailed issues; the second crops up at various places in the following discussion.

This introductory chapter will outline some of the ways in which thinking about each of the above issues is developing, or needs to develop, indicating the ways in which 'real-world' developments relate to the theoretical debate. In doing so it will introduce themes to be explored further in the body of this book.

The debate about 'top-down' and 'bottom-up' approaches to the study of implementation

The 'bottom-up' approach to the study of implementation provided a response to the 'top-down' studies which had shown how easily the aims of central initiatives were undermined at the local level (in particular the influential book by Pressman and Wildavsky (1973)). It suggested that it was more helpful to see new policy initiatives as developments which had to be accommodated by people already carrying out complex tasks at the grass roots (Elmore, 1978 and 1980; Hjern and Porter, 1981; Hjern and Hull, 1982; Barrett and Fudge, 1981). In doing so one might get away from a perspective which emphasised policy failure and tended to see local responses as perverse, towards one which recognised how difficult it was for implementers to take on these new complications for their tasks. It might also lead to the identification that the input from the top was in any case ambiguous, contradicting other inputs or containing very mixed messages (Barrett and Hill, 1984). Michael Lipsky's theoretical work on 'street-level bureaucracy' (1980) was particularly influential in emphasising the difficulties of handling complexity and excess demands at the 'bottom', which led to such workers in fact making 'policy'.

These findings provoked three different kinds of prescriptive response. One of these was the outlining of a variety of 'rules' for policy-makers designed to minimise those influences which interfered with the clear implementation of policy goals (Gunn, 1978; Hogwood and Gunn, 1984; Sabatier and Mazmanian, 1979). A second was to urge the actor or actors at the top to become deeply involved in the policy implementation process (Bardach, 1974). The third was to suggest that policy should really be made at the 'bottom', where the problem was really understood (Hjern and Hull, 1982; and, to a lesser extent, Elmore, 1980).

To the student of the policy process arguments in which descriptive and prescriptive objectives are mixed together are a source of difficulty (we will come to some other examples later in this chapter). It is one of the characteristics of this area of study that writers are eager to prescribe; indeed much of the research has been commissioned by clients who expect prescription. In the study of implementation this leads to discomforts when questions are raised about identification with the goals of the various parties. The top-down approach is the least ambiguous in this respect: it asks questions about why the *top* fails to impose its goals. Quite apart from probably being the researcher's paymaster, the top can often lay claim to legitimacy for its goals, deriving from democratic policy-making processes. By contrast, to identify with the bottom is to challenge such legitimacy. In terms of democratic theory this is a feasible, but more difficult objective. If institutions are involved, this may be a matter of claiming that a local or subordinate tier of government is the more appropriate locus for a democratic decision. If, however, it is specific local actors (as opposed to tiers of government) who are claiming to 'know best', there are difficulties most appropriately summed up in terms of questions about administrative and professional paternalism.

The second alternative outlined above, associated with the work of Bardach (1974), may partly solve this dilemma, but the difficulty here lies in the fact that many administrative arrangements involve a delicate balance between legitimacies at different levels, between central and local government in particular. There is also the discomfort that some of the most corrupt and totalitarian systems of administration have involved networks of party members as collaborators at various levels in the system.

While it seems most unlikely that policy-makers have paid attention to the academic debate about implementation, a range of actions during the 1980s suggest that there has been a search by the top for new approaches to the solution of implementation problems, through new ways to monitor the behaviour of lower-level actors. There have also been some examples of the deliberate dumping of such problems upon actors at lower levels.

First, there have been areas of policy where the follow-through from the top has been particularly thorough. The British example of the sale of council houses to their occupiers provides a case in point. It seems to have some of the characteristics which the implementation literature (see, for example, Gunn's prescriptions for successful implementation (1978)) suggests would make for difficulties. It is a policy directly implemented not by central government, but by local government. Many local authorities are, or were, hostile to the policy. They are required to carry out complex actions to implement the policy – advertising the right to buy, processing applications, providing access to loans and professional advice – and the policy has cost implications and limited financial benefits for the vendors (they retain only part of the proceeds and even these affect future grants).

Why then, after some initial skirmishes between central and local government (see Forrest and Murie, 1988), was this policy implemented very successfully? We can identify a variety of factors influencing this:

- The relative simplicity of the policy goals, so that expected results could be specified and non-implementation readily identified.
- The policy could depend upon tenants with an interest in buying (prices were markedly discounted according to length of tenancy) to push the implementation along (see further discussion below).

- Within the hostile local authorities there were nearly always Conservative councillors ready to expose deficient administration to central government.
- The action required was essentially the reduction of local responsibility: local authorities, although they initially had a new task to carry out, were in the long run partially relinquishing a task rather than developing one. Hence their willing compliance was not as essential as it is in many implementation situations where positive initiatives need to be taken.
- The policy has no cost implications for the central Exchequer.

But, perhaps more important than all these, what was involved here was a strong political commitment to enact a policy which was structured (through the discounts) to be directly popular to all who benefited. Those disadvantaged by the policy – homeless or ill-housed people who local authorities were being rendered less able to help – were a small, disorganised and probably non-participating group who were in any case only indirectly disadvantaged. The element of political will was underlined by the readiness of central government to show local authorities they meant business by moving in to take over direct supervision of the implementation process in one authority that they deemed to be deliberately 'dragging its feet' – not, it must be stressed, refusing to implement (the Norwich case, see Forrest and Murie (1988)).

The Thatcher era in Britain has been seen by Marsh and Rhodes (1992) as characterised as much by 'implementation gaps' as other eras in which governments have had 'radical' ambitions. They agree, however, that housing was an area of relative 'success' in achieving policy goals. It was one in which the implementation process was penetrated quite effectively. This penetration has been seen by some as involving, along the lines suggested in Bardach's analysis, the insertion of trusted allies into key roles. This is summed up by the title of Hugo Young's biography of Thatcher, *One of Us* (1989). However, Young's evidence, which particularly concerns influence upon civil service appointments, has been challenged (see Hennessy, 1989; Jordan and Richardson, 1987).

It is perhaps in their mistrust of local government that the Thatcher governments most clearly manifested their concerns about control of the implementation process. They undermined the old central–local partnership, particularly in the increasingly Labour-controlled cities, both through legal and financial controls and through devices designed to take power away. Surprisingly, in this area of policy Marsh and Rhodes stress implementation control failure. While it was certainly the case that policy went through many twists and turns, as controls were evaded or produced unexpected results, the centre persisted (and is still persisting after the fall of Thatcher) and has substantially undermined local power (see Glennerster *et al.*, 1991).

Some aspects of this British development have wider resonances, not necessarily involving simply the strengthening of the influence of the centre. A characteristic institutional innovation in this period has been the development of devices which combine strong central controls, particularly over finance, with considerable delegation. This is explored further in Chapters 2 and 3 by Degeling and Flynn. There has been a recognition, perhaps aided by new technology, that it is possible to solve some implementation control problems by a combination of strengthening some controls while weakening others. This may be seen as resolving the dilemmas embodied in the top-down/bottom-up debate by locating responsibility at the level at which it can most effectively be exercised. Hence the observations on Swedish *decentralisation* by Beckman in this book provide a contrast to British centralisation efforts (see Chapter 8). This contrast is further illustrated in Schartau's comparative examination of the management of Swedish and British education (Chapter 10). This contrast can also be explored in terms of a choice of levels. The central impulse in Britain, for the ideological reasons suggested above, has been to try to jump over local authorities and delegate to lower-level institutions (schools, etc.), while in the Swedish case local government has been increasingly seen as a crucial partner in the policy process.

There are other areas of public policy where it can be argued that problems about the relationship between policy and its implementation have been solved by the centre in more evasive ways. In the face of such dilemmas, a handy alternative is to displace complex goals by simpler ones. Consider, for example, policy concerns with crime. The new right gets into just as much difficulty as the old left when it sets out to attack the root causes of criminality. But there is a different, easier agenda available, disregarding causes but concentrating instead upon protecting property more effectively, creating defensible space for those of us with much to lose. Perhaps, here, a difference between the present and the recent past is that the earlier era saw 'displacement' as occurring as a series of unintended or unacknowledged consequences. Now policy-makers are more ready openly to replace complex long-term goals with simple short-term ones.

But this is not the only policy-making strategy which enables implementation problems to be evaded. Another is to delegate implementation responsibility to an organisation for which the central policy-makers deny responsibility. In this way policies as riddled with contradictions as any in the past may be enacted, with the blame for their ensuing problems shifted to organisations presented as outside central control.

The recent history of British central–local relations is one of strict control over local finance while complex implementation problems are delegated from the centre. The ensuing problems are presented by the centre as the result of local inefficiency rather than as consequences of contradictory central policies. In the area of social security policies this tendency has been most apparent (see the discussion of housing benefit and community care policies by Fimister and Hill in Chapter 5). This delegation is being accompanied by a recognition that clients themselves may be able to play a more positive role in monitoring implementation. An obvious example of this in the discussion above was the fact that the central resolve to force local authorities to sell council houses could be supported by giving tenants a 'right to buy' which they have incentives to exercise.

The notion of centrally specified rights occurs in other legislation and is a feature of the citizen's charters in Britain. Some of these rights are much vaguer than the 'right to buy' and may involve conflicts between individual rights not all of which can be enforced, such as parents' rights to choose schools for their children. Nevertheless their specification by central government does invite individuals to draw attention to what are taken to be shortcomings by implementers. Certainly in the current climate of British central–local relations citizens are encouraged to believe that, rather than there being deep policy dilemmas, intimately associated with national resource shortages, the main obstacle to securing rights to services is likely to be recalcitrant quasi-autonomous implementers of national policy. Again, an interesting contrast is provided by the chapters which deal with the Netherlands in this book, and particularly in Chapter 6 where Hupe examines situations in which Dutch citizens are involved in 'co-production' of policy outputs, rather than encouraged to operate in an individualistic way to counter the power of implementers, as in Britain. Hupe refers to similar phenomena in British 'neighbourhood offices', etc., but by the 1990s these have become sadly weakened by the central curbs on local government expenditure and autonomy.

The examination of the role of professionals in the policy process

One of the areas where the prescriptive element in the bottom-up approach to the study of implementation is particularly open to challenge is that of the power of professionals (see Degeling in Chapter 2). An extensive literature has examined the power of professionals in both the making and implementation of public policy (see various examinations of this issue in health services – Alford, 1975; Ham, 1992; and Klein, 1989 among many others – and the general analysis of it in relation to social policy – Wilding, 1982).

While for the health sector it has been seen principally as a top-down control problem, there has been an important vein of work which has looked at it as a problem from the (*very*) bottom up (Illich, 1977, for example). This has had echoes in the street-level bureaucracy work in public policy, and both Lipsky (1980) and Wilding (1982) end their books with a search for devices to ensure that professionals are more accountable to the public.

Certainly the power of professionals has not been merely an academic issue: both as a top-down issue and as a matter of concern for the vulnerable member of the public it has been, and remains, firmly on the public policy agenda. It is of value to compare and contrast these two ways of looking at this 'problem of professionalism' to see to what extent they come together in the practical measures adopted, and to what extent they lead to divergent and perhaps contradictory solutions.

Until the mid-1970s top-down control over professionals was principally an item on the political agenda of the left, a concern about preventing professionals from 'capturing' the welfare state. The issue of escalating costs put it on the agenda of the right too. Moreover, the intellectual right provided a policy theory, 'public choice' (Niskanen, 1971), to explicate the link between professionalism and escalating costs. The common denominator message derived from all this work was the need for controls to curb professional power, particularly professional dominance over spending decisions. In Chapters 2 and 3 Degeling and Flynn explore some of the ways in which they have been developed.

But, of course, public choice theory offers something more, speaking to the concerns of the public as clients of publicly employed professionals. It suggests that the absence of market constraints upon professionals *both* escalates the cost of their services *and* reduces their responsiveness to public needs. This theme will be explored further in the next section, where it will be suggested that there are some serious contradictions between these two objectives.

One of those contradictions which will be explored here, however, is that the public choice critique of the public sector does not only relate to service professionals, it embraces all bureaucratic employees. There is thus a problem that the current strong emphasis upon the need to control some categories of professionals such as doctors, social workers and teachers involves elevating the power of those with the skills, techniques, positions or predispositions to exercise that control. The long-run political issue is whether 'the cure is worse than the disease'.

Meanwhile, there are some important policy research agendas concerned with exploring the roles of those who manage professionals (see Chapters 9 and 10 by Nixon and Schartau), with one particularly interesting issue here being the extent to which these people themselves emerge from the profession they are required to control. Their key reference groups may then become other managers rather than members of their original profession. Then alongside these managers of professionals there are others who are responsible for the techniques used to monitor and control professional work (see Degeling in Chapter 2). Interestingly, these are also often regarded as professionals, but of rather different kinds – accountants, statisticians, computing experts. The contracting devices used to weaken professional monopolies (again, see further discussion in the next section) themselves heighten the importance of some of these managers and accountants, and also bring in another professional group – lawyers. We may perhaps describe this as the replacement of the dominance of 'service professionals' by a new élite of 'managerial professionals'. An alternative view is to see this as the emergence of 'corporate rationalisers' (Alford, 1975) to displace the previously dominant professionals in policy sectors like health and education. However conceptualised, this development still raises questions about the extent to which the alleged problems with traditional professionalism are effectively solved through the emergence of another 'élite'.

Hence some new issues about professional power are very much on the agenda. Meanwhile, there continues to be a lobby for a very different approach to control over professionals, through decentralisation and devices to increase grass-roots accountability. To explore this it is necessary to examine further some of the issues about street-level bureaucracy. This is done in the next section.

The development of some of the ideas about street-level bureaucrats and discretion

In other discussions of Lipsky's work, the author (Ham and Hill, 1993, ch. 8; Hill and Bramley, 1986, ch. 9) has raised questions about the extent to which the concept of street-level bureaucracy overemphasises the capacity of lowly officials to make policy for themselves. Certainly Lipsky is very concerned with the extent to which the street-level bureaucrat's role is a constrained one in terms of the availability of resources, but he gives rather less attention to other constraints upon action. There is a popular version of Lipsky's thesis which has come into use which emphasises the discretionary freedom of street-level bureaucrats. Yet in the study of administrative discretion it has come to be recognised that discretionary freedom is contained within a structure of varying degrees of rigidity. Dworkin's image of discretion as 'the hole in the donut' conveys this idea, in a slightly bizarre way (1977). Other writers have emphasised the extent to which discretion will be set in a framework of rules (Jowell, 1973) and those rules may set 'standards' for decision making (Galligan, 1986).

These approaches to discretion are particularly concerned with its hierarchical structuring. The literature on discretion has tended to explore the extent to which such structuring is feasible (see, for example, Davis, 1969, or Jowell, 1973), and there has been a widespread concern with the extent to which it is desirable (see Adler and Asquith, 1981). Yet there are two other issues here which have been given less attention.

One of these is the issue of the extent to which explicit hierarchical regulation of decision making may not occur because political or administrative authorities do not want to be seen as directly responsible for specific policy outcomes. The author wrote about this a long while ago in an analysis of discretion in income maintenance policy in terms of hierarchical avoidance of clearly taking an either hard or soft line on need (Hill, 1969). But in a more sinister way hierarchies may leave discretionary decision making to fall into a specifically biased pattern – for example, involving racism. They leave the responsibility for action they accept, but will not publicly condone, in the hands of subordinates. When such behaviour is challenged subordinates can take the blame. This is an aspect of the politics of delegated discretion which has been little explored. The case study by Fimister and Hill in Chapter 5 takes its exploration further.

The other neglected issue about the structuring of discretion concerns the extent to which it occurs, neither through hierarchical controls nor as a result of unilateral action by street-level bureaucrats, but is rather 'negotiated' (see Strauss (1978) on 'negotiated order') by the agency, and particularly by its low-level operational staff in the process of relating to the public. Several studies in this book explore this further. In Chapter 7 Haimes shows how a committee, set up to try to make policy in a complex and sensitive area of social life, did in fact negotiate a shared view of the boundaries to concepts of 'normality' in family life. In the process they delegated discretionary issues further down the line to professionals who would have to deal with actual decisions on the extent to which they would assist surrogacy. They may perhaps, however, find themselves negotiating these definitions with the people who seek their services, and Haimes is exploring this in further research.

In a very different policy context Hanf shows in Chapter 4 how the long-running debate about 'capture' of regulators by the regulated in environmental policy can be better handled by the notion of the 'co-production' of policy. Hupe applies the same notion in relation to issues about public assistance policy, more directly reorienting the way street-level bureaucracy theory has looked at human services (Chapter 6). In Chapter 8 Beckman, exploring yet another policy context, planning policy in Sweden, shows how traditional central approaches steering local activities have been modified to facilitate public–private negotiation processes at the local level.

The notion of co-production emerges perhaps from a distinctively Dutch political culture (see Hupe's discussion of this). Contemporary Swedish decentralisation has developed in a context in which local prerogatives have long been recognised (see Gustafsson, 1990). However, it is a theme which deserves wider attention inasmuch as it offers an approach to participative ways of controlling the activities of professionals. In Britain this approach has been championed by Stoker (in Stewart and Stoker, 1989) and by Hoggett (1991). It finds echoes in the political parties' rival attempts at formulating 'citizen's charters'. But it faces formidable difficulties in emerging strongly on the political agenda because of the dominance of the preoccupation with cost control. Its private-sector-inspired alternative, seeing the citizen as a 'customer' to be given marketed alternatives to choose, seems to outbid it because of its promise to attack the cost containment issue as well.

The concern about the extent to which 'public-sector' decision and management processes can be seen as different from private-sector ones

During the 1970s there was a gradual transformation of 'public administration' into 'the study of public policy', as authors urged that the policy delivery process should be seen as an 'open' rather than 'closed' system. This process involved bringing to bear upon the study of public administration various disciplines including the sociology of organisations (see Dunsire, 1973; Hill, 1972). In the course of doing this a distinction tended to be drawn between organisational behaviour in public organisations and organisational behaviour in private ones (particularly industrial firms). That distinction, which always involved difficulties, particularly in dealing with the wide range of cases where the two categories converged, has increasingly come under challenge.

That challenge is both an intellectual one and a political one. It is fruitful to observe the debate within organisational sociology between those who emphasise environmental constraints and contingencies and those who emphasise power (see the discussion in Clegg (1990)), and to recognise its application to the public sector. The debate about the usability of exchange theory for relationships between public-sector organisations, particularly provoked by Rhodes (1979), has been a useful one, while corporatist work has shown how important public-sector/private-sector exchanges may be (Grant, 1985; Cawson, 1978).

Manifestly in those areas of policy, such as planning (see Beckman in Chapter 8) and pollution control (see Hanf in Chapter 4), where public and private sectors interface this joint production of policy is an inevitable, and relatively uncontroversial, development. The position is rather different in those areas of public policy which had come to be seen, over the period between the 1940s and the 1970s, as very much the territory of the public sector. In many ways the challenge here is not merely a challenge to the waning influence of statist ideals; it is also a challenge to our notions of democratic accountability. The privatisation measures which have changed public monopolies into private monopolies seem as deliberately blind to the underlying control issues as the earlier nationalising acts. The old socialists claimed that the newly nationalised industries now belonged to the people; the modern privatisers proclaim that they are now answerable to the consumer. Are not both claims hollow? The interesting questions arise for policy analysis when organisational forms are adopted where some kind of competition seems to be feasible. How real are these?

It is instructive to start from a theme in organisation sociology: the growth of large enterprises absorbing smaller ones and integrating their own semi-autonomous units (see Chandler, 1977). This was a process under which, according to Williamson

(1975), market failures or market control problems made it expedient to replace 'markets' by 'hierarchies'. The new right argues that now the process must be reversed. While there are grounds for suspicion that they apply this argument more zealously to public monopolies than to private ones, there is a vein in post-Fordist theory which suggests that new technologies offer the opportunity to return to more loosely coupled organisational forms (Stoker in Stewart and Stoker, 1989; Bagguley, 1991). The central question, then, is can this be done in a way which really enhances efficiency and really heightens the scope for public accountability?

The advocates of markets argue that their great virtue is that self-interest, which is (it is argued) in any case the dominant human motive, can reign supreme, and the 'hidden hand' will solve our social distribution problems. Much of the argument for the introduction of market, or quasi-market, arrangements is based upon a critique of non-market processes in which little attention is given to the extent to which markets may manifest similar weaknesses. Setting these on one side, however, it is important to consider here the implications for public policy outputs inherent in putting self-interest into so central a role in the motivation system.

It is argued, by Tullock (1976) and others, that bureaucratic behaviour has the characteristics of market behaviour. Bureaucrats, and professionals, in the public services are in a monopoly, or quasi-monopoly, position in which they can enlarge their 'enterprises' and their rewards without check from competitive forces. However, let us not forget that this is just a theory which has been used to justify action but has been little tested by research. Let us also not forget that this theory comes from the United States where the public service ethic is weak and market values are powerful influences on all behaviour. British critics have suggested that empirical evidence here provides little support for the theory. A particularly full analysis of this issue has recently been supplied by Dunleavy, who suggests that the notion of 'bureau maximising' should be rejected and replaced by recognition that there are opportunities for 'bureau shaping' by bureaucrats, which may manifest themselves in a variety of consequences for the public (Dunleavy, 1991). More concretely, it is suggested that we can find many examples of public servants winning acclaim and advancement by being cutters, reorganisers and privatisers!

It may be conceded, as it is by Dunleavy, that in some special circumstances the bureau-maximising theory can be sustained. The point to be made here is that it is more applicable to a department explicitly encouraged to engage in quasi-market behaviour in an 'enterprise culture' (see the discussion of aspects of this by Nixon in Chapter 9), than it is in the traditional bureaucratic context. In which case, to follow the logic of the theory, the constraints of competition become all the more important. But can those constraints really be built in? Or is the reality of quasi-markets not perhaps a brief phase when all appears to be open to competition (at potentially enormous public cost as old resource allocation arrangements are abandoned), followed by an era in which the initial 'winners' engage in a range of behaviour designed to protect their interests and prevent future market entrants? In this context, moreover, we must not forget that in many public services market entry costs are considerable. Hospitals or universities are seldom set up as speculative ventures! There may also be considerable 'exit' costs for consumers who want to change their market preferences. Old people do not 'buy' residential care on a regular basis like sacks of potatoes; they try to make decisions which will last for the rest of their lives. There are related constraints to prevent public customers changing their contractors for public services.

Some rather similar considerations apply with another argument deployed to some effect by the critics of bureaucratic modes of provision: the argument about 'perverse incentives'. Again, there is certainly no wish here to be seen as unconcerned about perverse incentives. A particularly valuable feature of this approach has been its contribution to the exposure of hidden incentives. Nevertheless may not the problem of perverse incentives be heightened in a system in which *incentives* are given a central role?

Market systems are commended as ones in which individuals have incentives to minimise their costs and maximise benefits to their customers. The problem is that this may mean *externalising* costs, and ensuring there are no externalised benefits. Dunleavy has provided a masterly analysis of the implications of this for public services (1986). Examples of externalised benefits are perhaps less obvious than externalised costs. They are, however, very important in the public sector – including such exemplary employment practices as equal opportunities policies and compassionate treatment of employees in difficulties ('community care within the organisation'?). Some of the issues about participation, inherent in the co-production notion as explored by Hupe, may fall into this category too.

Externalised costs are obviously enormously important in many public service sectors. For example, central to the problems of relationships between health and social care is the extent to which they pass costs on to each other. Those, like Enthoven (1985) in his influential little pamphlet on the British health service, who point to perverse incentive problems as pervasive in our system and advocate quasi-market solutions to these problems skate too easily over the issues about externalised costs. Quality control in health and social care is so difficult that it is all too easy to reduce costs by passing them on elsewhere – to the individual, the family and the community. In a world of performance indicators with expensive accountants to count and cost all that can be counted and costed, so many other real 'costs' can be overlooked. In Chapter 2 Degeling indicates some concerns of this kind.

Again, however, let us try to give the 'market' school of thought the benefit of the doubt. Let us assume that they can do a good job here at identifying costs and benefits. What that means in terms of public policy is that they will be good at identifying *needs*. However, we know that the concept of 'need' makes no sense in the language of markets, where the corresponding concept is 'demand' – need backed by the resources to pay. In health and community care it is, of course, the government which often provides the resources where a need has been established. Now the point of this piece of elementary policy analysis is to ask what happens when there are agencies aiming, along the lines indicated by public choice theory (Tullock, 1976), to maximise the size and scope of their activities and constrained by sophisticated measurement to quantify need effectively and to absorb implicit costs? The answer is surely, in a world of health and social care, where need in the absolute sense is likely far to exceed resources, that they get a great deal better than they already are at demonstrating the need for their services. Is there an argument here for a quasi-market system? If there is one here, it is one that challenges the claim that market processes will also reduce costs. It implies that the political arena will be filled more than ever before by a clamour of clever arguments for more screening, more spare-parts surgery, more cosmetic surgery and, perhaps also, more effective care for neglected groups.

These reflections are important for the 'rational' use of indicators (discussed by Degeling), and we will return to this theme in the next section. They also give us pause for thought about the very different kinds of control crisis found by Flynn in Britain and Holland. Are the two countries, and many others, really responding to the same 'contingencies' in ageing societies, the rising costs of health care? And if they are, why should a comparatively low-cost system like Britain's adopt ideas from a high-cost system like that of the United States? Or have we here the copying of the latest public policy fashions, spreading ideas in a comparatively mindless way across a world where domestic policy is becoming internationalised?

Inasmuch as there are common themes between the countries represented in this book they are perhaps rather more about the consequences than the causes of some of the parallel developments. One such theme concerns cultural and value changes. Privatisation, real or unreal, needs to be seen as involving value changes in which altruism is being undermined. This is already weakened within caring services. Will it be further eroded by the creation of an ethos of competition and entrepreneurship? Already fragile arrangements for planning and public consultation are being weakened. The processes under which individuals try to maximise their own 'empires', externalise their costs and internalise their benefits, processes which it is acknowledged are hard to control, are being reinforced.

The debate about the extent to which policy decision processes can be described as rational or incremental

The last of the specific issues to be explored in this chapter involves revisiting an old theme in the study of the policy process, on which in many respects it might be more appropriate to say like a newspaper editor 'this correspondence is now closed'. It has been shown that a great deal of misunderstanding has occurred in the course of the debate between the rational model theorists and the 'incrementalists' because of the extent to which both sides claim to be both prescriptive and descriptive. In fact the 'rational' school is much stronger on the prescriptive side and 'incrementalism' offers a good description of the way most policy change occurs (Smith and May, 1980). However, it has become clear from recent contributions by Goodin (1982) and Gregory (1989) that the use of 'rational' to describe one side of the debate sows considerable confusion because of the ambiguity of that word. Hence the implication of Gregory's arguments is that it is surely not rational to try to fly in the face of political realities.

Why, however, reopen the subject here? A recent book by Harrison, Hunter and Pollitt (Harrison *et al.*, 1990) has re-examined the incrementalist argument in a way which draws attention to various neglected parts of the debate. They take from Lindblom the idea of separating 'incremental politics', 'incremental analysis' and 'partisan mutual adjustment'. The distinction between the first two reminds us that, as far as the prescriptive debate is concerned, one can conceive of a process of examination of policy options which is reasonably comprehensive – 'satisficing' to meet Simon's limited criteria for 'rationality' – in the context of a political decision process which is essentially incremental. Therefore, when the terms are used descriptively one may distinguish the analysis process from the outcome.

But while Harrison and his colleagues have usefully reminded us of the case for the separation of analysis and politics in relation to the rationalism/incrementalism debate, it is important to remember that there is a 'politics' of analysis. This is a theme which has been picked up in a range of recent writing on policy analysis as a prescriptive art (see Heineman *et al.*, 1990). Choices about analytical data and indices are likely to be politically informed choices. Data are not necessarily neutral, but may advantage particular interests. This is a theme which is very pertinent to Degeling's chapter. Similarly, forms of analysis are linked with specific professional groups within the policy process. The increasing power of the accountants is linked with the growth of the use of financial audits as a data source for decision making. The power of the economists derives from acceptance of their kind of data (Ashmore *et al.*, 1989). Knowledge is a weapon in conflicts over policy making and implementation, but the fashioning and provision of that weapon is not a neutral process.

Harrison and his colleagues describe Lindblom's concept of 'partisan mutual adjustment' (PMA) as 'fragmented or greatly decentralised political decision making where policies are the resultants of attempts at mutual persuasion by the interests concerned, and outcomes (whether incremental or not) "happen" rather than being the decision of some single or unitary authority. PMA is therefore "to some extent a substitution of politics for analysis" ' (Harrison *et al.*, 1990, p. 9; the internal quotation is from Lindblom, 1979, p. 524). Harrison and his colleagues argue that PMA does not occur in the British health service; rather 'doctors dominate' (p. 154).

Such a conclusion is partly challenged by Flynn's contribution to this book (Chapter 3). But in addition other contributions to the book explore other forms of PMA. Hanf's discussion of regulatory policy in Chapter 4 examines the kind of interaction between regulators and the regulated which makes the latter to some degree co-producers, exploring the extent to which street-level bureaucrats develop shared 'rules' in collaboration with their publics which determine limits to PMA. In Chapter 6 Hupe explores PMA and co-production in relation to service delivery. There is an important reminder for British students of the policy process that we may have a culture and a power structure in which PMA is inhibited, by contrast with the Netherlands, and that we may have just lived through an era in which, under the influence of Mrs Thatcher, that inhibition may have been enhanced.

However, there are problems with the concept of partisan mutual adjustment. There are severe interpretative problems about distinguishing between patterns of domination and patterns of negotiation. Hanf's chapter reminds us how often the negotiated settlements of pollution control are alternatively interpreted as regulatory weakness in the face of the power of polluting enterprises. These interpretative difficulties are enhanced by the extent to which mutual adjustment systems operate in contexts of powerful dominant value systems, a theme explored by Haimes in Chapter 7.

Conclusions

This chapter introduces a range of important contemporary issues for the study of public policy. These are the debate about approaches to the study of implementation, the exploration of roles played by professionals in the policy process, issues about the structuring of street-level decision making, the extent to which there is or can be fusion between public and private sectors, and the debate about rationalism and incrementalism in public policy decision processes.

Throughout the discussion of these issues there tend to surface from time to time, as in almost all writing about policy processes, issues about prescription. Thus, the top-down versus bottom-up debate is partly a debate about how policy *is* made and partly about how it *should be* made, and the same theme is picked up again in arguments about street-level bureaucracy and discretion and in the discussion of incrementalism. Arguments about the privatisation of public services, and about the extent to which managerialist ideas from the private sector can be imported into the public sector, are heavily charged with feelings about the extent to which these developments should occur. This collection is principally concerned with analysis rather than with prescription. But there is a need to recognise how these two get tangled together from time to time, and to acknowledge that the authors may have biases deriving from strong feelings about the underlying ideological issues.

In particular, issues about accountability run through the discussion, and it must be recognised that in the societies discussed here the context is democracy. Public accountability is more than managerial accountability writ large.

While the contributions in this book come from various countries and deal with varied policy areas, the link between them is a shared concern among the authors about exploring the policy process, and particularly some of its detailed manifestations. The themes explored in this introductory chapter are picked up in various ways in the chapters that follow. No attempt has been made to impose a uniform framework on the case-study chapters, and there is no requirement that every chapter should refer to every one of the themes. Comparison occurs through the exploration of a shared pool of ideas in different countries and different policy sectors. In the process interesting cultural and constitutional contrasts are brought out, which seem to enhance, for example, co-production in the Netherlands and decentralisation in Sweden – phenomena which seem to be weak in the United Kingdom. These may be contrasted with preoccupations which the countries examined seem to have in common – for example, concerns with ways of controlling expenditure and problems about professional power – and ideas about ways to deal with administrative problems which travel increasingly fast around the world.

The book aims to broaden understanding of the policy process and sharpen up the tools used to analyse it, in the recognition that ours is a subject which deals with issues and ideas shared across national boundaries.

References

Adler, M., and S. Asquith (eds) (1981) *Discretion and Welfare*, London: Heinemann.

Alford, R. (1975) *Health Care Politics*, Chicago, Ill.: University of Chicago Press.

Ashmore, M., M. Mulkay and T. Pinch (1989) *Health and Efficiency: A sociology of health economics*, Milton Keynes: Open University Press.

Bagguley, P. (1991) 'Post-Fordism and enterprise culture', in R. Keat and N. Abercrombie (eds), *Enterprise Culture*, New York: Routledge.

Bardach, E. (1974) *The Implementation Game*, Cambridge, Mass.: MIT Press.

Barrett, S., and C. Fudge (eds) (1981) *Policy and Action*, London: Methuen.

Barrett, S., and M. Hill (1984) 'Policy, bargaining and structure in implementation theory', *Policy and Politics*, 12, pp. 219–40.

Cawson, A. (1978) 'Pluralism, corporatism and the role of the state', *Government and Opposition*, 13 (2), pp. 188–9.

Chandler, A. D. (1977) *The Visible Hand: The managerial revolution in American business*, Cambridge, Mass.: Harvard University Press.

Clegg, S. (1990) *Modern Organizations*, London: Sage.

Davis, K. C. (1969) *Discretionary Justice*, Baton Rouge, La.: Louisiana State University Press.

Dunleavy, P. (1986) 'Explaining the privatization boom: public choice versus radical approaches', *Public Administration*, 64 (1), pp. 13–34.

Dunleavy, P. (1991) *Democracy, Bureaucracy and Public Choice*, Hemel Hempstead: Harvester Wheatsheaf.

Dunsire, A. (1973) *Administration*, London: Martin Robertson.

Dworkin, R. (1977) *Taking Rights Seriously*, London: Duckworth.

Elmore, R. (1978) 'Organisational models of social program implementation', *Public Policy*, 26 (2), pp. 185–228.

Elmore, R. (1980) 'Backward mapping: implementation research and policy decisions', *Political Science Quarterly*, 94, pp. 601–16.

Enthoven, A. C. (1985) *Reflections on the Management of the NHS*, London: Nuffield Provincial Hospitals Trust.

Forrest, R., and A. Murie (1988) *Selling the Welfare State*, London: Routledge.

Galligan, D. J. (1986) *Discretionary Powers*, Oxford: Clarendon Press.

Glennerster, H., A. Power and T. Travers (1991) 'A new era for social policy: a new enlightenment or a new Leviathan?', *Journal of Social Policy*, 20 (3), pp. 389–414.

Goodin, R. E. (1982) *Political Theory and Public Policy*, Chicago, Ill.: University of Chicago Press.

Grant, W. (ed) (1985) *The Political Economy of Corporatism*, London: Macmillan.

Gregory, R. (1989) 'Political rationality or incrementalism? Charles E. Lindblom's enduring contribution to public policy making', *Policy and Politics*, 17 (2), pp. 139–53.

Gunn, L. (1978) 'Why is implementation so difficult?', *Management Services in Government*, November, pp. 169–76.

Gustafsson, G. (1990) 'Swedish local government: reconsidering rationality and consensus', in J. J. Hess (ed.), *Local Government and Urban Affairs in International Perspective*, Baden Baden: Nomos Verlagsgesellschaft.

Ham, C. J. (1992) *Health Policy in Britain* (3rd edn), London: Macmillan.

Ham, C., and M. Hill (1993) *The Policy Process in the Modern Capitalist State*, Hemel Hempstead: Harvester Wheatsheaf.

Harrison, S., D. J. Hunter and C. Pollitt (1990) *The Dynamics of British Health Policy*, London: Unwin Hyman.

Heineman, R. A., W. T. Bluhm, S. A. Peterson and E. N. Kearny (1990) *The World of the Policy Analyst*, Chatham, NJ: Chatham House.

Hennessy, P. (1989) *Whitehall*, London: Secker and Warburg.

Hill, M. J. (1969) 'The exercise of discretion in the National Assistance Board', *Public Administration*, 47, pp. 75–90.

Hill, M. J. (1972) *The Sociology of Public Administration*, London: Weidenfeld and Nicolson.

Hill, M., and G. Bramley (1986) *Analysing Social Policy*, Oxford: Basil Blackwell.
Hirschman, A. O. (1970) *Exit, Voice and Loyalty*, Cambridge, Mass: Harvard University Press.
Hjern, B., and C. Hull (1982) 'Implementation research as empirical constitutionalism', in B. Hjern and C. Hull (eds), *Implementation Beyond Hierarchy*, special issue of *European Journal of Political Research*.
Hjern, B., and D. O. Porter (1981) 'Implementation structures: a new unit of administrative analysis', *Organisational Studies*, 2, pp. 211–27.
Hoggett, P. (1991) 'A new management in the public sector', *Policy and Politics*, 19 (4), pp. 243–56.
Hogwood, B. W., and L. A. Gunn (1984) *Policy Analysis for the Real World*, Oxford: Oxford University Press.
Illich, I. (1977) *Limits to Medicine*, Harmondsworth: Penguin.
Jordan, A. G., and J. J. Richardson (1987) *British Politics and the Policy Process*, London: Unwin Hyman.
Jowell, J. (1973) 'The legal control of administrative discretion', *Public Law*.
Klein, R. (1989) *The Politics of the NHS* (2nd edn), London: Longman.
Lindblom, C. E. (1979) 'Still muddling, not yet through', *Public Administration Review*, 39, pp. 517–26.
Lipsky, M. (1980) *Street-Level Bureaucracy*, New York: Russell Sage.
Marsh, D., and R. A. W. Rhodes (1992) *Implementing Thatcherite Policies*, Milton Keynes: Open University Press.
Niskanen, W. A. (1971) *Bureaucracy and Representative Government*, New York: Aldine-Atherton.
Pressman, J., and A. Wildavsky (1973) *Implementation*, Berkeley, Calif.: University of California Press.
Rhodes, R. A. W. (1979) *Public Administration and Policy Analysis*, Farnborough: Saxon House.
Sabatier, P., and D. Mazmanian (1979) 'The conditions of effective implementation: a guide to accomplishing policy objectives', *Policy Analysis*, 5, pp. 481–504.
Smith, G., and D. May (1980) 'The artificial debate between rationalist and incrementalist models of decision-making', *Policy and Politics*, 8 (2), pp. 147–61.
Stewart, J., and G. Stoker (eds) (1989) *The Future of Local Government*, London: Macmillan.
Strauss, A. (1978) *Negotiations*, San Francisco, Calif.: Jossey-Bass.
Tullock, G. (1976) *The Vote Motive*, London: Institute of Economic Affairs.

Wilding, P. (1982) *Professional Power and Social Welfare*, London: Routledge and Kegan Paul.
Williamson, O. E. (1975) *Markets and Hierarchies*, New York: Free Press.
Young, H. (1989) *One of Us: A biography of Mrs Thatcher*, London: Macmillan.

CHAPTER 2

Policy as the accomplishment of an implementation structure: hospital restructuring in Australia

Pieter Degeling

Background

The last 15 years have witnessed significant shifts in the agenda of health policy in Australia, Britain and the United States, as is evident in both the priorities being pursued and the implementation structures used. Until the mid-1970s, the primary issue was improving access to the expanding curative benefits claimed for medical science. More recently the focus has moved to medical accountability, and what can be done to manage demand for acute care services and to contain costs.

Implementation of the earlier access model was seen variously to depend on the focused application of public and private funds, the distribution and further development of physical plant and medical technology, and the availability of suitably qualified clinical staff. The ultimate effectiveness of the health care system, as registered in what happened to patients, was claimed to be guaranteed by the technical proficiency of doctors and the autonomy and discretionary powers they derived from their professional status. These factors, when combined with the accountability systems operating within the medical profession, would, it was assumed, ensure not only that doctors acted as patients' advocates, but also that patients benefited from the latest development in medical science.

The organisational media used in delivering acute care exhibited many of the characteristics of what has been termed a bottom-up approach to policy implementation. This model proceeds from the argument that implementation is most effective when the organisational arrangements used in service delivery give room for manoeuvre to direct service providers (Lipsky, 1971, 1976; Weatherley and Lipsky, 1977; Prottas, 1978, 1979) and assist them to address and negotiate issues that emerge in service encounters (Hanf, Hjern and Porter, 1978; Hjern and Porter, 1981; Elmore, 1979–80). Accordingly, when designing implementation structures, policy-makers should begin 'not with statements of intent, but with a statement of the specific behaviour at the lowest level of the implementation process that generates the need for a policy' (Elmore, 1979–80, p. 604).

The advantages claimed for bottom-up implementation are very similar to medicine's justifications for its position in acute care delivery. Medicine regards itself as the primary reservoir of knowledge and expertise about disease and illness and about the clinical and organisational aspects of curative care provision. Its claim to autonomy is realised in everyday encounters between doctors and their patients. In certifying illness, ordering tests, prescribing treatments, referring patients to their specialist colleagues and authorising hospital admissions, doctors claim that their decisions should remain immune from constraints that outsiders to the doctor–patient encounter seek to impose for reasons of organisational convenience or resource efficiency. Their patient-advocacy role, it is claimed, requires doctors to diagnose and treat patients solely according to personal expert judgement; it is only by remaining outside the claimed pathologies of hierarchy that doctors can discharge their ethical responsibilities.

In the period since 1970, significant aspects of this bottom-up approach have come into question. Among other matters, medicine's claim to autonomy is increasingly being judged in terms of perceived shortcomings in the profession's capacity to regulate itself, doubts about the efficacy of many of the diagnosis and treatment regimes ordered by many doctors, and the growing impost of acute care delivery on an already strained public purse. There is a growing body of evidence which demonstrates that patients with similar symptoms are likely to be treated differently depending on where they live and/or the age and educational background of their doctor. Apart from pecuniary interest, factors affecting doctors' diagnoses and treatment have been shown to include their knowledge of recent clinical developments;

a desire to establish a reputation in a particular field of practice; a propensity to interpret death as personal failure; unwillingness to accept the limits of medicine; and finally, a perceived need to establish defensive positions against the possibility of malpractice litigation.

For central policy-makers, the impact of this range of non-clinical factors on medical decision making is ultimately registered not only on the bodies of patients but also in the increasing resource demands that acute hospital services are placing on stretched health budgets (Thompson *et al.*, 1975; McMahon *et al.*, 1986; Yodor and Connor, 1982). The perceived prevalence of overservicing, together with anticipated expansions in demand for curative services resulting from an ageing population and further developments in medical technology, has heightened awareness of the resource implications of medical practice (Bates and Lapsley, 1985). For players in central policy circles, established methods for managing demand, such as waiting lists and prices to consumers, are regarded as inadequate for the task. These outcomes, when combined with evidence of the class bias in the distribution of medical services (and the level of resourcing that would be required to redress this bias), have reinforced the view that issues arising from medicine's capacity to influence service demand and cost can no longer be ignored (Palmer, 1986; Palmer and Short, 1989; Wennberg *et al.*, 1980).

Currently, the preferred solutions for addressing these issues reflect a top-down concern for bolstering hierarchy and strengthening the instrumental character of implementation (Dror, 1968; Van Horn and Van Meter, 1976; Van Meter and Van Horn, 1975; Sabatier and Mazmanian, 1980a, 1980b; Sabatier, 1986a, 1986b). In justifying their stance, central policy-makers advance reasons which mirror views advanced by proponents of the top-down perspective. Both question the discretionary powers and consequent autonomy of professionals and direct service providers on the grounds that they undermine necessary relationships of authority, responsibility and accountability both within a representative system of government (Hogwood and Gunn, 1984; Linder and Peters, 1987) and within hospitals (Fetter and Freeman, 1986; MacMahon *et al.*, 1986). Recognising the implications of street-level autonomy for implementation, current versions of the top-down approach emphasise goal clarity as a crucial factor in policy formation, and the need to set in place mechanisms for monitoring and managing performance at the bottom (Sabatier, 1986a, 1986b).

Medicine's response to the claimed primacy of political–administrative authority over its ethical responsibility to patients closely resembles Elmore's conclusion that such assertions are ultimately 'based on distrust' (Elmore, 1979–80, p. 610), which in the main is unwarranted. Uncritical acceptance of this standpoint, the medical argument runs, provides justification for the ultimate bureaucratisation of medicine and a resultant application of what is termed 'cookbook medicine', to the detriment of patient care. Like Elmore, the medical profession makes much of trust; the relationship between patient and doctor is described in these terms and the profession fends off criticism by reference to medicine's scientific basis and the range of mechanisms internal to the profession which ensure ethical behaviour (Friedson, 1970a, 1970b, 1986; Willis, 1989).

While this defence may be rhetorically effective, it denies accumulating evidence about shortcomings in both the clinical and ethical dimensions of medical practice. Moreover, in mobilising the notion of trust, both Elmore and the profession suppress consideration of issues arising from the power–knowledge dimensions of, for example, medical practice. That more than issues of trust are involved here becomes apparent when we consider how the pursuit of scientific medicine can contribute to casting patients as mere objects of knowledge and intervention, and remove from them any capacity for shaping the service they receive. Recognition of the depowering effects built into what doctors term 'accepted medical practice' raises questions about the limitations of bottom-up strategies in situations where service providers are central to implementation, but at the same time are also at the core of the problem that a policy is seeking to address.

Defining the problem and searching for solutions

In more economically straitened times, medical accountability is increasingly being defined primarily in financial terms (Alford, 1975; Starr, 1982; Mechanic, 1986; Mooney, 1986; Palmer and Short,

1989). In the absence of significantly increased levels of resourcing, medicine's continued immunity from accountability will mean longer queues outside hospital and/or that inequities produced through rationing-by-price will become more blatant. The likely political damage arising from either outcome has contributed to the attention being given to the adoption of more output-oriented and financially driven approaches in the management of hospital services and in the review of medical practice.

The politics of health in Australia has been characterised as 'a strife of interests' (Sax, 1984) in which the Commonwealth (federal) and State governments have been 'slowly taking control' (Crichton, 1990) not only of the organisation and management of health care, but also, in more recent times, of the details of medical practice. In terms of current divisions of governmental responsibility for the financing of health care, the Commonwealth funds and administers Medicare, a universal health insurance scheme, and also provides the bulk of the finance for hospital services, although the day-to-day administration of hospitals lies with State health departments.

Governmental concern about the interconnections between medical autonomy, the cost of health care and the issue of hospital efficiency first surfaced in 1974 following the federal Labor government's establishment of Medibank, an earlier universal health insurance scheme. Administrative arrangements associated with the fees and payment component of Medibank brought to light evidence of overservicing, particularly in the diagnostic area. The production of this kind of data and subsequent debates about its implications in the media and in political–administrative circles have contributed to maintaining the prominence of medical accountability on health care agendas.

The responses of Commonwealth and State authorities have varied in focus and have operated at a number of levels. With respect to medicine specifically, the moral and political force of both the federal and state parliaments have been brought to bear by way of a number of inquiries by Parliamentary Accounts Committees into overservicing and the referral and billing practices of doctors (Australia: Georges, 1985). In addition, depending on the political hue of the government of the day, Commonwealth and State authorities have either attempted to strengthen the regulatory mechanisms applicable to medicine or encouraged the profession voluntarily to extend its involvement in quality assurance and peer review activity (Crichton, 1990, p. 88). In the short term neither strategy has proved to be effective. Initiatives on self-regulation drew little more than rhetorical support from the profession, while resort to powers available within Commonwealth and State regulations was interpreted as being little more than civil conscription. By 1984 sections of the profession in New South Wales were in open revolt, which led to a strike on the part of some medical specialities. The bitterness engendered by this euphemistically termed 'doctors' dispute' continues to confound relations between sections of the profession and government (Daniel, 1990).

On the hospital front, a number of official inquiries (parliamentary and ministerial) have prompted moves directed at strengthening organisation structures and improving management accounting and information systems (Australia: Jamison, 1981; Australia: Pennington, 1984). New administrative structures have either abolished or reduced the independence of hospital boards, thus bringing hospitals more directly under departmental and hence ministerial control. In the same vein, state health authorities have acted to cap hospital budgets and institute a system of service agreements which extend their control over hospital managers: nowadays, bringing the hospital 'in on budget' has become a major preoccupation (Palmer and Short, 1989, p. 86).

This end is construed as being more readily achievable through implementing methods and techniques that have been developed by disciplines such as management science and decision theory, operations research and information science and accounting. The resulting classification and information systems, when combined with the data storage, retrieval and management capacity of modern information technology, are projected as significantly extending top management control. In particular, these information systems are promoted as enabling management first to map and survey the total web of activity integral to service provision, and second, to derive standards against which the efficiency and effectiveness of individual clinical units can be assessed (Feinglass and Salmon, 1990).

The adoption of this top-down approach marks a significant departure from conventional hospital organisation. As noted earlier, the organisational arrangements and resource management methods conventionally used in curative care settings generally were structured to support the diagnostic and therapeutic aspects of a patient's encounter with the doctor. In essence, the faith placed in medical science and the assumed technical proficiency and professional character of medical practice meant that hospitals were largely regarded as facilitative mechanisms which enabled doctors to apply the latest developments in medical science to pathologies displayed by individual patients.

For the promoters of a top-down approach to hospital management, however, an outcome of traditional hospital organisation was that doctors were not held accountable for either the clinical efficacy or the resource implications of their practices. Significantly, it is these dimensions of curative care provision that are the focal points for the current hospital reform programme. In effect, the prominence now being accorded to creating visibilities for the therapeutic and resource outcomes of clinical practice recognises that the behaviour 'at the lowest level of the implementation process that generates the need for a policy' (Elmore, 1979–80, p. 604) is no longer simply the patient's encounter with the doctor, but also includes the doctor's accountability for the therapeutic efficacy of her or his practices and the resource implications that flow from these. In effect, as noted earlier, the introduction of this additional dimension has meant that clinical departments within hospitals are now conceived not just as media for delivering curative care, but also as media through which the accountability of doctors can be realised.

The casemix development programme

The most recent Commonwealth initiative on these fronts has focused on the utilisation of diagnosis-related groups (DRGs) in funding and managing hospitals. The term 'diagnosis-related groups' refers to an in-patient classification system developed by researchers at Yale University as a medium for mapping the clinical 'products' of a hospital. In this view, the central activity of a hospital is the sustained and systematic production of sets of 'diagnostic and therapeutic regimens judged by clinicians [as the end producers and managers of treatment] to be effective in returning [patients] to a desired state of health' (Fetter and

Hines, 1988). Hence a hospital is depicted as a multi-product service organisation producing a mix of treatment outputs such as hysterectomies, colectomies, treatments of hypertension, respiratory neoplasms and myocardial infarctions among others. When grouped and aggregated, these constitute the hospital's casemix.

With over 10,000 entries, the International Classification of Diseases indicates the full range of possible hospital treatment products. These have been clustered into about 480 groups. Proponents of the system argue that its benefit lies in its capacity to provide information which can be used in resource allocation, in management decision making and in constituting management control systems which can be focused on treatment production. For example, because DRGs group patients in terms of the treatments they receive, they provide means for establishing information systems which can collect and aggregate information about the quantum and types of diagnostic and therapeutic services delivered by a hospital, individual clinical units and/or individual clinicians, and also about resource usage patterns that have resulted.

Information constituted by using DRGs provides a basis for establishing casemix accounting and budgeting systems at hospital and clinical department levels. A casemix accounting system will enable management to relate the financial flows of these hospitals directly to the number of products (i.e. treated patients) of individual clinical departments. This enables managers to map and then determine the distribution of hospital expenditures (costs) classified by type of expenditure for each product as defined by the DRG system. Furthermore, by using a casemix management system, managers will also be able to compare costs by DRG between similar institutions (and/or clinical units) and to analyse cost variances that come to light. DRG-specific cost information generated in this way, when combined with forecasts of patient volume classified by DRG, also provides means for predicting the resource needs of a hospital and/or its clinical units. In this way, an allegedly more 'information-based' approach to budgeting and resource allocation becomes available.

Alternatively, in management decision making and control, a Case Mix Management Information System (CMMIS) will provide information about trends in a hospital's casemix which can be used in service planning both within a hospital and in networking services between hospitals. Furthermore, when similar information is obtained from other hospitals, it becomes possible to establish industry norms for individual treatment regimens (i.e. DRGs). These norms can then be used to evaluate the relative effectiveness of the regimens being pursued by individual clinical units.

Information systems which can provide this form of information and at this level of detail will enable clinicians and managers to engage in conversations about both the efficiency and effectiveness of the patient-treatment regimens used in individual clinical units, for example. A CMMIS provides information which makes available the means for a much more robust approach to utilisation review and quality assurance. The system will enable managers to highlight what are termed 'outliers', where resource usage has varied significantly from the industry norm. These cases can then be investigated more closely to establish the reasons for their unusual characteristics.

Clinical directorates: a new implementation structure

Management information systems similar to those outlined above are being introduced in a number of teaching hospitals in the Sydney metropolitan area. Two of these hospitals have redesigned their organisation structures along casemix lines. The new structure is justified in terms of its claimed capacity to overcome dysfunctions commonly attributed to conventional hospital organisation structures. As illustrated in Figure 2.1, hospitals are conventionally locales in which members of distinct authority structures are loosely linked in the provision of services. The separateness of medicine, nursing, allied health and administrative and hotel services, recognised in the formal authority structure of most hospitals, attests to the past capacity of these occupational groups to stake out and preserve their control over particular aspects of treatment provision. Paradoxically, while wards are the key production units of the hospital, they are the least significant in the way that authority and power are located, resources are distributed and managed, and information is gathered and reported.

Proponents of reform argue that this orientation towards function and profession, as well as the relative absence of medicine in day-to-day management, has produced outcomes which are deleterious to hospital efficiency and effectiveness. For example, existing structures produce plural bases for exercising

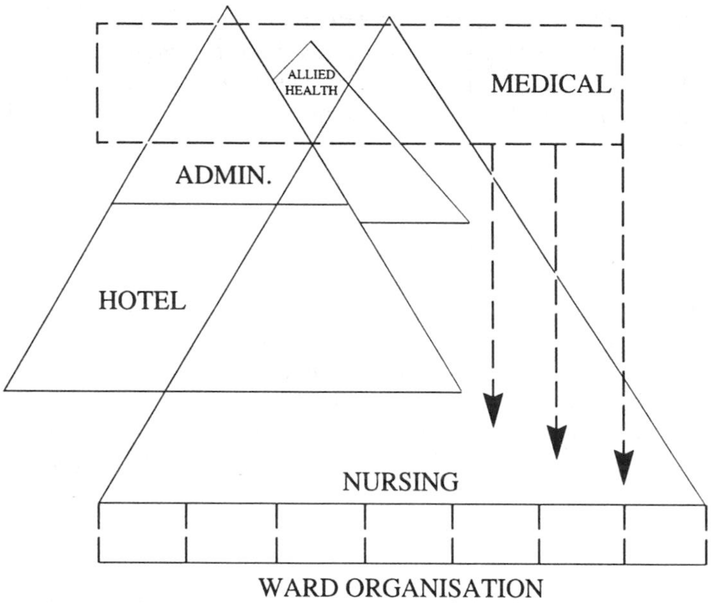

Figure 2.1 Conventional hospital organisational structure.

authority and the emergence of a negotiated order which is characterised by the virtual absence of points for managerial leverage and a vacuum of accountability and control. Under existing organisational arrangements and practices, the argument goes, hospitals are administered rather than managed. The activities of hospital administrators (even when they are called managers) have been producer oriented rather than consumer/product oriented (McMahon and Newbold, 1986; Feinglass and Martin, 1990). More particularly, hospital administrators perform a diplomatic organisational maintenance role. They smooth out internal conflicts, and are preoccupied with mediating the competing claims of individual professional groups and with providing resources and facilities that professionals say they require. This preoccupation with day-to-day problem solving has meant that there is little commitment (by either administrators or individual professional groups) to strategic planning or to implementation of plans. Change, if it occurs, has tended to be incremental rather than strategic, usually consisting of little more than slight marginal adjustments to the status quo.

In an attempt to overcome these shortcomings, the new structure embodies two design principles. First, in keeping with the view that the production of bundles of patient treatments (grouped on DRG lines) is the core activity of a hospital, primacy of place is given to clinical directorates such as medicine, surgery, obstetrics and gynaecology, which produce specialist treatments as final products. Second, specific recognition is given to the centrality of doctors in designing and managing these final products. Whereas previously clinicians maintained an arm's-length relationship with the organisational and resourcing dimensions of acute care provision, the new arrangements require that they become directly involved in management.

As Figure 2.2 shows, the new structure establishes two lines of responsibility and authority. Heads of departments such as

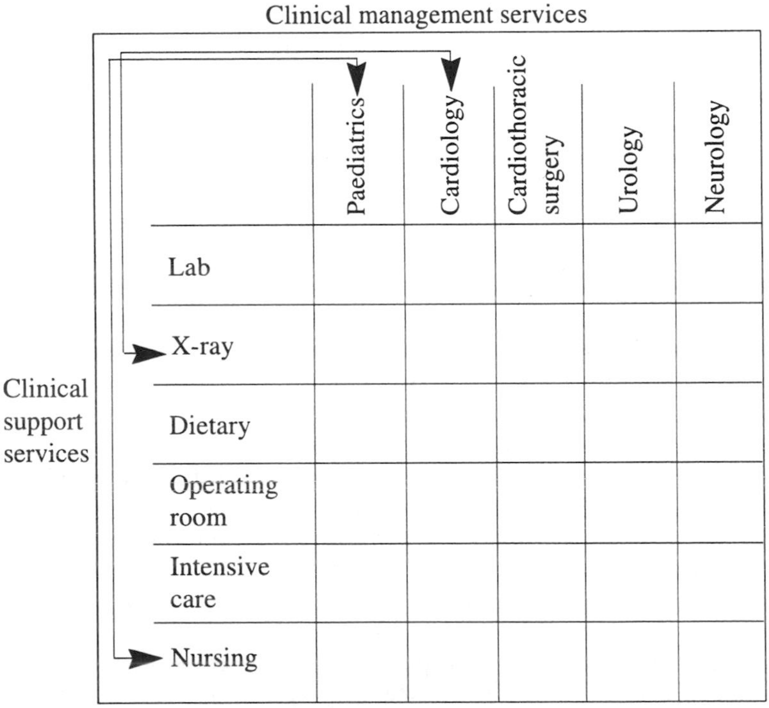

Figure 2.2 A clinical matrix management structure. *Source:* Fetter and Freeman (1985).
Note: Arrows outside of the matrix indicate negotiations between product designers and managers of the intermediate products.

pharmacy, pathology and hotel services are responsible for the efficiency of production process through which intermediate products such as laboratory tests and meals are produced. In turn the conversion of these intermediate products into sets of therapeutic services becomes the primary responsibility of heads of clinical directorates constituted along established differentiations within medicine, as shown in the diagram. It is these final product units which are construed as performing the core activities of the hospital (i.e. the production of bundles of patient treatments such as appendectomies and hysterectomies) and which are projected as becoming the main providers and users of information generated by CMMIS. Furthermore, clinical directorates and the clinical sub-specialities within them constitute the principal identities in the casemix accounting and budgeting systems described earlier. In each of the hospitals, practising medical clinicians have been appointed as heads of final product departments. They are supported in this role by a business manager and a nurse manager.

Accomplishing the new implementation structure

The benefits and advantages claimed for a DRG-based management system have not guaranteed its smooth implementation. The reasons for this, in part, are to be found in the way that the new structure (and the practices and ways of talking it promotes) threatens significant aspects of hospital culture. For example, many hospital employees have interpreted the shift to a more managerially oriented and finance-driven approach as a denial of the qualitative and social dimensions of care provision. In addition, they see the transformation of care into a commodity which is defined in terms of its costs as an attack on what they regard as the 'moral community' of their hospital.

What is important here is that the 'treatment production' view integral to the DRG system and given primacy by its implementation is only one of a number of ways of thinking and talking about a hospital. Doctors, nurses, administrators and other occupational groups, as well as groups in the community in general, also identify their hospital as the following:

- A medium for realising the social dimensions of care.
- A locale for pursuing teaching and research.

structure provides managers and medical clinicians with means for undermining hard-won gains on professional and industrial fronts. The new structure, they claim, will re-establish medicine's dominance over nursing and provide doctors and administrative staff with both a rationale and means for questioning and ultimately negating nursing's emerging autonomy.

Professional and industrial nursing organisations are responding to the possibility of these developments on a number of fronts. Bodies such as the NSW Royal College of Nursing have held a number of public seminars, in the course of which the pros and cons of casemix management for nursing have been explored by eminent nurse academics and nurse administrators from within Australia and overseas. The College has also provided funds for documenting alternative organisational structures which would deliver the benefits of casemix management without reducing the professional and organisational standing of nursing. Professional educational activities such as these have been synchronised with more overtly political campaigns involving leaders of nursing unions and senior nurse managers. Included here are the widespread dissemination of a nursing perspective on narrowly management-focused casemix initiatives; work stoppages in individual hospitals; joint representations by the Royal College, senior nurse administrators and the union to the Department of Health and the minister's office; and ultimately, the threat of state-wide industrial action. To date the issue has not been resolved, but it can be expected that the final outcome will accommodate nursing concerns.

Medicine's response to casemix-based management

As with nursing, medicine's reactions to the new arrangements are mixed, although for significantly different reasons. In contrast to nurses, doctors on the whole welcome the move to establish clinical directorates as focal points for organising and managing the hospital. Among other outcomes, the new structure is seen by many doctors as providing an organisational basis for restoring their ultimate authority over what takes place in the diagnosis and treatment of patients. In addition, establishing clearly defined specialist clinical units, each with its own dedicated resources (including staff, beds and money), is seen by some specialities

- A primary reference point for clinical referral networks.
- A venue for building professional careers.
- A terrain in which industrial awards and agreements are given expression.
- A component of the local service welfare network.
- A reflector of community values and expectations.
- A vehicle for demonstrating community spirit and private beneficence.
- A component of the local economy.

The availability of these 'identities' and the way they are continually mobilised by people within and outside hospital settings is indicative not only of the broad range of players who can claim to have an interest in the hospital game, but also of the variety of values, meanings and rules which they can call on to stake their claims. The structuring effect of some of these values and meanings and rules, as well as their capacity to throw into question attempts to give pre-eminence to a 'treatment production' definition of a hospital, becomes apparent when we consider the reactions of nursing and medical staff to the changes in train in their hospitals.

Nursing reactions

The reactions of nurses to the new arrangements are mixed. Most welcome the information that becomes available following the introduction of casemix information systems, arguing that these will enable nurses for the first time to make visible the full extent of nursing's contribution to acute care provision. Among other matters included here is the further elaboration of patient classification systems which document patient dependency by DRG. The information which results will enable nurses to demonstrate the nursing workforce requirements (expressed in terms of numbers of nurses and skill mix) that result from reductions in the average length of stay (ALOS) by patients in acute care hospitals. Nurses point out that, in so far as improving the efficiency and effectiveness of hospital-based services brings about reductions in ALOS, it also increases the intensity of nursing work. As ALOS is reduced, the volume of patients receiving treatment increases along with their nursing dependency, which in turn should imply an increase in the nursing workforce. Nurses argue that past experience demonstrates that, in the absence of information about increased workloads, nursing resources will not be increased and nursing labour power will once again be exploited by 'medicine' and 'the administration'.

On a more positive note, nurses argue that the availability of casemix information improves the planning and co-ordination of nursing services to the benefit of both patient care and hospital efficiency. For example, information systems which make visible the number and skill mix of nursing resources that are required for particular DRGs will enable nursing management to allocate nursing resources to where they can be used to best effect. Clinical departments which are staffed according to the dependency levels of the patients they treat experience lower complication rates, reduced usage rates of diagnostic, therapeutic and ancillary services, improved co-ordination in the use of expensive equipment, and ultimately reduced lengths of stay. In a similar vein, other nursing studies have demonstrated how the availability of casemix information will enable critical review of existing work demarcations between nurses, allied health staff, clerical staff and doctors, and will expose where changes can and should be introduced to the benefit of both patient care and overall hospital efficiency.

Its positive response to the information-creating capacity of casemix methodologies is evidence of nursing's internal coherence and its emerging managerial and professional sophistication. These same factors, however, have caused nurses to oppose significant aspects of the organisation design that are being introduced into hospitals in the name of casemix management. Prior to the introduction of clinical matrix structures, the nursing division of each hospital was a highly structured professional bureaucracy with well-established traditions of nursing, holding its ground against encroachments by other blocs such as the administration or medicine. Nurses continue to be the only occupational group which provides a 24-hour clinical service to patients and which, through the controls that nurses exercise at ward level, organises and co-ordinates the full range of non-medical services that are entailed in patient treatment. In response to what is regarded as the targeting of nursing in past budget-cutting exercises, nursing divisions in hospitals developed their own budgeting, personnel

and management information systems in ways which established and reinforced their independence from the administration and strengthened their bargaining position.

On a broader front, over the past ten years nurses have become much more articulate about their professional standing. The commencement of tertiary-level nurse education in 1983 has taken the profession out of the apprenticeship model which had limited its development. In the course of this process, an emerging generation of nurse academics is developing a rhetoric and body of knowledge for nursing which is independent of medical knowledge. In addition, the technical basis of nursing practice is being elaborated and to varying degrees now covers matters which were previously the sole preserve of doctors, such as nursing diagnosis, nursing acuity and dependency measures, nursing patient histories and nursing protocols.

Finally, up until the beginning of 1992, the capacity of nursing to protect and advance its interests was bolstered by what was termed the 'nursing shortage problem' – in other words, the exit of qualified nurses to other, more attractive forms of employment and the apparent inability of health authorities to recruit entrants into the profession. The nursing shortage, together with medicine's increasing dependence on a skilled nursing workforce, has done much to extend and reinforce nursing's industrial muscle, and the profession's willingness to flex this muscle is demonstrated in the increasing militancy of nursing unions.

When viewed against this background, the reactions of senior nurse managers, union officials and leaders of professional bodies to organisational proposals which give primacy of place to medically qualified directors of newly established clinical departments is hardly surprising. They argue that, at best, this arrangement places first-line nursing managers in the ambiguous position of having to answer to two sources of authority: their director of nursing and the medical director of their clinical unit. At worst, the new structure signals the beginning of the demise of the nursing division as an organisational force and as the primary professional reference point for hospital-based nurses.

Nurses consider that the realisation of either of these possibilities will reduce their capacity to compete for resources within the hospital, and that an already overburdened workforce will be further exploited. In addition, nurses take the view that the new as reducing the capacity of other specialities to colonise their resource base – a practice which, in the past, had been the source of much intra-medical conflict. Many doctors also take the view that the availability of casemix information will provide a better basis for service planning (both within specialities and between them) and will ensure that, in the future, resources will be allocated (either to individual hospitals or to individual clinical departments within a hospital) not in terms of historical accretion but in terms of currently demonstrated performance and need.

While individual doctors recognise that under the new arrangements not all specialities will obtain added resources, they nevertheless believe that past methods of resourcing worked against the interests of their particular speciality and that the new system will provide means for redressing this. In addition some doctors argue that the adoption of casemix funding will, in the long term, enable medicine to demonstrate that the level of overall government funding for health services is inadequate. With either of these possibilities doctors express the view that responsibility for making the resource case for individual clinical departments, a hospital and, in the longer term, the acute health care system as a whole will to a large degree fall on people who take on the headship of newly established clinical directorates.

However, the benefits claimed to flow from the introduction of casemix management are not restricted to resource allocation. As indicated earlier, the interest on the part of central policy-makers in casemix methodologies lies in their potential for making visible the resource usage patterns that result from the diagnostic and therapeutic practices of individual doctors. This aspect of the casemix programme calls into question strongly held views about medical autonomy and medicine's immunity from management control, even when the manager concerned is a medical colleague. Accordingly, the possibility that CMMIS can be used to create visibilities regarding the resource usage patterns that result from the diagnostic and therapeutic practices of individual doctors is regarded with apprehension.

It is expected that incentives for using CMMIS in this way are likely to increase following the introduction of casemix budgeting systems. As outlined earlier, under casemix budgeting the funding of a clinical department will be tied to an agreed level of output expressed in terms of a casemix profile. This linking of funds to output will structure relations not only between the manager of a clinical directorate and the general management of the hospital, but also between the manager and the clinical staff of his or her department. The level of funding that a clinical unit attracts (in any given year) will depend in part on its past performance in meeting output targets. This, together with the possible establishment of *virement* arrangements (under which units will be able to retain savings resulting from improvements in their efficiency), is likely to place pressure on the manager of a clinical directorate to take a more direct interest in the resource implications of medical practice. Furthermore, the newly established casemix clinical and management information system will provide the information required for doing this.

The organisational and ideological bases for mounting resistance to initiatives such as these are readily to hand. In most hospitals, medical staff are a loosely linked coalition of autonomous practitioners who are variably integrated into the organisation of their hospital. Some are intermittent members (e.g. visiting medical officers) and some are full-time staff (e.g. specialists and academics). As noted earlier, relations within medicine are claimed to be based on collegiality rather than hierarchy. In so far as issues of accountability and control arise, the appropriate mechanisms for handling these are seen to be available in the profession's commitment to science; the operation of the profession's own accountability systems; and the doctors' ascription to a common value system which gives primacy to the interests of patients. In this regard attempts to establish hierarchy (through, for example, the co-optation of some doctors into management) as well as attempts to constitute systems of control and methods of surveillance which are commonly associated with bureaucratic organisations (e.g. CMMIS) are seen by most doctors as being antithetical to the profession's standing and proper functioning.

In justifying their opposition to attempts to bring them within the ambit of managerially determined performance criteria, most doctors make reference to their patient advocacy role and the indeterminate nature of the signs and symptoms exhibited by patients. They claim that the conjunction of these two factors requires that their treatment practices should remain immune from managerial direction and control. In a similar vein, clinicians are concerned to ensure that the evaluation of clinical practice is

- A primary reference point for clinical referral networks.
- A venue for building professional careers.
- A terrain in which industrial awards and agreements are given expression.
- A component of the local service welfare network.
- A reflector of community values and expectations.
- A vehicle for demonstrating community spirit and private beneficence.
- A component of the local economy.

The availability of these 'identities' and the way they are continually mobilised by people within and outside hospital settings is indicative not only of the broad range of players who can claim to have an interest in the hospital game, but also of the variety of values, meanings and rules which they can call on to stake their claims. The structuring effect of some of these values and meanings and rules, as well as their capacity to throw into question attempts to give pre-eminence to a 'treatment production' definition of a hospital, becomes apparent when we consider the reactions of nursing and medical staff to the changes in train in their hospitals.

Nursing reactions

The reactions of nurses to the new arrangements are mixed. Most welcome the information that becomes available following the introduction of casemix information systems, arguing that these will enable nurses for the first time to make visible the full extent of nursing's contribution to acute care provision. Among other matters included here is the further elaboration of patient classification systems which document patient dependency by DRG. The information which results will enable nurses to demonstrate the nursing workforce requirements (expressed in terms of numbers of nurses and skill mix) that result from reductions in the average length of stay (ALOS) by patients in acute care hospitals. Nurses point out that, in so far as improving the efficiency and effectiveness of hospital-based services brings about reductions in ALOS, it also increases the intensity of nursing work. As ALOS is reduced, the volume of patients receiving treatment increases along with their nursing dependency, which in turn should imply an increase in the nursing workforce. Nurses argue that past experience demonstrates that, in the absence of information about increased workloads, nursing resources will not be increased and nursing labour power will once again be exploited by 'medicine' and 'the administration'.

On a more positive note, nurses argue that the availability of casemix information improves the planning and co-ordination of nursing services to the benefit of both patient care and hospital efficiency. For example, information systems which make visible the number and skill mix of nursing resources that are required for particular DRGs will enable nursing management to allocate nursing resources to where they can be used to best effect. Clinical departments which are staffed according to the dependency levels of the patients they treat experience lower complication rates, reduced usage rates of diagnostic, therapeutic and ancillary services, improved co-ordination in the use of expensive equipment, and ultimately reduced lengths of stay. In a similar vein, other nursing studies have demonstrated how the availability of casemix information will enable critical review of existing work demarcations between nurses, allied health staff, clerical staff and doctors, and will expose where changes can and should be introduced to the benefit of both patient care and overall hospital efficiency.

Its positive response to the information-creating capacity of casemix methodologies is evidence of nursing's internal coherence and its emerging managerial and professional sophistication. These same factors, however, have caused nurses to oppose significant aspects of the organisation design that are being introduced into hospitals in the name of casemix management. Prior to the introduction of clinical matrix structures, the nursing division of each hospital was a highly structured professional bureaucracy with well-established traditions of nursing, holding its ground against encroachments by other blocs such as the administration or medicine. Nurses continue to be the only occupational group which provides a 24-hour clinical service to patients and which, through the controls that nurses exercise at ward level, organises and co-ordinates the full range of non-medical services that are entailed in patient treatment. In response to what is regarded as the targeting of nursing in past budget-cutting exercises, nursing divisions in hospitals developed their own budgeting, personnel and management information systems in ways which established and reinforced their independence from the administration and strengthened their bargaining position.

On a broader front, over the past ten years nurses have become much more articulate about their professional standing. The commencement of tertiary-level nurse education in 1983 has taken the profession out of the apprenticeship model which had limited its development. In the course of this process, an emerging generation of nurse academics is developing a rhetoric and body of knowledge for nursing which is independent of medical knowledge. In addition, the technical basis of nursing practice is being elaborated and to varying degrees now covers matters which were previously the sole preserve of doctors, such as nursing diagnosis, nursing acuity and dependency measures, nursing patient histories and nursing protocols.

Finally, up until the beginning of 1992, the capacity of nursing to protect and advance its interests was bolstered by what was termed the 'nursing shortage problem' – in other words, the exit of qualified nurses to other, more attractive forms of employment and the apparent inability of health authorities to recruit entrants into the profession. The nursing shortage, together with medicine's increasing dependence on a skilled nursing workforce, has done much to extend and reinforce nursing's industrial muscle, and the profession's willingness to flex this muscle is demonstrated in the increasing militancy of nursing unions.

When viewed against this background, the reactions of senior nurse managers, union officials and leaders of professional bodies to organisational proposals which give primacy of place to medically qualified directors of newly established clinical departments is hardly surprising. They argue that, at best, this arrangement places first-line nursing managers in the ambiguous position of having to answer to two sources of authority: their director of nursing and the medical director of their clinical unit. At worst, the new structure signals the beginning of the demise of the nursing division as an organisational force and as the primary professional reference point for hospital-based nurses.

Nurses consider that the realisation of either of these possibilities will reduce their capacity to compete for resources within the hospital, and that an already overburdened workforce will be further exploited. In addition, nurses take the view that the new structure provides managers and medical clinicians with means for undermining hard-won gains on professional and industrial fronts. The new structure, they claim, will re-establish medicine's dominance over nursing and provide doctors and administrative staff with both a rationale and means for questioning and ultimately negating nursing's emerging autonomy.

Professional and industrial nursing organisations are responding to the possibility of these developments on a number of fronts. Bodies such as the NSW Royal College of Nursing have held a number of public seminars, in the course of which the pros and cons of casemix management for nursing have been explored by eminent nurse academics and nurse administrators from within Australia and overseas. The College has also provided funds for documenting alternative organisational structures which would deliver the benefits of casemix management without reducing the professional and organisational standing of nursing. Professional educational activities such as these have been synchronised with more overtly political campaigns involving leaders of nursing unions and senior nurse managers. Included here are the widespread dissemination of a nursing perspective on narrowly management-focused casemix initiatives; work stoppages in individual hospitals; joint representations by the Royal College, senior nurse administrators and the union to the Department of Health and the minister's office; and ultimately, the threat of state-wide industrial action. To date the issue has not been resolved, but it can be expected that the final outcome will accommodate nursing concerns.

Medicine's response to casemix-based management

As with nursing, medicine's reactions to the new arrangements are mixed, although for significantly different reasons. In contrast to nurses, doctors on the whole welcome the move to establish clinical directorates as focal points for organising and managing the hospital. Among other outcomes, the new structure is seen by many doctors as providing an organisational basis for restoring their ultimate authority over what takes place in the diagnosis and treatment of patients. In addition, establishing clearly defined specialist clinical units, each with its own dedicated resources (including staff, beds and money), is seen by some specialities retained within the profession and that it should continue to be based solely on clinical criteria. Many clinicians go on to argue that a significant extension of clinician involvement in hospital management will embroil clinicians in ethical dilemmas which cannot be readily resolved as they attempt to mediate conflicts between the interests of the patients and organisational concerns such as resource management and cost containment. Furthermore, many clinicians take the view that a direct involvement in hospital management by clinicians is wasteful of scarce clinical resources and marks an unwarranted retreat from the much more skilled field of clinical practice by those clinicians who choose this career route.

In summary, a number of medical staff are interpreting their hospital's involvement in the casemix reform programme in terms of its likely effects on what they claim as their 'clinical freedom'. They take the view that attempts to utilise the supervisory and disciplining potential of CMMIS will need to be resisted. They further argue that utilising DRG performance targets in setting budgets for clinical departments (and the possibility that the subsequent performance of a clinical department will be assessed purely in quantitative terms) denies the significance for resource consumption of variations in patient severity. These doctors project that, as funds become more constrained, diagnosis/treatment protocols will not only be enforced but will become institutionalised – a development which ultimately will work to the detriment of both individual patients and the future development of medicine. Finally, the pursuit by clinician managers of a proactive approach to managing is being interpreted in some clinician circles as an unwarranted violation of the norms of collegiality and as potentially signalling a dangerous abrogation of authority.

When viewed in terms of medicine's demonstrated capacity to resist, thwart and undermine past reforms which cut across its interests, it is not surprising that heads of newly established clinical directorates are defining their new roles in terms which are much more limited than those projected by reformers. In this regard, most clinician-managers have concentrated on the resource acquisition potential of casemix management and have played down their medical supervision and accountability capacities. In justifying this stance, many directors express the view that the clinical and management information systems being introduced as yet lack the capacity claimed for them by their promoters, arguing that the information supplied is either inaccurate or not timely. Alternatively, some directors are of the opinion that the DRG methodology itself requires further refinement before it can be used in the way that reformers intend. Furthermore, they question the need to extend surveillance, and cite benefits that derive from existing accountability systems within their hospital and/or the profession.

Among others included here are existing approaches to utilisation reviews; peer reviews; medical audits; death reviews; tissue, infection control and drug reviews; patient satisfaction reviews; and quality assurance activity. These systems are presented as performing functions similar to those that would result from a fully developed CMMIS and as having the added advantage of not inviting wholesale opposition from medical staff. In addition many directors of clinical units share the misgivings of their medical colleagues about the effects that a wholesale adoption of casemix methodology would produce in both the collegiate structure of medicine and its internal coherence. The limitations that heads of clinical departments are placing on their newly assigned management responsibilities suggest that many of the accountability and internal efficiency and effectiveness issues which provided the initial motivation for developing casemix-based management will remain beyond critical review.

Discussion

The introduction of a casemix-based approach to hospital management has placed under threat significant aspects of the negotiated order which has characterised each of the participating hospitals. When viewed from a perspective which takes account of the full range of 'identities' (and related values, meanings and rules) that people in hospital settings can call on – in defining, organising and justifying their work; in staking their claim to resources; in advancing and protecting the standing of their profession; and in assigning responsibility and authority – it becomes clear that hospitals are much more than media for the production of patient treatment. For players with a stake in the game (i.e. nurses, doctors, local community bodies, unions, medical researchers), hospitals are arenas in which allocations of valued resources are routinely structured, contested and renegotiated. These players recognise that their capacity to influence these processes will be determined to a large degree by the hospital identities routinely accorded recognition. The players further recognise that preservation of identities which favour their interests and concerns will depend on the continued enactment of rules, settlements and agreements reached in past (often hard-fought) contests. It is not surprising, then, that reforms which erode and/or erase these are variously avoided, evaded and resisted.

The New South Wales experience with introducing casemix management mirrors what is occurring in other settings. Medicine's capacity to resist changes which threaten its place in the negotiated order of hospitals is well documented (Saltman and Young, 1981; Young and Saltman, 1983; Begun, 1985; Glandon and Morrisey, 1986; Flynn, 1992). More particularly, studies in Britain and the United States have also reported hesitancy on the part of clinician-managers to utilise the supervisory and disciplining potential of casemix management. For example, hospital managers in the United States are not fully utilising the controlling potential of the information systems that have been introduced into their hospitals in recent years, despite the evident potential of these systems for strengthening their position (Feinglass and Martin, 1990). In so far as the incorporation of a DRG methodology into the mechanism used to pay hospitals for services to Medicare patients has had any effects on management strategy in the United States, these have been concentrated largely on the revenue-raising side of a hospital's operation (Weiner *et al.*, 1987). In a similar vein, experience with resource management reforms in the United Kingdom suggests that heads of clinical departments are reluctant to subject their professional colleagues to the managerial prerogatives that have become available to them under the Griffith reform programme and/or by way of subsequent 'resource management' initiatives (Steele, 1985; Brooks, 1986; Harrison, 1988; Harrison and Schulz, 1989; Pollitt *et al.*, 1988; Ham and Hunter, 1988).

It is apparent, then, that the introduction of DRG-based management cannot be achieved by managerial fiat nor will implementation be achieved by outside experts authoritatively pronouncing new rules or promoting new ways of thinking and talking. As with attempts to introduce change in other organisational settings, the proposals are not compelling in themselves. Rather, the new arrangements and systems are being assessed by players in the game in terms of how they will advance or restrict the capacity of identifiable players to pursue interests, concerns and meanings particular to them. Under these circumstances, proposals for reform only have force to the extent that those who propound and promote them are able to establish coalitions of support behind them. (Degeling and Colebatch, 1984; Colebatch and Degeling, 1986; Dunphy and Stace, 1988).

These findings raise questions about the conceptual and practical adequacy of much of the implementation studies literature. As outlined in the introductory section of this chapter, the lines of debate between bottom-up and top-down perspectives are drawn largely by the interests and concerns that each side represents, and by the resulting differences in the organisation designs they each promote. Both the interests that are to be recognised and the organisation designs regarded as necessary for implementation are presented in either/or terms. But this preoccupation with organisation design is puzzling, particularly when account is taken of the antagonists' shared misgivings about the efficacy of past exercises in organisation design. For example, both agree that the formal authority structures of many organisations (presumably the product of past attempts at organisation design) cannot guarantee management's control over implementation.

Agreement on this point, however, has not led either side to question the cause–effect relationships that they impute, for example, to the future promulgation of top-down design principles. On the contrary, the beneficial and/or baleful outcomes variously attributed to the top-down approach reflect a prior assumption that the future design and promulgation of a set of rules and procedures is tantamount to their enactment. The large body of evidence which demonstrates the folly of this assumption transforms the top-down design principles into little more than a set of proverbs which are invoked as articles of faith. Alternatively, strict adherence to a bottom-up position entails not merely faith that service providers will not abuse their discretionary powers, but also subscription to the contradictory conclusions that hierarchy is determinate of action (viz. the pathologies) but at the same time will be circumvented (viz. emergent discretion).

The realisation that the design principles offered by either side do not satisfy the tenets of 'good science' (i.e. internal consistency and empirical support) does not, however, negate their significance in implementation. Rather, as with proverbs generally, it invites examination of both the conditions of their invocation and the effects that this produces. The conceptual basis for doing this is provided by the sociological literature which proceeds from an 'action' perspective (Silverman, 1971). This literature focuses, among other matters, on the contingent and contested make-up both of organisations and of the processes entailed in their constitution and maintenance. Examples of this approach include organisation as: an ensemble of relationships (Crozier and Friedberg, 1980); a negotiated order (Strauss *et al.*, 1963; Day and Day, 1977); a contested terrain (Perrow, 1979; Pfeffer, 1981; Pettigrew, 1973); and a mobilisation of identities (Colebatch and Degeling, 1986).

Within the 'action' perspective, the primary object of study becomes 'organising' rather than 'organisation'. Analysis proceeds from the conviction that the composition of organisations cannot be determined either by definition or simply by managerial direction. Rather, the structural composition of an organisation is the product of structuring and contest among a wide range of people, each seeking recognition for what are often disparate and contending interests and concerns. In highlighting the essentially political dimensions of organising, attention is given to the structuring effects of institutionalised frameworks of meaning, rules and values, that players either enact in taken-as-given ways or call on strategically in organising their relations with one another.

The institutionalised character of many of these frameworks of meaning renders them available to being read and mobilised as if they were 'texts'. The term 'texts' is used here as a heuristic device which, following Boland (1989), refers to the way that discourse, language and human action are intertwined and embedded in domains of social practice. Texts provide canons of interpretation that are supported by history, tradition and common usage and are regarded as true and compelling. Individual texts signify and authorise particular versions of what is real and complete, possible and permissible, and what is worthy of attention. In addition to providing legitimation for its version of the 'real', a text also provides a basis for finding other constructions erroneous, arbitrary and/or utopian. In this way, the strategic mobilisation of different texts contributes to structuring relationships and frames the focus of negotiation and bargaining.

Perhaps it is here that the significance of the design principles enunciated by the top-down and bottom-up approaches to implementation is to be found. Each perspective draws on a number of texts whose standing is generally taken as given. For example, the top-down perspective expresses values commonly associated with the so-called Westminister system of representative government. In so doing, it references and legitimates the authority and control over policy conventionally attributed to ministers and, by implication, their senior managers. Similarly, its espousal of a realist/objectivist view of the world draws support from the legitimacy attributed to instrumental science in industrial societies, which in turn justifies the top-down model's programmatic view of control. In combination, these attributes provide textual bases both for asserting the claims of hierarchy and for legitimating the rational/instrumental prescriptions offered to bolster hierarchy as the remedies for gaps in implementation (Dillon, 1976).

In contrast, the design principles espoused by the bottom-up perspective echo attributes commonly claimed for and by professions. These claims draw support from the taken-as-given and hence textual standing generally accorded to the ethical and disinterested application of licensed expert knowledge in resolving issues and problems which are inherently ambiguous and hence indeterminate. The values and meanings which underpin the authority and autonomy of professions are manifested not only in the ideology of profession, but also in legislation and in the organisational practices promoted for their governance, namely collegiality rather than hierarchy. As with the bottom-up perspective's faith in the man or woman on the spot, the resulting autonomy of professions is projected as guaranteeing their capacity to act ethically as champions of their clients.

When viewed in this way, the significance of positions staked out in the debate between bottom-up and top-down perspectives is found in the rationales and scope for action that their espousal provides for the contenders. Each perspective embodies and promotes a particular construction of interests and concerns which is projected as 'true and real'. In doing so, each perspective provides justifications for the dispositions of particular participants towards implementation and for denying the reality and truth status of others. Furthermore, in asserting the values and meanings which need to be embodied in implementation, each perspective, as a text, provides legitimation for its version of the structure of authority required to accomplish implementation and for questioning other versions. In this way, the strategic mobilisation of individual texts variously contributes to defining the issues and problems that are to be the focus of negotiation; framing the meanings and interests that are to be recognised; specifying the actors who can be involved and their relative standing; and authorising the rules which are to govern relationships between contestants and allies.

What is important here is that engagement in the top-down/ bottom-up debate is not restricted to students of implementation. Administrators and professionals are not inert objects of study; they are conscious of and articulate about the processes in which they are engaged, and have a practical interest in the 'realities' embodied in models offered as 'best-fit' solutions to implementation. Being aware of the multiple 'realities' that can be mobilised, they recognise that their room for manoeuvre will be a product of, among other matters, the texts variously taken as given or strategically mobilised in negotiating and bargaining. It is not surprising, then, that in organising their relationships with others they act to reinforce and/or mobilise texts which, given their positions and related interests and concerns, support and advance their construction of 'the real' and mitigate the structuring effects of alternative texts.

The structuring capacity of individual texts, however, is not determinate. The simultaneous mobilisation of multiple texts means that organising becomes an essentially dialectical process in which the determining capacity of individual texts is likely to be diffused. In the course of these processes, relationships might be 'restructured', though not necessarily changed, as the organisation (as product of structuring and contest) comes to exhibit institutional arrangements and practices which are loosely linked to what was proposed by the contestants. In Bourdieu's terms, the structuring of relations which results will be such that even those who are in a position of dominance 'cannot say, even with the advantage of hindsight, how the formula was found, and are astonished that institutions can exist as they do' (Bourdieu, 1981).

What is being suggested here resonates with Braybrooke and Lindblom's typification of the outcomes of policy as 'partisan, mutual adjustment' (1963). For example, the fact that clinicians, with some success, are resisting attempts to constitute management control over them does not mean that the reforms have had no effect. On the contrary, there is mounting evidence suggesting that clinicians are becoming more amenable to strengthening mechanisms for self-regulation. In part, these initiatives are motivated by a growing realisation that, if the profession does not act to elaborate and bolster its own regulatory mechanisms, it will have external regulations imposed on it. When seen in this light, the significance of promoting top-down structures and procedures comes to lie not in their direct enactment, but in the degree to which their promotion encourages other players to move from entrenched bargaining positions. In effect, by adopting a more instrumental and directive stance, players in central policy circles have influenced the expectations of many clinicians and encouraged them to adopt strategies which, while bolstering their claim to autonomy, also contribute to producing outcomes sought by central policy-makers.

But the adjustments which result from an attempt to restructure organisational relations are not restricted to outcomes which as desired end states, justified the changes that are being introduced by top management. As noted by Bourdieu (1981), restructuring often produces unforeseen outcomes. For example, while the primary rationale for introducing casemix management was to increase medical accountability, its effects are registered most immediately in its impact on nursing. Significantly, managing the politics that the challenge to nursing occasioned has been a major preoccupation of senior management in both the participating hospitals.

However, in addition to readily observable but unintended effects such as these, others are likely to derive from the reform programme dependence on accounting, operations research and economics and systems analysis. Utilisation of these disciplines is neither neutral nor benign. Each constitutes the world using a vocabularly of economic/financial numbers whose use in mapping service provision empties out other values and meanings and leads to services being defined solely in terms of their resource implications. More particularly, defining services to patients as products which, depending on their resource usage patterns, are grouped into product lines (DRGs) calls into play other modes of signification, namely the hospital as a multi-product firm that requires product/market-focused management for its survival. Not only does the incorporation of this mode of signification into the fabric of health care delivery deny the social and subjective dimensions of care provision, it also has the capacity to displace the significance of social and economic causation of disease (Chua and Degeling, 1991).

Moreover, the resulting commodification of health care makes permissible and possible the reconstitution of health care delivery along market lines. The coincidence of resort to the market as a solution to health care organisation in both Britain and Australia, and the increasing colonisation of health care by accounting and economic discourses, is not only noteworthy in its own right, but also demonstrates how constituting medical accountability in financial terms may produce outcomes well beyond those canvassed by the proponents of the top-down and bottom-up perspectives.

References

Alford, R. R. (1975) *Health Care Politics: Ideological and interest group barriers to reform*, Chicago, Ill., and London: University of Chicago Press.

Australia (1974): Hospitals and Health Services Commission, *A Report on Hospitals in Australia*, Canberra: AGPS.

Australia (1981): Commission of Inquiry into the Efficiency and Administration of Hospials (Chairperson, J. H. Jamison) *Final Report*, Vols 1–3, Canberra: AGPS.

Australia (1984): Committee of Inquiry into Rights of Private Practice in Public Hospitals (Chairperson, D. Pennington) *Final Report*, Canberra: AGPS.

Australia (1985): Commonwealth Parliamentary Public Accounts Committee Report (Chairperson Sen. G. Georges), Canberra: AGPS.

Bates, E., and H. Lapsley (1985) *The Health Machine: The impact of medical technology*, Ringwood, Melbourne: Penguin.

Begun, J. W. (1985) 'Managing with professionals in a changing health care environment', *Medical Care Review*, 42(1), pp. 3–10.

Boland, R. (1989) 'Beyond the objectivist and the subjectivist: learning to read accounting as text', *Accounting, Organisations and Society*, 14(5–6), pp. 591–604.

Bourdieu, P. (1981) 'Men and machines', in K. Knorr-Cetina and A. V. Cicourel (eds), *Advances in Social Theory and Methodology*, London: Routledge and Kegan Paul.

Braybrooke, D., and C. E. Lindblom (1963) *A Strategy of Decisions*, New York: Free Press.

Brooks, R. (ed.) (1986) *Management Budgeting in the NHS*, Keele Health Services Manpower Review.

Chua, W. F., and P. J. Degeling (1991) 'Information technology and accounting in the accomplishment of public policy: a cautionary tale', *Accounting Management and Information Technologies*, 1(2), pp. 109–39.

Colebatch, H. K., and P. J. Degeling (1986) 'Talking and doing in the work of administration', *Public Administration and Development*, 6, pp. 339–56.

Crichton, A. (1990) *Slowly Taking Control? Australian governments and health care provision, 1788–1988*, Sydney: Allen and Unwin.

Crozier, M., and E. Friedberg (1980) *Actors and Systems: The politics of collective action*, London: University of Chicago Press.

Daniel, A. (1990) *Medicine and the State: Professional autonomy and public accountability*, Sydney: Allen and Unwin.

Day, R., and J. Day (1977) 'A review of the current state of negotiated order theory: an appreciation and a critique', in J. K. Benson (ed.), *Organisational Analysis: Critique and innovation*, London: Sage.

Degeling, P. J., and H. K. Colebatch (1984) 'Structure and action as constructs in the practice of public administration', *Australian Journal of Public Administration*, 43(4), pp. 320–31.

Dillon, G. M. (1976) 'Policy and dramaturgy: a critique of current conceptions of policy making', *Policy and Politics*, 5(5), pp. 47–62.

Dror, Y. (1968) *Public Policy-Making Re-Examined*, San Francisco, Calif: Chandler.

Dunphy, D. C., and D. J. Stace (1988) 'Transformational and coercive strategies for planned organisational change: beyond the OD model', *Organisation Studies*, 9, pp. 317–34.

Elmore, R. F. (1978) 'Organisational models of social program implementation', *Public Policy*, 26(2), pp. 185–228.

Elmore, R. F. (1979–80) 'Backward mapping: implementation research and policy decisions', *Political Science Quarterly*, 94(4), pp. 601–16.

Feinglass, J., and G. J. Marru (1990) 'The Financial impact of physician practice style on hospital resource use', Unpublished working paper, Centre for Health Services Research and Policy, Northwestern University.

Feinglass, J., and J. W. Salmon (1990) 'Corporatization of medicine: the use of medical management information systems to increase the clinical productivity of physicians', *International Journal of Health Sciences*, 20, pp. 233–52.

Fetter, R. B., and J. L. Freeman (1986) 'Diagnosis related groups: product line management for hospitals;, *Academy of Management Review*, 11(1), pp. 41–54.

Fetter, R. B., and J. L. Freeman (1985) 'Diagnosis related groups: a product oriented approach to hospital management', in R. B. Fetter, J. D. Thompson and J. R. Kimberley (eds), *Cases in Health Policy and Management*, Homewood, Ill.: Richard D. Irwin, Inc.

Fetter, R. B., and H. Hines (1988) 'The management of hospitals under prospective payment', *Second International Conference on the Management and Financing of Hospital Services*, Sydney, 18–20 February, p. 147.

Friedson, E. (1970a) *Profession of Medicine: A study of the sociology of applied knowledge*, New York: Harper and Row.

Friedson, E. (1970b) *Professional Dominance: The social structure of health care*, Chicago, Ill.: Aldine.

Friedson, E. (1986) *Professional Powers: A study of the institutionalisation of formal knowledge*, Chicago, Ill.: University of Chicago Press.

Gardner, H. (ed.) (1989) *The Politics of Health: The Australian experience*, Melbourne: Churchill Livingstone.

Glandon, G. L., and M. A. Morrisey (1986) 'Redefining the hospital – physician relationship under prospective payment' *Inquiry*, 23(2) pp. 166–75.

Grant, C., and H. Lapsley (1989) *The Australian Health Care System, 1988*, Australian Studies in Health Service Administration, Kensington: University of New South Wales.

Ham, C., and D. J. Hunter (1988) *Managing Clinical Activity in the NHS*, London,: Kings Fund Institute.

Hanf, K., B. Hjern and D. O. Porter (1978) 'Local networks of manpower training in the Federal Republic of Germany and Sweden' in K. Hanf and F. W. Scharpf (eds), *Interorganizational Policy Making*, Beverly Hills, Calif., and London,: Sage.

Harrison, S. (1988) *Managing the NHS*, London,: Chapman and Hall.

Harrison, S., and R. I. Schulz (1989) 'Clinical autonomy in the UK and the US', in G. Freddi and J. W. Bjorkman (eds), *Controlling Medical Professionals*, London: Sage.

Hjern, B., and D. O. Porter (1981) 'Implementation structures: a new unit of administrative analysis', *Organisation Studies*, 2(3), pp. 211–27.

Hogwood, B. W., and L. A. Gunn (1984) *Policy Analysis for the Real World*, Oxford,: Oxford University Press.

Linder, S. H. and G. Peters (1987) 'A design perspective on policy implementation: the fallacies of misplaced prescription', *Policy Studies Review*, 6(3), pp. 459–74.

Lipsky, M. (1971) 'Street-level bureaucracy and the analysis of urban reform', *Urban Affairs Quarterly*, 6(4), pp. 391–409.

Lipsky, M. (1976) 'Towards a theory of street-level bureaucracy', in W. D. Hawley and M. Lipsky (eds.), *Theoretical Perspectives on Urban Politics*, Englewood Cliffs, NJ: Prentice Hall.

McMahon, L. F., R. B. Fetter, J. L. Freeman and J. D. Thompson (1986) 'Hospital matrix management and DRG-based prospective payment', *Hospital and Health Service Administration*, 31, pp. 62–74.

McMahon, L. F. and R. Newbold (1986) 'Variation in resource use within diagnosis-related groups: the effect of severity of illness and physician practice', *Medical Care*, 24, pp. 388–97.

Mechanic, D. (1986) *From Advocacy to Allocation: The evolving American health care system*, New York: Free Press.

Mooney, G. (1986) *Economics, Medicine and Health Care*, Brighton.: Wheatsheaf.

Palmer, G. R. (1986) 'The economics of financing hospitals in Australia', *Australian Economic Review*, 3, pp. 60–72.

Palmer, G. R., and S. Short (1989) *Health Care and Public Policy: An Australian analysis*, Melbourne: Macmillan.

Perrow, C. (1979) *Complex Organisations: A critical essay*, New York: Random House.

Pettigrew, A. M. (1973) *The Politics of Organisational Decision Making*, London: Tavistock.

Pfeffer, J. (1981) *Power in Organisations*, Boston, Mass.: Pitman.

Pollitt, C., S. Harrison, D. Hunter and G. Marnoch (1988) 'The reluctant managers: clinicians and budgets in the NHS', *Financial Accountability and Management*, 4(3), pp. 213–33.

Pressman, J. L., A. Wildavsky (1973) *Implementation: How great expectations in Washington are dashed in Oakland*, Berkeley, Calif.: University of California Press.

Prottas, J. M. (1978) 'The power of street level bureaucrat in public service bureaucracies', *Urban Affairs Quarterly*, 13(3), pp. 285–312.

Prottas, J. M. (1979) *People Processing: The street level bureaucrat in public service bureaucracies*, Lexington, Mass.: D. C. Heath.

Sabatier, P. A. (1986a) 'Top-down and bottom-up approaches to implementation research: a critical analysis and suggested synthesis', *Journal of Public Policy*, 6(1), pp. 21–48.

Sabatier, P. A. (1986b) 'What can we learn from implementation research?' in K. Kaufmann, G. Majone and V. Ostrom (eds), *Guidance, Control and Evaluation in the Public Sector*, Berlin: Walter de Gruyter.

Sabatier, P., and D. Mazmanian (1980a) 'The conditions for effective implementation: a guide to accomplishing policy objectives', *Policy Analysis*, 5(4), pp. 481–504.

Sabatier, P., and D. Mazmanian (1980b) 'The implementation of public policy: a framework for analysis', *Policy Studies Journal*, 8(4), pp. 538–60.

Saltman, R. B., and D. W. Young (1981) 'The hospital power equilibrium: an alternative view of the cost containment dilemma', *Journal of Health Politics, Policy and Law*, 6(3), pp. 391–418.

Sax, S. (1984) *A Strife of Interests: Politics and policies in Australian health services*, Sydney: Allen and Unwin.

Silverman, D. (1971) *The Theory of Organisations*, London: Heinemann Educational Books.

Starr, P. (1982) *The Social Transformation of American Medicine*, New York: Basic Books.

Steele, R. (1985) 'Clinical budgeting and costing', in *NHS Management Perspectives for Doctors*, King Edward's Hospital Fund for London.

Strauss, A. L., L. Schatzman, K. Bucher, D. Erlich and M. Sabschin (1983), 'The hospital and its negotiated order' in E. Freidson (ed.), *The Hospital in Modern Society*, Glencoe, Ill.: Free Press.

Thompson, J. D., R. B. Fetter and C. Mross (1975) 'Casemix and resource use', *Inquiry*, pp. 43–9.

Van Horn, C. E., and D. S. Van Meter (1976) 'The implementation of intergovernmental policy', in C. O. Jones and R. D. Thomas (eds.), *Public Policy Making in a Federal System*, Beverly Hills, Calif.: Sage.

Van Meter, D. S., and C. E. Van Horn (1975) 'The policy implementation process: a conceptual framework', *Administration and Society*, 6(4), pp. 446–88.

Weatherley, R., and M. Lipsky (1977) 'Street-level bureaucrats and institutional innovation: implementing special-education reform,' *Harvard Educational Review*, 47(2), pp. 171–97.

Weiner, S. L., J. H. Maxwell, H. M. Sapolsky, H. M. Dunn and W. C. Hsaio (1987), 'Economic incentives and organisational realities: managing hospitals under DRGs', *Milbank Quarterly*, 64(4), pp. 463–87.

Wennberg, J. E., J. P. Bunker and B. Barnes (1980), 'The need for assessing the outcome of common medical practices', *Annual Review of Public Health*, 1, pp. 277–95.

Willis, E. (1989) *Medical Dominance: The division of labour in Australian health care*, Sydney and London: Allen and Unwin.

Yodor, J. L., and R. A. Connor (1982) 'Diagnosis related groups and management', *Topics in Health Care Financing*, Summer, pp. 29–42.

Young, D. W., and R. B. Saltman (1983) 'Prospective reimbursement and the hospital power equilibrium: a matrix-based management control system', *Inquiry*, 20(1), pp. 20–3.

CHAPTER 3

Restructuring health systems: a comparative analysis of England and the Netherlands

Rob Flynn

This chapter discusses the implementation of policies of restructuring in the Dutch and English health systems. First, some basic conceptual issues about the nature of restructuring, about policy implementation and about comparative analysis are considered. The chapter then reviews substantive material about the characteristics of major changes in the financing, planning and provision of medical services in the Netherlands and in the English National Health Service. Finally, some general observations are made about the implications of cross-national studies of policy implementation.

Restructuring

The term 'restructuring' is used here not as a simple synonym for reorganisation in administrative structures and decision-making procedures, but to indicate much broader shifts in underlying objectives, institutional arrangements and working practices. Reorganisations may reallocate existing roles and functions among different agencies while preserving established goals and values. They are commonplace occurrences within commercial enterprises and the public sector as methods of reacting to perceived changes in the internal and external organisational environment.

Here 'restructuring' in the public sector is used to refer to the creation of new roles and functions, ultimately reflecting fundamental changes in ideology about the nature of state–society relations, and the scope of government intervention. It therefore implies a significant modification (or reinterpretation) of goals and values, a concomitant redefinition of agencies' purposes and responsibilities, and the creation of new patterns of inter- and intra-organisational relationships. While reorganisation might involve some changes in relationships of authority and power between interdependent agencies, restructuring requires a radical redistribution of power, and a realignment of interests. Restructuring is thus not mere reform; it is rather (in Kuhnian terms) a 'paradigm-shift' affecting, indeed altering, the entire system of policy making and implementation.

Various writers have described restructuring as: changes in the composition of welfare state expenditure and functions (Robinson, 1986); economic and industrial change associated with 'disorganised capitalism' leading to transformations in the social structure (Lash and Urry, 1987); a series of interrelated changes in the economy, culture and the state (Hamnett *et al.*, 1989); as a new type of government ('the contract state') and a new form of policy making (Dunsire and Hood, 1989); and as a post-Fordist modernisation process (Hoggett, 1990). Here 'restructuring' refers to systemic and societal change in general, but also includes alterations in the goals, apparatus and processes of public policy making.

This immediately raises the difficult question of assessing whether reforms are 'really' fundamental, whether they actually bring about distinctively new forms of policy making and lead to significant changes in practice. This will be a matter for empirical enquiry, and there will inevitably be theoretical debate about whether there have been profound changes, and about the relevance of alternative causal factors. In the first instance, researchers do not have to rely on a priori assumptions that 'real' restructuring (rather than incremental reform) is taking place, because there will be sufficient evidence already available to indicate that extraordinary changes are under way. This is likely to be reinforced by ideological claims by protagonists that current events and future plans constitute a transformation in previously established tasks, objectives and regimes (cf. Degeling's stress on the mobilisation of interests around 'texts' and rationales for implementation: see Chapter 2).

The other important question raised is whether, given that restructuring comprises an all-embracing and systemic set of interrelated changes, it is methodologically necessary to investigate restructuring *tout ensemble*. Of course, it is unrealistic to claim that it is possible to provide a complete analysis of restructuring – just as it is impractical to attempt a wholly comprehensive analysis of a discrete policy system. What *is* possible, though, is to concentrate on key elements and strategic issues, and to examine selectively important changes in the arena of policy making and their implications for different groups and interests.

Restructuring within any policy sector is therefore of particular relevance to analysts of implementation, precisely because it consists of the reconstruction of institutional relationships and activities, oriented towards new priorities and objectives. It remains to be seen whether the implementation of restructuring is inherently different from any other type of policy implementation process. For present purposes it is sufficient to note that it constitutes an important and interesting example of large-scale policy making and implementation (in Hupe's terms, following Dror, a 'meta-policy': Hupe, 1990), and one which, because of its putative all-inclusiveness demands close scrutiny.

Policy implementation

In studying public policy, and comparing different national systems, basic assumptions must be made about the nature of 'policy' and 'implementation'. It is impossible to pursue this in any depth here, but it is argued that the most appropriate and realistic approach to such questions rejects consensual, formal/legal-rational and mechanistic models of organisational decision making. Instead, organisational goals and policies are regarded as contingent outcomes of bargaining and conflict among competing groups and coalitions.

Authoritative decisions to pursue specific objectives can be pragmatically taken as indicators of policy intentions, but they are in themselves often ambiguous, even contradictory, and frequently contested. Non-élite organisational members (and by extension, hierarchically subordinate agencies), through their everyday activities and variable degrees of regulated discretion, may create policy too. This may co-exist with, modify or perhaps subvert the commands or requirements of superordinates.

To an unknown extent, particular issues and options may be pre-empted or taken for granted as impermissible: action as well as non-action reflects the constraints of structurally embedded values and interests. 'Policy' exists in the everyday working assumptions and operating procedures of established custom and practice. Moreover, despite appearances, and formal as well as commonsensical claims to the contrary, policy and implementation are not separate categories, nor phases in a linear sequence. Rather, they are emergent properties – problematic, more or less open to dispute and negotiation, depending on the mobilisation of resources and the differential capacity of actors to secure relative autonomy, and to exercise influence.

Here, then, we are following the 'processual' or 'action' approach to policy implementation promoted by Barrett and Fudge (1981), Ham (1980), Ham and Hill (1984), Ham (1981) and others. It includes (or perhaps is subsumed by) radical organisational theory which argues that all organisations, as assemblages of practices and reifications of interests, are simultaneously the object and the result of social struggle, and are the embodiment of power relations (Clegg, 1989a, 1989b). Consequently, policy and implementation, like organisations, are 'locales of politics' in which control, among all actors and at all levels, is contested in varying ways.

The major difficulty is how to move beyond these metaphors, and operationalise this approach in empirical research. One severe problem is in specifying the boundaries of inquiry: in investigating a particular type of policy, must we examine *all* aspects of policy determinants, content and outcomes, and must we include *all* possible actors and agencies? Selective case studies risk accusations of being unrepresentative and incomplete; they also raise the spectre of all investigations of the use of power – the problem of infinite regress. Further, most writers stress the necessity to move beyond simple [*sic*] description, to connect organisational decision making with 'structural interests', and to link different levels of analysis. How this is to be accomplished remains unclear.

The inherent complexity of the processes seems to defy the possibility of a single, overarching theory, but in the meantime it also presents formidable obstacles to empirical work. Perhaps we should not be surprised to learn that:

> there is no theory of implementation that commands general agreement: researchers continue to work from diverse theoretical perspectives and to employ different variables to make sense of their findings . . . Implementation researchers are not in agreement about what constitutes the subject of their inquiry . . . [There is] a welter of views concerning the principal components and the operation of the implementation process itself. (O'Toole, 1986, pp. 182–3)

More positively, O'Toole has argued that theoretical advances are possible by using concepts such as 'implementation structures' (Hjern and Porter, 1981), by attempting to synthesise so-called top-down and bottom-up perspectives, and by drawing eclectically on a variety of concepts from different disciplines to understand 'multi-actor systems'. This merely echoes much earlier exhortations simultaneously to document actors' assumptive worlds and discretionary decision making *and* to examine the content and operation of policy within and between organisations *and* to locate these processes within a broader analysis of the state and structures of power (Ham and Hill, 1984).

However, in the absence (and improbability) of a coherent, integrated and universal theory which can account for all types of action/non-action, which explicates the relation between structural constraints and individual discretion, and which unravels the linkages between agencies and institutions at different levels, we must be more modest and pragmatic. Our studies might aspire to discover the conceptual and methodological Holy Grail of comprehensiveness, but it is probable that our endeavours will be very limited, partial and provisional. That this is so need not be regarded as a failure, because ultimately these questions about the interdependence of levels bedevil *all* sociological (and social scientific) theory: they concern the relation between human action and social structure, what Giddens has referred to as a paradoxical duality, a dialectic of power and control which is intrinsically contingent and indeterminate (Giddens, 1979, 1982; see also Alford and Friedland, 1985).

Comparative analysis

Given that there are these unresolved theoretical difficulties in studying even one policy sector within one society, it is inevitable that there will be further problems when undertaking *comparative* analysis of policy implementation cross-nationally. It is well known that, quite apart from the availability of data, there are always difficulties in 'standardising' units for comparison, in determining whether apparently similarly described organisations and services, for example, actually share common features, and in deciding whether particular features are culturally specific, and if so, why. Descriptions of institutions and occupations in two or more countries (for example, hospitals and doctors) may appear identical, but the organisation of production and system of resourcing and remuneration may mean that their power and significance is very varied. Policies (and policy processes) which superficially seem similar may have quite different meanings and consequences in different societies.

Nevertheless, as Higgins (1981, 1986) has pointed out, all genuinely social scientific explanations entail comparison, and comparative analysis is essential in order to avoid 'ethnocentrism' in theory and practice. If we seek to make generalisations, we must search for comparisons and validation from many cases; if we are looking for alternative (or improved) ways of accomplishing certain tasks, we must consider a wide range of options. Notwithstanding the methodological obstacles, comparative research is worthwhile and necessary to make our theories robust; the realistic solution is to be as rigorous as possible, given the limitations, and to be cautious in interpreting findings.

Comparative social policy as a field of intellectual inquiry has expanded rapidly in the last decade, and comparative analysis of health systems has been an area of special growth. Widespread concern with securing continually improving standards of health and, associated with this, anxiety about rising costs in all developed economies have been instrumental in stimulating much academic work using international comparisons (see, for example, OECD, 1987; Maxwell, 1981; Raffel, 1984; Schieber and Poullier, 1987; Schieber *et al.*, 1991).

However, there have been some doubts about the value of some of this literature, in relation to the gross simplifications which tend to emerge, the validity of data and the lack of a body of theory (Atteveld *et al.*, 1987). Wilensky and his colleagues (1987) have been highly critical, arguing that most of the available studies are too descriptive and not analytical, and that little progress has been made in explaining cross-cultural variation in health care provision. Wilensky *et al.* suggest that there needs to be 'systematic evaluation of how various institutional structures shape the degree of government involvement in health care provision' (p. 418), and recommend that comparative research should 'examine the ways in which similarities and divergences in institutional context and structural forces explain variations in health policy, health systems, and their effects on real health' (p. 422).

This suggestion provides a convincing rationale for pursuing cross-national studies of the organisation of health care systems, but again there are further caveats to be noted about undertaking analysis of the health policy sector.

Analysing health policy implementation

There are innumerable studies of many different aspects of health service organisation and health policies. In the British social scientific literature, health economics, political science and medical sociology have all been very prolific in their investigations of the workings of the National Health Service (NHS). However, it is probably correct to observe that most 'policy analysis' has been informed by those working within a political science and/or public administration tradition (one classic study is Klein (1983)). What is noticeable about most of the outstanding recent studies is the frequent repetition of the need to integrate descriptions of decision making with analyses of power relations, and an implicit recognition that, to date, our research has not yielded such integration.

A decade ago, Ham (one of the leading British scholars in this field) noted that there had been few attempts to understand health policy from what he termed a 'policy analysis perspective', and that there was a need for a multi-disciplinary approach to understanding the 'black box' of policy implementation, linking actors' beliefs and actions with the overall distribution of power (Ham, 1981). Haywood (1983) emphasised the importance of bargaining and organisational politics in policy processes, and stressed the necessity to recognise conflict and the use of power as normal rather than pathological (see Haywood and Aleszewski, 1980; Lee and Mills, 1982). Later, Ham (1985) was critical of descriptive studies which did not account for how policies developed and who influenced what was decided; he castigated studies of single issues, single organisations and single levels of policy making as deficient. Thus, in his view:

> there is a gulf between writers who concentrate on the detailed processes of decision-making in health care organisations and those who direct their attention to the role of the state and its implications for health services. Very rarely are the two levels of analysis combined . . . there is a need to relate micro theories of the policy process to macro theories of the state. (Ham, 1985, p. 2)

More recently, Harrison and his colleagues (1990) adopted a 'bargaining' model in explaining the dynamics of British health policy, and attempted to focus explicitly on the structure of power relations by combining neo-élite and neo-Marxist theories. However, they acknowledged that (as other writers such as Ham and Hill have argued previously), policy cannot be explained in terms of any *one* theory, and that different theories are appropriate for different levels of analysis. Most importantly, they concluded that there is little consensus about how to use and operationalise such hierarchically ordered sets of theories.

Similarly, in a review of British medical sociology (a subdiscipline which encompasses epidemiology, studies of the phenomenology of health and illness, ethnographic accounts of doctor–patient interactions, and studies of professional knowledge and power (see Turner, 1987)), Hunter (1990) argued for more sociological research on the policy process. In particular he suggested that sociologists should concentrate on the organisation and management of health services if we are to obtain a better understanding of the impact of provider discretion and resource use in health care. Again, he too noted that no single social science discipline was sufficient (because policy analysis requires multidisciplinary responses), and he advocated research of the 'middle-range type' to bridge the gap between existing approaches.

Thus there is convergence about themes and problems associated with analysing health policy implementation. But despite this consensus, there does not seem to be any obvious agreement as to *how* this coherent, integrated, multi-level explanation is to be achieved. It remains an elusive ideal-type: its importance and value is that it can serve as a reference point for our research and theory.

It therefore seems reasonable to argue that, although *comparative* health policy analysis should strive towards meeting these intellectual objectives, in practice there may be profound problems in devising empirically grounded explanations of cross-national patterns. In comparing the implementation of health policies in different societies it may be impossible to conduct research or obtain secondary data for all 'levels' or all relevant actors, and logistic and resource constraints make original fieldwork even more difficult than usual. How, then, can comparative health policy analysis proceed? Altenstetter and Bjorkman (1981, p. 29) have suggested that 'comparative studies . . . of the implementation of health plans start by mapping actors, structures, and the contextual environments as preconditions for generalisations'. The remainder of this chapter is one attempt to begin such an exercise, looking at the institutional context within which the restructuring of health services has occurred in England and the Netherlands.

Health care has been absorbing growing proportions of economic resources in most countries. Advances in medical treatment and technology, increases in the proportion of elderly people in the population and general increases in demand have led to increased costs. The economic crisis of the 1970s and subsequent recession led to a fiscal crisis in western welfare states and government attempts to reduce public expenditure. Retrenchment and cost control in health care systems became a central objective for many governments, and there have been widespread efforts to reform and reorganise the financing and delivery of health care services, particularly in the intramural (hospital) sector. In England and the Netherlands, more far-reaching attempts have been made to restructure their health systems.

During the 1980s, the process of restructuring consisted of four interrelated elements. First, programmes of measures to control and reduce costs, and to improve cost efficiency, were introduced in both countries. Second, there have been parallel developments in central government interventions in planning and finance. Third, there have been similar moves to restrict the degree of influence enjoyed by medical professionals. Finally, in both countries there has been a major shift in policy towards the creation of a market system of regulated competition among health service providers. The next sections give a brief overview of these interconnected trends.

Cost containment

It has been argued that cost containment and cut-backs are easier to implement, and are more effective, in centralised public systems like the National Health Service (NHS) in England, and conversely more difficult and less effective in fragmented and mixed systems like that in the Netherlands (see Abel-Smith, 1984; Maxwell, 1981). In the former, health care is comprehensive, universal, free at the point of consumption and funded out of general taxation, with predominantly state ownership of facilities and state employment of medical and nursing staff. In the latter, 'social insurance' model, there is compulsory social insurance paid by employers and employees through non-profit sick funds for groups below a specific income level, and private insurance for those above that level. The funding and provision of health services takes place through a mixture of private (non-profit) institutions, with government regulation. Expenditure in both countries is very high, and increased rapidly until the mid-1980s: in 1983 total health spending comprised 8.6 per cent of GDP in the Netherlands, and 5.9 per cent in the UK (OECD, 1987; Schieber *et al.*, 1991). However, recently, governments in both countries have taken various measures to reduce the rate of growth, restrict supply and demand, and improve efficiency.

Space prevents a detailed description of the retrenchment policies pursued, and they have been analysed extensively elsewhere (Flynn and Simonis, 1990). However, there are five key areas affecting the supply of medical services where virtually identical measures were adopted in the NHS and in the Netherlands. For example, capital developments – investment in new buildings and equipment – have been stringently controlled and limited by central government. Various directives and financial mechanisms have been used to regulate the distribution and volume of new facilities, especially in the acute hospital sector.

Second, there has been a common adoption of so-called efficiency savings – introduced in 1981 in the NHS, and 1984 in the Netherlands. These comprised a variety of methods to improve productivity and reduce operating costs in all spheres of medical and non-clinical activity – for example, rationalisation of hospital units, changes in the employment, wages and conditions of ancillary staff, privatisation of certain functions, and improvements in the use of energy and estate.

Third, there have been deliberate and substantial reductions in the number of hospital beds. In England, there have been large annual declines in the number of hospital beds (40,000 between 1980 and 1986) due to several reasons (and partly compensated for by increased throughput of patients). But it is widely known that recent underfunding compelled many health authorities to close beds, wards and some clinical units, solely in order to remain within cash-limited budgets. Since the early 1980s, Dutch governments have tried to impose compulsory bed reductions (one plan required a reduction of 8,000 beds in the period 1982–9), but there have been widescale disagreements among hospitals, sick funds, provinces and the central health ministry about how these can be achieved. Despite bargaining over financial incentives, these bed and cost reduction targets have not yet been fully met.

Fourth, there have been similar measures to limit the supply of high-technology medicine, and attempts to regulate the numbers and remuneration of medical and nursing personnel. This has been more 'successful' in the centralised NHS than in the Dutch health system.

Finally, there have been similar attempts to control clinical costs in hospitals by introducing cash-limited prospective budgets. In the Netherlands this represented a major departure from the former 'open-ended' regime, in which insurers were obliged to reimburse doctors and hospitals for treatments provided. Complex budgeting procedures were introduced in 1983, and now an elaborate system of calculating prices, tariffs and production agreements involving hospitals, the insurers and central regulatory bodies is in place. In the NHS, control over local budgets has always been highly bureaucratised and centralised. Despite this, chronic 'overspending' continued, leading to annual budget crises in many authorities. Since 1983 several different schemes have been tried to increase central control over local expenditure, and measures have been introduced to make clinicians directly responsible for resource use.

When comparing retrenchment in the Netherlands and England it is apparent that, although they have very different organisational and financial structures, similar goals and strategies have been pursued. It is also evident (though not possible to document here) that, because of more complex arrangements for planning, finance and service delivery in the Dutch system, cost control and cut-backs were more difficult to accomplish there than in the NHS (see Ham *et al.*, 1990).

The paradox of centralisation

In the Netherlands, responsibility for financing, planning and delivering health services is dispersed among a number of different institutions within a corporatist framework. In the view of successive Dutch governments this has resulted in excessive costs, excess capacity and lack of co-ordination. The most recent remedy is simplification of the bureaucracy, and increased competition between insurers, general practitioners and hospitals. In the English NHS there has been (until recently) a highly centralised, hierarchical structure in which the government decided policy and resource allocation, and determined capacity through strict cash limits. In response to widespread political concern about 'underfunding' and cut-backs, the Thatcher and Major governments introduced market mechanisms in the provision (but so far not the funding) of services, to obtain better cost effectiveness and quality from the general practitioners, hospital specialists and local health authorities (see Day and Klein, 1991).

Recently in both countries there has been a fundamental questioning of existing arrangements for the funding and provision of health care. Some of the impetus for this reappraisal has come from changes in the nature and volume of medical needs, and changes in the pattern of care, but much of the pressure for reform has originated in political demands for enhanced efficiency in the use of resources as well as government determination to control (or reduce) expenditure.

Throughout the 1970s and 1980s, in both the Netherlands and England, there were very similar debates about the need for greater planning and co-ordination, and frequent attempts to improve administrative, budgeting and management structures.

One major concern has been the redistribution of functions (and balance of power) between various levels of government and health care agencies and providers. Faced with rising unemployment, budget deficits and inflation, right-of-centre coalitions in the Netherlands embarked on economic and social policies which were very similar to Thatcherism in Britain. In the 1980s there have been complete reassessments of government functions, reorganisation of state services, privatisation measures, deregulation, decentralisation and retrenchment across the entire range of welfare (see Brenton, 1982; Flynn, 1986; Hupe, 1990, and this volume, Chapter 6; Idenburg, 1985; Sociaal en Cultureel Planbureau, 1984, 1986; Venema and Verbaan, 1984).

The role played by government in health policy, finance and provision is different in the two countries, and this has affected the degree to which centralisation and decentralisation have been attempted. Historically, both the financing and provision of health care in the Netherlands have been carried out by private voluntary associations, reflecting the influence of political, religious and social 'pillarisation' in Dutch society. There is no national health service provided by the state. All citizens are required to belong to a health insurance scheme: 62 per cent of the population belong to the social insurance system, and 38 per cent (higher income-earners) belong to private (for-profit and non-profit) insurance schemes. Primary and hospital medical treatment is provided by independent practitioners and hospitals are owned and managed by private non-profit, non-governmental bodies. Medical professionals and hospitals have contracts with different sick funds and private insurers, and their tariffs are negotiated centrally through national bodies, within government financial guidelines. The planning of facilities (and levels of provision) is supposed to be co-ordinated by provincial (regional) and municipal authorities, but this has been ineffective because of the plurality and independence of providers and financiers.

As in other policy sectors, health care is financed and delivered through so-called 'private initiative' institutions – most notably the sick funds. These enjoy considerable legal and political autonomy, and are subject to only a loose and indirect form of central regulation, organised through a complex *corporatist* framework (see Baakman *et al.*, 1989). The Dutch government became acutely concerned about the apparent uncontrolled growth in health expenditure during the 1970s, and voiced particular criticisms of the lack of planning in health service facilities. As a result, there have been a series of moves which represented a major modification in the degree of central intervention (Simonis *et al.*, 1988).

One crucial development was the 1974 government memorandum (Structuurnota Gezondheidszorg) about the structure of health services and the role of private institutions *vis-à-vis* central and local government. New mechanisms to influence the supply, financing and costs of services were established, and these significantly enlarged central government influence. At the same time, provincial authorities and municipalities were given new powers and responsibilities to plan and co-ordinate local medical facilities. To date their influence has not been very effective in the overall pattern of services locally.

Two serious problems have persisted. The planning of hospital capacity was not a task for central government, and so its influence (through regional plans, and investment permits) was generally regarded as ineffective. Second, the costs of medical services were also difficult to control centrally because of the complex negotiating machinery for tariffs.

The fundamental problem for Dutch governments was (and still is) how to achieve overall control of expenditure when the institutions responsible for planning, finance and provision are separate, quasi-autonomous and located at various levels (national, regional, local). In principle, there has traditionally been a policy of 'functional decentralisation' in the Dutch system. From the mid-1970s, however, there was increased *centralisation* through greater government influence over financial frameworks regulating prices, tariffs and costs. As hospitals, sick funds and insurers have negotiated with each other and with the provincial authorities about the planning of capacity, their decisions have been constrained by increasingly rigid government guidelines. The principle of decentralisation has been displaced by *ad hoc* retrenchment measures, particularly those affecting the supply and volume of intramural care (Flynn and Simonis, 1989, 1990).

Disputes about the structure and allocation of functions and responsibilities in the National Health Service in England have continued since its creation in 1948. There have been two major structural reorganisations (in 1974 and 1982) and many administrative reforms, and continuous arguments about their effectiveness. The most important point is that, because the NHS is national, comprehensive and funded out of general taxation, it is ultimately the responsibility of *central* government. Although there are important areas for local discretion, Regional and District Health Authorities are in practice *agencies* of central government. Their members and chairpersons are appointed by the minister, not elected, and they are legally and financially accountable to Parliament through the minister. Until very recently, local planning, service provision and resources were subject to central government directives, and constrained by central financial allocations.

Despite this hierarchical chain of command (reinforced by general management after 1983), there has always been bargaining and conflict within the system. Key policy issues such as the failure to move resources away from acute medicine towards care of the mentally ill and mentally handicapped, and preventative health care, demonstrate that central government priorities have not always been implemented locally. The central government is dependent on local health authorities and medical professionals to carry out its legislation, but compliance with central objectives is mediated by a complex of local political interests, professional lobbying and pre-existing patterns of provision. However, until 1991, the NHS planning system, and an extensive set of procedures and instruments for financial allocation and budgeting (to ensure an equitable distribution of resources between different areas and care groups, and to control expenditure), provided the basis for enforcing central directives. One dominant principle has been that there should be maximum delegation downwards, and maximum accountability upwards. However, as pressures to impose even stricter financial and managerial control in the NHS intensified in the late 1970s and 1980s, the tendency to centralisation was evident in a variety of different measures (see Harrison, 1988; Day and Klein, 1989; Nichols, 1989).

During the 1980s there was an explicit move towards a more directive, interventionist management style by the Department of Health, particularly as central government emphasised efficiency in resource use and value for money. Districts and regions were compelled to improve their own productivity and efficiency, to undergo evaluation through numerous 'performance indicators', and to achieve specific output targets (see Allen *et al.*, 1987; Birch and Maynard, 1988; Day and Klein, 1985; Pollitt, 1985). While general management had been claimed to encourage devolution, managerial enterprise and local autonomy, government responses to a series of expenditure crises from 1986 demonstrated that front-line managers' operational control was severely limited by central intervention (see Flynn, 1991). Tension surrounding accountability and central–local relations, and conflicts over central government intervention, have thus intensified because of the effects of financial cut-backs. There have been significant changes in the management system and attempts to alter the NHS organisational culture, but these too have been confounded by renewed forms of centralisation (NHSTA, 1987).

Therefore in both the Dutch and English health care systems there has been a similar, paradoxical trend. In the traditionally pluralistic, fragmented Dutch system, central governments have sought to bring about greater co-ordination and control while maintaining (or claiming to maintain) the independence of private initiative institutions. In the NHS, despite measures intended to promote greater managerial flexibility and innovation, retrenchment policies have demanded local conformity with central instructions, and centralisation has continued to flourish. In both countries radical proposals to resolve this paradox have emerged, involving extensive deregulation and managed competition in a quasi-market system. However, before reviewing these proposals it is necessary to consider another crucial issue – professional medical autonomy – which has a direct relevance to the implementation of health policy in all systems.

Regulating medical autonomy

In almost all industrialised societies, medical professionals and other health workers play a crucial role in the delivery of services. The degree to which professionals possess technical autonomy – and its institutionalisation through the doctrine of clinical freedom – is variable in different health systems. However, in most countries there have been increasing attempts to challenge, and restrict, medical authority, and these efforts have intensified where cost control has been a dominant governmental objective (see Freddi and Bjorkman, 1989). The increased influence of consumerism, political insistence on greater accountability and demands for improved efficiency and effectiveness have combined and led to various developments designed to reduce medical power in resource allocation and health policy in both the Netherlands and England.

In the Netherlands, medical professionals have traditionally been relatively very powerful. General practitioners and hospital specialists are independent, though licensed by the state; their income is mainly derived from fees received from the sick funds and private insurers, which are legally required to make contracts with doctors registered in their areas. It seems generally accepted that the expansion of health care facilities in the 1960s and 1970s was 'supplier induced' and resulted in duplication, an uneven spatial distribution of resources and excess capacity within intramural institutions. The financial system (fee-for-service) rewarded increased output and gave an incentive to increase referrals and treatments, because hospitals and specialists were automatically reimbursed by the sick funds and insurers. Various Dutch governments tried to regulate supply, prices and costs, but medical professionals exerted countervailing influence through their national representative bodies, and especially through the 'corporatist' machinery for finance and planning – the Central Council for Health Care Charges (COTG), the Sick Funds Council (ZFR) and the Council for Hospital Facilities (CvZ) (see Baakman *et al.*, 1989; Groot, 1987; Lapre, 1988; Rutten, 1987; Van den Ven, 1987).

Recently, however, medical dominance has been threatened and constrained at various points in the system. For example, the government has required hospitals to work within externally determined annual prospective budgets (fixed by the Central Council for Health Care Charges) which limit clinical activity. There have also been limits placed on the number of doctors in training, government-imposed ceilings on hospital specialists' incomes, and various measures to strengthen professional standards and quality audit, all involving external monitoring and surveillance.

Historically, the influence of doctors within the NHS has also been very strong, but current government policies are expected to restrict their professional autonomy. General practitioners (and the Family Health Service Authorities) enjoy a form of delegated discretion in the provision of most primary care, and GPs are the 'gatekeepers' who refer patients for hospital treatment. They have substantial autonomy, based on their position as independent contractors within the NHS, and (until recently) have not had limits placed on their expenditure, except for restrictions on the type of drugs which may be prescribed. However, hospital doctors (consultants or 'clinicians') are responsible for decisions which consume the most (and the most expensive) medical resources, and they *have* experienced increasing regulation by health service managers (see Flynn, 1992a).

The long-established principle of 'clinical freedom' gave consultants (and GPs) complete responsibility for the care of a patient, authority to decide how a patient is to be treated and an ethical duty to provide the best possible treatment. Hospital doctors' clinical decisions determine bed numbers, nurse staffing levels, operating theatre time, and use of diagnostic and therapeutic equipment, and services, drugs and other supplies. They also affect the type and quantity of ancillary or supporting services needed (paramedical staff, administrators, catering, cleaning and other domestic staff, etc).

However, consultants are not formally accountable to managers. They work within professional guidelines laid down by national colleges and professional bodies, and are nominally supervised by local Medical Executive Committees, composed of representatives of specialities organised in 'divisions'. It is widely acknowledged that doctors have not been fully integrated into general management schemes, and cannot be directed by non-medical managers. Governments and NHS administrators have regarded this as a major problem for some time, but concern intensified as the crisis of NHS funding worsened. The 1983 Griffiths Report argued that doctors must be integrated with management because of their determinant role in the use of resources. The Social Services Committee report on the future of the NHS also argued that clinical freedom had to be exercised within resource constraints (House of Commons, 1988).

Such 'managerial' views have now become orthodox, and are being implemented in measures adopted as a result of the 1989 NHS review. However, there has been opposition from consultants to the extension of management control, objections to 'resource management' (clinical budgeting) because it interferes with clinical freedom, and conflicts about the introduction of 'medical audit' (professional peer review of clinical practice). It is well known that, until recently, medical professionals in the NHS have constituted a powerful interest group, and have been very influential in policy making and implementation. That dominance is now under threat. For example, Flynn (1988, 1991) has described how district managers, finance directors and planners claimed that one of their most urgent priorities was the need to control clinical activity and to exert stronger managerial control over doctors. But the doctors interviewed criticised the extension of managerial authority and were unwilling to participate in the *financial* management aspects of clinical decisions (see also Pollitt *et al.*, 1988).

However, such incorporation (or co-option) is exactly what central government has demanded. Doctors are now required to take greater responsibility for the budgetary consequences of their medical decisions, through schemes such as resource management. Information technology enables doctors to assess the workload, staffing, drugs and supplies and other costs of treatments, and they are then expected to adjust their behaviour to maximise efficiency. To date these schemes have not been very successful because of technical difficulties and medical opposition (see Brooks, 1986; Pollitt *et al.*, 1988; Steele, 1985). Nevertheless, they provide the mechanism to reduce clinical autonomy, which is likely to be further curtailed as demands for greater accountability and quality control grow (see Harrison, 1988; Harrison and Schultz, 1989; Harrison *et al.*, 1989a; Kings Fund Institute, 1988).

Thus producers or providers of medical services in England and the Netherlands are undergoing increased extra-professional control by institutional managers, and by those responsible for the allocation of financial resources. If retrenchment and cost containment policies continue, then inevitably more attempts will be made to limit or reduce the extent of medical autonomy. In both countries, government commitments to improve efficiency, effectiveness and quality through 'market' reforms will also necessarily entail the restriction of professional power. Such a strategy will encounter considerable opposition from doctors and their professional associations. It also raises questions about bureaucratic accountability and the role of the newly empowered managerial cadres. Whose interests are represented by the *managers* of funding, purchasing and providing agencies? Will managers become a new élite rather than merely a countervailing influence in health policy making? These issues, however, are not unique to England or the Netherlands: in all advanced industrial societies there is a growing tension between medical professional power and managerial control (Baakman *et al.*, 1989; Degeling, this volume, Chapter 2; Flynn, 1992a; Freddi, 1989).

Marketisation

Faced with escalating costs, professional opposition and apparent bureaucratic inertia, new right governments in both countries have turned towards radical market solutions. In 1987 the Dekker Committee on the structure and financing of health care in the Netherlands published its report, entitled *Willingness to Change*. In 1989 a ministerial committee convened by the Prime Minister carried out a 'review' of the NHS and issued a White Paper entitled *Working for Patients* (Department of Health, 1989). Both addressed the problem of increased demand and limited resources, and both recommended major structural changes to introduce a form of regulated competition. These changes will have important consequences for the organisations and personnel involved in funding, planning and delivering medical services, and for consumers of those services. It is therefore valuable to compare the main arguments and proposals, and briefly to assess their policy implications.

The Dekker Report

The Dekker Committee's terms of reference explicitly referred to the necessity to achieve substantial reductions in (total) health care costs, and to control growth in the volume of services. Linked to this was the claim that there was a need for deregulation and a reduction in bureaucracy. The report argued that expansion in the 1960s had produced inefficient and uneven provision, and that the planning and financial systems were fragmented and unco-ordinated. The committee's solution to these problems was to reduce government regulation and to introduce market mechanisms. 'Efficiency' was to be achieved by making users and providers more cost conscious; by reforming the insurance system so that there was greater competition between insurers; and by establishing competition between hospitals, specialists and GPs.

The existing system was believed to encourage GPs to refer too many patients to hospitals unnecessarily. Hospitals, and their contracted specialists, were said to have an incentive to carry out excessive (and expensive) treatments. Consequently, there was an oversupply of facilities and services, with inflated costs. The committee accordingly recommended substantial reductions in the number of hospital beds (and hospitals). It also decided that hospitals and medical staff would work within externally fixed budgets, and that there should be a policy of 'substitution' from intramural (hospital) care to primary care. The most fundamental reform involved the merger of the sick funds and private health insurers, and the introduction of a single insurance scheme comprising a compulsory basic package of cover for most medical services (other services are regarded as a voluntary element to be paid for separately). Dekker proposed that the basic insurance package will be financed from income-related premiums; supplementary insurance will be funded by flat-rate premiums, which will vary in price between insurers, thus encouraging competition.

The Dutch government responded positively to the Dekker proposals and introduced legislation to implement the main recommendations (see Ministry of Welfare, Health and Cultural Affairs, 1988; 1990). The government endorsed the committee's diagnosis of the 'problems' and agreed with its suggestions for restructuring – expanding the role of market forces and reducing government regulation, changing the basis of the insurance system and stimulating competition between doctors, hospitals and insurers. However, the government acknowledged that, because health care could not be driven and determined solely by market forces, it must retain its powers to intervene in price and budget negotiations. Central government has maintained its right to control costs by defining the content of the basic insurance package, by deciding the level of income-related premiums and by fixing expenditure ceilings on new developments. At the same time the government proposed that it would withdraw from detailed, decentralised planning. In future the distribution and supply of medical services is expected to become the direct responsibility of health care providers and insurers. Thus 'functional regionalisation' and 'quality' are to be determined by the operation of the market and 'self-regulation'.

The NHS review and the internal NHS market

The NHS review and 1989 White Paper were a response to unprecedented public concern and political controversy about funding during 1987/88. The White Paper asserted that there was a 'need for change' because of rising demand, and a need for reform in the organisation and delivery of health care because of disquiet about variations in performance. Two main objectives were identified: to obtain better choice for patients; and to provide greater satisfaction and rewards for NHS employees (Department of Health, 1989, pp. 3–4). Three other central aims were listed: to extend patient choice, to delegate responsibility and to secure the best value for money (p. 102). The measures now being implemented constitute the most fundamental change in the structure of the NHS since 1948, and have led to widespread professional criticism and political opposition (Day and Klein, 1991).

Major changes in the financing and organisation of the hospital and general practitioner service are geared towards the introduction of an 'internal market' in the NHS. Doctors, health authorities and hospitals will be required to buy and sell medical services and make contracts with each other, on behalf of patients. General practitioners in fund-holding practices will have a fixed budget and will arrange contracts with hospitals in their area or in other health authority areas, to purchase specified services for their referred patients. GPs and District Health Authorities will purchase health care services from 'self-governing' NHS hospital trusts, directly managed NHS hospitals or private hospitals, using a variety of different types of contract (see Department of Health, 1989, Working Papers 1–8). The basic aim is to make general practitioners compete with other GPs and to make hospitals compete with other hospitals. Managers and GPs will seek out the best available services at the best (lowest) prices. Since money will 'flow' with the patients, more resources will go to those doctors and hospitals providing the most efficient service. It is presumed that GPs and hospitals will become more responsive to their 'customers', and that professionals and institutions will improve patient choice and quality of service.

There are numerous specific changes which cannot be detailed here. Large self-managed hospitals will enjoy greater autonomy in relation to capital borrowing, employment conditions and wages, and specialisation of provision. Hospital consultants will be required to hold budgetary responsibility, to be accountable to unit managers and to participate in 'medical audit' of their clinical practices. Health authorities and units will undergo further changes in management and organisation to make them become more like commercial business enterprises.

Not surprisingly, there has been sustained opposition from the general practitioners, hospital doctors and nursing staff. Many GPs are opposed to cash-limited budgets and restricted drug budgets. They are concerned that they might have to refuse treatment to some patients because their treatment is too expensive and will exhaust their budget allocation. GPs also claim that patient choice will be reduced in the internal market because most GPs cannot refer their patient to a specialist or hospital preferred by the GP, but only to one with whom the health authority has agreed a contract.

There are doubts about whether *comprehensive* medical services can be provided in each locality because self-governing hospitals may prefer to concentrate on 'profitable' specialties to the neglect of other services. The government has insisted that all hospitals must provide emergency and 'core' services, but local District Health Authorities have discretion to determine what this 'core' will consist of when negotiating contracts. District and Regional Health Authorities' tasks and roles in this new system are also problematic. They are expected to monitor the effectiveness and performance of GPs and hospitals, but their overall function and powers are unclear. 'Marketisation' of the NHS is thus likely to proceed unevenly, and its ultimate effects are difficult to predict (see Flynn, 1992b). Ironically, one possibility is that marketisation may encourage cost escalation, as production units profilerate and struggle to maximise revenue. Service providers may extend the range of treatments, upgrade facilities and offer enhanced salaries to recruit professional staff, thereby increasing total costs across the health care system. In the NHS internal market, the number of interest groups bidding for resources will increase, but the aggregate effects on expenditure, as indeed on other aspects of health care, are as yet unknown.

Conclusions

There are clear similarities in governmental problem definitions and recommended strategies for the Dutch and English health systems. The creation or extension of market influences (in provision) is regarded as the primary solution to the growth in costs. Efficiency is expected to improve if providers are given competitive incentives, and if at the same time medical professionals in both systems are subjected to tighter control in connection with clinical budgets and quality. In each country, the implementation of a managed market necessitates a fundamental transformation in arrangements for funding and providing medical, especially hospital, services. In both cases of restructuring, however, there are unresolved questions about how to reconcile competition with regulation (Ham *et al.*, 1990).

The convergence in policy between countries with dissimilar health systems, but similar right-of-centre governments, is remarkable in itself. It is extremely difficult to identify the causes of such convergence. Similarities in policy undoubtedly reflect the influence of new right precepts in both countries' governments. The coincidence may also be a result of mutual learning and international borrowing and diffusion of ideas – policy copying. The ideology and practice of organisational restructuring in their welfare states also share a common affinity with a more widespread modern phenomenon – what might be termed the hegemony of 'managerialism' (see Pollitt, 1990), Finally, of course, the imperative of cost containment may in itself be an objective where, inexorably, common means (marketisation) are adopted to limit supply and restrain demand, irrespective of national context and institutional differences.

Perhaps the most important point for students of policy

implementation to note is that ostensibly similar measures are being attempted within very different institutional structures, to achieve virtually identical objectives. In the NHS the crucial problem is the creation of an internal market within a formerly professionally dominated but cash-limited and centrally planned system. In the Netherlands the main task is the introduction of a regulated market within an organisationally fragmented, pluralistic structure in which finance, planning and service delivery are controlled by different bodies with different competences and powers.

Of course, in both cases the outcome will depend on struggles between different interest groups in the health sector, and on national economic and political debates. It is argued here that, while the implementation of restructuring will be problematic and contentious in both countries, it is likely that marketisation will evolve relatively more quickly within the Dutch system. This is mainly because there has always been a mixed economy of health with numerous institutional actors, and because central government intervention has been diffuse and indirect. Moreover, the pillarised nature of Dutch society and politics underpins and reinforces such pluralism, and emphasises self-help and a minimal state. There is a long tradition of encouraging voluntary action and promoting 'non-state' agencies in the public sector, which both explains and facilitates decentralised and quasi-market arrangements (see Hupe, this volume, Chapter 6).

By contrast, the NHS market is relatively less likely to flourish, not merely because of widespread support for welfare state values (universalism, comprehensiveness, equity and need), but more particularly because (compared with the Netherlands) the system has been (relatively) highly centralised, hierarchical and integrated. Paradoxically, it might be assumed that in such a situation new policies might be more easily executed. However, NHS marketisation and restructuring entails the abandonment of central planning, the encouragement of decentralisation and self-regulation, and the acceptance of diversity. This, together with the separation of 'provider' and 'purchaser' functions within health authorities, and the introduction of competition between GPs, hospitals and contractors, represents a reversal of many long-established policies and practices. Indeed, it requires such a complete alteration of assumptions and operating procedures for *all* actors (commentators refer to a total change in organisational culture) that there are profound doubts and uncertainties among disinterested experts about whether it will succeed (Harrison *et al.*, 1989b; Pettigrew *et al.*, 1991).

Thus there are a number of interrelated trends – cost control mechanisms, changing forms of central intervention, managerial encroachment on professional medical autonomy, and marketisation – which cumulatively constitute a restructuring process in England and the Netherlands. One of the most difficult analytical problems is that to investigate one aspect of this process it is necessary to examine other elements simultaneously. Returning to the earlier discussion, it is obvious that it is extremely difficult to achieve a comprehensive description of an entire health system, and yet it is inadequate to focus on one component without also placing it in its context. *Comparative* research reveals this dilemma very starkly. Notwithstanding the strictures of other scholars about the need to link accounts of actors' beliefs and actions with theories of the state and power relations, comparative policy analysis almost unavoidably lends itself to institutional description. A processual or 'action' model of policy implementation, and an awareness of the political nature of all inter- and intra-organisational life, are undoubtedly valuable heuristic devices, but in comparative cross-national research they remain methodologically problematic. Some writers have referred to implementation research as a 'mapping' exercise. Without stretching the analogy too far, it must be remembered, and accepted, that there are many different maps, on different scales, for different purposes. The 'action/structured bargaining approach' aspires to design a three-dimensional model or perhaps a hologram of the policy process. Comparative analysis, at the institutional level, may only be able to produce outline sketches, but these are useful in their own right, as well as necessary preliminaries for further detailed research.

Note

This chapter is based on research funded by the Netherlands National Hospital Institute, 1987–9, and involved collaborative work between the author and Dr J. B. D. Simonis (University of Utrecht). Further details of the project and findings are reported in Flynn (1988) and Flynn and Simonis (1989, 1990). I am indebted to Jan Simonis for background information, but I must stress that I am solely responsible for this analysis, and for any errors or mistranslations in it.

References

Abel-Smith, B. (1984) *Cost Containment in Health Care*, London: Bedford Square Press/NCVO.

Alford, R. R., and R. Friedland (1985) *Powers of Theory*, Cambridge: Cambridge University Press.

Allen, D., M. Harley and G. T. Makinson (1987) 'Performance indicators in the NHS', *Social Policy and Administration*, 21 (1), pp. 71–84

Altenstetter, C., and J. W. Bjorkman (1981) 'Planning and implementation: a comparative perspective on health policy', *International Political Science Review*, 2 (1), pp. 11–42

Atteveld, L., C. Broeders and R. Lapre (1987) 'International comparative research in health care', *Health Policy*, 8, pp. 105–36.

Baakman, N., J. Van der Made and I. Mur-Veeman (1989) 'Controlling Dutch health care' in G. Freddi and J. W. Bjorkman (eds), *Controlling Medical Professionals*, London: Sage.

Barratt, S. and Fudge, C. (1981) 'Examining the policy–action relationship' in S. Barrett and C. Fudge (eds), *Policy and Action*, London: Methuen.

Birch, S., and A. Maynard (1988) 'Performance indicators', in R. Maxwell (ed.), *Reshaping the National Health Service*, Oxford: Policy Journals/Transaction Books.

Brenton, M. (1982) 'Changing relationships in Dutch social services', *Journal of Social Policy*, 11 (1), 59–80.

Brooks, R. (ed.) (1986) *Management Budgeting in the NHS*, Keele: Health Services Manpower Review.

Clegg, S. R. (1989a) 'Radical revisions: power, discipline and organizations', *Organization Studies*, 10 (1), pp. 97–115.

Clegg, S. R. (1989b) *Frameworks of Power*, London: Sage.

Day, P. and R. Klein (1985) 'Central accountability and local decision-making', *British Medical Journal*, 290, 1676–78.

Day, P. and R. Klein 'The politics of modernization', *Milbank Quarterly*, 67 (1), pp. 1–34.

Day, P. and R. Klein (1991) 'Britain's health care experiment', *Health Affairs*, 10 (3), pp. 39–59.

Dekker Committee on the Structure and Financing of Health Care in the Netherlands (1987) *Willingness to Change* (Bereidheid tot Verandering), Rijswijk.

Department of Health (1989) *Working for Patients*, Cm 555, London: HMSO.

DHSS (1983) (Griffiths) *Report of the NHS Management Inquiry*, London: DHSS.

Dunsire, A., and Hood, C. (1989) *Cutback Management in Public Bureaucracies*, Cambridge: Cambridge University Press.

Flynn, R. (1986) 'Cutback contradictions in Dutch housing policy', *Journal of Social Policy*, 15 (2), 223–36.

Flynn, R. (1988) *Cutback Management in Health Services* (Report for the Netherlands National Hospital Institute), Salford: University of Salford.

Flynn, R. (1991) 'Coping with cutbacks and managing retrenchment in health', *Journal of Social Policy*, 20 (2), pp. 215–36.

Flynn, R. (1992a) *Structures of Control in Health Management*, London: Routledge.

Flynn, R. (1992b) 'Managed markets: consumers and producers in the NHS', in R. Burrows, and C. Marsh (eds), *Consumption and Class*, London: Macmillan.

Flynn, R., and J. B. D. Simonis (1989) *Cost Control and Retrenchment in the Health Care Systems of the Netherlands and England*, Utrecht: ISOR.

Flynn, R., and J. B. D. Simonis (1990) 'Cost containment in health care: a comparison of policies in the Netherlands and England', *Public Policy and Administration*, 5 (3), pp. 48–62.

Freddi, G. (1989) 'Problems of organizational rationality in health systems' in Freddi and Bjorkman (1989).

Freddi, G., and J. W. Bjorkman (eds) (1989) *Controlling Medical Professionals*, London: Sage.

Giddens, A. (1979) *Central Problems in Social Theory*, London: Macmillan.

Giddens, A. (1982) 'Power, the dialectic of control and class structuration' in A. Giddens and G. MacKenzie (eds), *Social Class and the Division of Labour*, Cambridge: Cambridge University Press.

Groot, L. M. J. (1987) 'Incentives for cost-effective behaviour: a Dutch experience', *Health Policy*, 7, pp. 175–88.

Ham, C. (1980) 'Approaches to the study of social policy-making', *Policy and Politics*, 8 (1), pp. 55–71.

Ham, C. (1981) *Policy-making in the National Health Service*, London: Macmillan.

Ham, C. (1985) *Health Policy in Britain* (2nd edn), London: Macmillan.

Ham, C., and M. Hill (1993) *The Policy Process in the Modern Capitalist State* (2nd edn), Hemel Hempstead: Harvester Wheatsheaf.

Ham, C., R. Robinson and M. Benzeval (1990) *Health Check*, London: Kings Fund Institute.

Hamnett, C., L. McDowell and P. Sarre (1989) 'Introduction', in Hamnett *et al.* (eds), *The Changing Social Structure*, London: Sage.

Harrison, S. (1988) 'The workforce and the new managerialism' in R. Maxwell (ed.), *Reshaping the NHS*, Hermitage: Policy Journals/ Transaction Books.

Harrison, S., and R. I. Schultz (1989) 'Clinical autonomy in the UK and the US', in Freddi and Bjorkman (1989).

Harrison, S., D. Hunter, G. Marnoch and C. Pollitt (1989a) 'General management and medical autonomy in the NHS', *Health Services Management Research*, 2 (1), pp. 38–46.

Harrison, S., D. Hunter, I. Johnston and G. Wistow (1989b)) *Competing for Health*, Leeds: Nuffield Institute for Health Service Studies.

Harrison, S., D. Hunter and C. Pollitt (1990) *The Dynamics of British Health Policy*, London: Unwin Hyman.

Haywood, S. (1983) 'The politics of management in health care', *Journal of Health Politics, Policy and Law*, 8 (3) pp. 424–43.

Haywood, S., and A. Aleszewski (1980) *Crisis in the Health Service*, London: Croom Helm.

Higgins, J. (1981) *States of Welfare*, Oxford: Basil Blackwell and Martin Robertson.

Higgins, J. (1986) 'Comparative social policy', *Quarterly Journal of Social Affairs*, 2 (3), 221–42

Hjern, B., and D. O. Porter (1981) 'Implementation structures', *Organization Studies* 2 (3), pp. 211–27.

Hoggett, P. (1990) *Modernisation, Political Strategy and the Welfare State*, Bristol: School for Advanced Urban Studies.

House of Commons (1988) Social Services Committee Fifth Report, *The Future of the NHS*, Cm 613, London: HMSO

Hunter, D. (1990) 'Organizing and managing health care', in S. Cunningham-Burley and N. P. McKeganey (eds), *Readings in Medical Sociology*, London: Routledge.

Hupe, P. L. (1990) 'Implementing a meta-policy', *Policy and Politics*, 18 (3), pp. 181–91.

Idenburg, P. A. (1985) 'The Dutch paradox in social welfare' in C. Jones and M. Brenton (eds), *The Yearbook of Social Policy in Britain 1984–85* London: Routledge and Kegan Paul.

Kings Fund Institute (1988) *Managing Clinical Activity in the NHS*, London: Kings Fund Institute.

Klein, R. (1983) *The Politics of the National Health Service*, London: Longman.

Lapre, R. M. (1988) 'A change of direction in the Dutch health care systems', mimeo, Rotterdam University.

Lash, S. and Urry, J. (1987) *The End of Organised Capitalism*, Cambridge: Polity Press.

Lee, K., and A. Mills (1982) *Policy-Making and Planning in the Health Sector*, London: Croom Helm.

Maxwell, R. J. (1981) *Health and Wealth*, Lexington, Mass: Lexington Books.

Ministry of Welfare, Health and Cultural Affairs (Netherlands) (1988) Summary of the Policy Document *Change Assured* (Verandering Verzekerd: Kabinetsstandpunt Commissie Dekker), Rijswijk.

Ministry of Welfare, Health and Cultural Affairs (1990) *Health Insurance in the Netherlands*, Rijswijk.

NHSTA/Templeton College (1987) *Managing for Better Health* (Eight Issue Studies on District General Managers), National Health Service Training Authority and Templeton College, Oxford.

Nichols, R. M. (1989) 'Central–local relationships in the aftermath of Griffiths', *Health Services Management Research* 2 (1), pp. 58–63.

OECD (1987) *Financing and Delivering Health Care*, Paris: Organisation for Economic Co-operation and Development.

O'Toole, L. J. (1986) 'Policy recommendations for multi-actor implementation', *Journal of Public Policy*, 6 (2), pp. 181–210

Pettigrew, A., E. Ferlie, L. Fitzgerald and R. Wensley (1991) 'The leadership role of the new health authorities', *Public Money and Management*, Spring, pp. 39–43.

Pollitt, C. (1985) 'Measuring performance: a new system for the NHS', *Policy and Politics* 13 (1), pp. 1–15.

Pollitt, C. (1990) *Managerialism and the Public Service*, Oxford: Basil Blackwell.

Pollitt, C., S. Harrison, D. Hunter and G. Marnoch (1988) 'The reluctant managers: clinicians and budgets in the NHS', *Financial Accountability and Management*, 4 (3), pp. 213–233.

Raffel, M. W. (ed.) (1984) *Comparative Health Systems*, London: Pennsylvania State University Press.

Robinson, R. (1986) 'Restructuring the welfare state', *Journal of Social Policy*, 15 (1), pp. 1–21.

Rutten, F. F. H. (1987) 'Market strategies for publicly financed health care systems', *Health Policy*, 7, pp. 135–48.

Schieber, G. J., and J. P. Poullier (1987) 'Recent trends in international health care spending', *Health Affairs*, 7, 3, pp. 105–12.

Schieber, G. J., J. P. Poullier and L. M. Greenwald (1991) 'Health care systems in twenty-four countries', *Health Affairs*, 10 (3), pp. 22–38.

Simonis, J. B. D., G. Morssinkhof and A. Wouda (1988) *Overheidsinterventie in de Gezondheidszorg* (Report for the Netherlands National Hospital Institute), Utrecht: University of Utrecht.

Sociaal en Cultureel Planbureau (1984) *Sociaal en Cultureel Rapport 1984*, Rijswijk.

Sociaal en Cultureel Planbureau (1986) *Sociaal en Cultureel Rapport 1986*, Rijswijk.

Steele, R. (1985) 'Clinical budgeting and costing', in King Edward's Hospital Fund for London, *NHS Management Perspectives for Doctors*, London: KEHF.

Turner, B. S. (1987) *Medical Power and Social Knowledge*, London: Sage.

Van den Ven, W. P. M. M. (1987) 'The key role of health insurance in a cost-effective health care system', *Health Policy*, 7, pp. 253–72.

Venema, F., and W. C. Verbaan (1984) 'Ombuigingen bij WVC en VROM', *Beleid en Maatschappij*, xi (5), pp. 138–42.

Wilensky, H., G. Luebbert, S. Reed-Hahn and A. Jamieson (1987) 'Comparative social policy' in M. Dierkes, H. Weiler and A. Berthoin-Antal (eds), *Comparative Policy Research*, Aldershot: Gower.

CHAPTER 4

Enforcing environmental laws: the social regulation of co-production

Kenneth Hanf

Social rules and co-operative enforcement

The proof of the pudding, we are told, is in the eating. Consequently, the 'real meaning' of environmental policy is determined by the impact of regulatory activities on the actual behaviour of the target firms. In this sense the primary 'function' of environmental law is to influence the behaviour of firms and consumers in a manner conducive to protecting the quality of the environment. The most common means of doing this is still some form of direct regulation, i.e. commands or prohibitions laid down by the government circumscribing the choices available to the targets of regulation. It is assumed, in pursuing these objectives, that the enforcement activities of government officials are of some consequence for ensuring that compliance will in fact be forthcoming.

In recent years, study after study – both in the United States and Europe – has concluded that what actually gets done with regard to pollution control policy is quite often considerably less than what was promised. Not surprisingly, the recognition of this state of affairs has led to an interest in finding out why, when viewed from the perspective of national policy-makers, policies as they are carried out by officials in the field often fail to have the intended impact. In searching for an answer to this question, a good deal of attention has been focused on alleged shortcomings in the implementation process and the organisations that are responsible for carrying out these policies.

What environmental regulations specifically require of the regulated firm is usually spelled out in a sequence of separate steps. Few concrete behavioural rules are found in the legislation itself; rule making is normally a post-parliamentary activity, with its results contained in various executive orders; and, ultimately, specific conditions with regard to concrete cases are found in conditional permits issued by regulatory authorities. Obviously, the intended behavioural effect will, in the last analysis, only be realised if the firms in fact fulfil these legal obligations. In order to ensure that this will indeed be the case, the government is authorised to undertake a variety of activities to check up on whether or not they are doing what is required of them. On the basis of the information provided by such monitoring activities, actions can be initiated to force violators to mend their ways and to provide visible examples to encourage others to maintain the desired behaviour so as to avoid a similar fate. It is this set of activities for securing compliance that is meant by the term 'enforcement'.

Viewed from the top, enforcement is usually seen as a process of subdividing a comprehensive mission into ever more specific operational tasks. From this perspective, achieving effective enforcement is considered to be a question of 'structuring and controlling the exercise of choice' (Diver, 1980, p. 261). An appropriate top-down enforcement policy would consist of a 'set of rules, increasingly specific as one descends the hierarchical ladder, for allocating resources among, and specifying the content of various surveillance and prosecutorial tasks' (p. 261).

On the other hand, if we approach things from the bottom, the process of enforcement looks quite different. The bottom referred to here is the local implementation front: that is, the point at which general programmes and the specific members of the intended target group interact directly with respect to a specific case of regulation. Although such a bottom-up analysis takes as its point of departure the formal division of administrative labour, it makes no a priori assumption regarding the ultimate role played by a formally mandated organisation or, for that matter, regarding the relative weight or importance of any particular public or private actor involved.

Such a bottom-up approach draws attention to the important features of the everyday context within which individual officials make the various choices through which enforcement policy is defined with regard to the concrete activities being regulated. It also suggests a broader perspective for incorporating the multi-actor character of this process into the analysis. Particularly important in this connection is the fact that the different participants in this 'production process' are locked together in interdependent relationships. The strategies and choices of the inspectors and prosecutors, which form the core of enforcement in the narrower sense, are based on the expected reactions of other actors, either in the form of inputs to or support for their own actions, or in the form of predictions about the subsequent behaviour of others shaping the immediate decisions of the actor in question. For example, in deciding how to deal with a detected violation, an inspector will anticipate the likelihood that a public prosecutor will, in fact, act on the citation he or she writes. Indeed, whether or not a state of affairs will be defined as constituting a 'violation' may also depend on what the inspector believes will happen once she or he has reported it.

Consequently, the typical enforcement situation is characterised by various kinds of interdependence that join the different actors. Not only do they depend on others for the resources needed to do their job; what they do also depends on prior actions by others or calls forth responses from others which, in turn, affect their own position. More generally, the final output of enforcement activities is, in important ways, a joint product in so far as no one actor is in a position to produce it directly on its own. This in turn means that these decisions result from interactions among different actors, and, further, that the product must be explained in terms of the characteristics of the interaction processes as such and not of the individual actors alone. It is, in short, the structure and dynamics of these interactions among interested public and private parties that will determine both the amount of (regulatory) activity and the quality of the outputs produced: that is, how strict or lenient the decisions are; whether or not sanctions are applied; and which interests are favoured.

Contrary to the traditional model of regulatory policy, this perspective would expect regulated subjects to be treated selectively, and in an important sense unequally, due to the fact that the enforcement of regulations occurs through bargaining instead of according to the consistent, even-handed application of general decision rules. Under such conditions, the real content of a regulation is determined through the interactions between the control agency and the target group in question, by which the conditions defining the conduct constituting compliance with the regulation are fixed.

Approaching regulatory enforcement from this general perspective draws attention to the fact that neither pollution nor violations of a regulation are self-evident. The behavioural meaning of these terms will be defined conjointly by enforcement agents and the regulated activities. 'Pollution' and 'compliance' are the outcomes of organised, sometimes lengthy social processes. In this sense, it is the routine behaviour of pollution control officers, as they interact with other actors, that is the 'reality of pollution control law' (Hawkins, 1984, p. 101). In real terms, it is not the legislation that determines what deviant behaviour is, but rather the inspectors and the investigative officials who do. It is these officials who create cases of violation of environmental law. Consequently, the process of regulation is not simply one where the regulators command and the regulated obey. On the contrary, '[a] market is created, as it were, in which bureaucrats and those subject to regulation bargain over the precise obligations of the latter' (Peacock, 1984, p. 3).

This chapter takes these fundamental characteristics of regulatory enforcement as given, and sketches the general context within and the process through which enforcement officials – viewed as 'street-level bureaucrats' – make decisions, in interaction with other actors, regarding the substantive meaning of environmental law in concrete enforcement situations. Drawing on recent experience with environmental policy in the Netherlands, some light is shed on what it is that regulatory officials do when they 'enforce the law' and on the factors that determine how they will behave in performing this task. The ways in which these officials cope with both the discretion and indeterminacy of the work situation in which they operate is especially interesting. In considering the social rules that govern the way in which they interpret and respond to the enforcement situations they confront, this chapter suggests how Lipsky's analysis of street-level bureaucrats might be improved by considering more the social and organisational context within which these bureaucrats act as well as their interactions with both the firms being regulated and other interested parties through which decisions regarding enforcement are 'co-produced'.

Lipsky is right in saying that the bottom line of public policy emerges out of the everyday decisions of individual street-level bureaucrats; he does not go far enough, however, in explicitly analysing the social structures through which the routines and rules governing these decisions are constructed.

The inter-organisational character of regulatory enforcement

Enforcement of environmental regulations involves a complex set of interrelated activities carried out by a number of separate governmental actors. The Dutch government has officially defined enforcement as carrying out inspections (monitoring) and, where necessary, applying (or threatening to apply) administrative law and criminal law sanctions to ensure that general as well as individually specified legal rules and regulations are complied with. The activities involved in both inspecting firms and investigating suspected violations mark the transition from rule giving (primarily through conditional permits) to the taking of actions to compel recalcitrant firms to come into compliance. Monitoring activities signal conditions that need to be dealt with, and in this way provide the occasion and information necessary for subsequent stages of the enforcement process.

Over the last fifteen years much has been written in the Netherlands about the inadequacies of environmental law enforcement. There have been complaints that the laws have been enforced in the wrong way, not strictly enough or, on the contrary, too inflexibly and too harshly; the instruments for enforcing the laws have been found to be too weak or, conversely, not appropriate for the types of violation confronted. Enforcement officials are not well trained in the formalities of issuing justiciable citations (thereby making it difficult to prosecute violations successfully), while police officials who have this skill lack the technical expertise required to analyse the evidence needed to support a case. Furthermore, there is a communication gap between the public prosecutor's office and the officials with investigative powers working in the administrative agencies. And to top it all off, the variety of actors performing inspection and investigative functions creates confusion and uncertainty regarding who is responsible to whom and for what.

Enforcement appears to be problematic in the Netherlands as a result of the way in which responsibility for these tasks is spread over a number of governmental actors. Dutch environmental law consists of a number of sectoral laws (for which different ministries are responsible), which are, for the most part, implemented through a decentralised system of administration. As a result of administrative decentralisation, each level tends to give its own accent to this environmental policy. Corrective steering of this decentralised policy by the central government is only marginally and indirectly possible.

This highly fragmented and complex state of affairs (as far as the number of actors involved and the division of labour among them is concerned) is also characteristic of enforcement activities. In the Dutch system of environmental management the national government takes the lead with regard to policy planning, legislation, rule making and standard setting (with a certain amount of room for further actions by other levels of government within these national parameters); in turn, sub-national governments are responsible for issuing permits and enforcing the general and specific rules and regulations. In the last analysis, it is the management of the regulated firms that has the primary responsibility for taking the control or remedial actions within their enterprises required by the regulations. At the same time, it is felt that in the context of preventative control these firms should be supported by the government with advice and information and otherwise aided in complying with the law.

Nevertheless, the governmental authority charged with the implementation of a particular law is ultimately responsible for seeing that the objectives of the laws are realised, that the regulations are complied with. To this end, these authorities are empowered by the different laws to take certain actions and, where necessary, to impose sanctions. In the Netherlands a distinction is made between the political authority at a given level of government (the mayor and the other magistrates, or the provincial executive committee) and the administrative apparatus that does the technical analysis and advising for these authorities. Administrative law sanctions are imposed by the political authorities, on the recommendation of their enforcement officials. This is important since these political executives are often reluctant to use formal sanctions, and, anticipating this reluctance, administrative officials will not be too hasty to make such recommendations. In any case, this kind of 'dependency' between different actors has important consequences for the way in which laws are enforced.

Decisions on whether to proceed with an enforcement action are, then, taken by the government authority on the level at which a law is implemented. In essence this means that the institutional focus of the decision-making process with regard to enforcement of environmental law is those administrative authorities at the level of the provinces, municipalities and local water boards charged with carrying out the permitting policy under a given environmental law. These authorities are responsible for enforcing the conditions they have bargained out with the permit holder.

The enforcement tasks at these levels are carried out by administrative officials who have formally been appointed as inspectors and been given the requisite powers for controlling compliance. Critics argue that this arrangement can lead to significant problems whenever the official involved fulfils the role of both policy-maker, in the sense that he or she advises and negotiates on the permit conditions, and inspector. It is the job of these inspectors to carry out periodic inspections of firms to see that they are operating in conformance with the conditions of their permits and general environmental regulations.

There is a second group of officials working within these administrative agencies whose job it is to carry out the necessary investigations in those cases where there is reasonable suspicion that a punishable offence has been committed. These investigative officials within the administrative units are inspectors who have been granted special legal powers to carry out police-like investigations. This is the first step in preparing a case for prosecution under the criminal law provisions of the environmental act in question. After gathering sufficient evidence, a formal citation can be issued on the basis of which the public prosecutor will take further action. These investigative officials – who, by the way, may in fact be one or the other inspector wearing another hat – are appointed by the Minister of Justice upon the recommendation of the political authority responsible for enforcing a given law. In their investigative capacity these officials function as part of the public prosecutor's office; as members of a particular administrative agency, they are under the direction of their hierarchical superior and, ultimately, the political authority.

The situation is complicated further by the fact that, along with the administrative authorities, criminal justice authorities, with their own independent responsibilities and prerogatives, fulfil certain tasks in connection with the enforcement of environmental law. Most important in this respect is the attempt to involve regular police officials in the investigation of environmental violations, both in terms of a signalling function towards the administrative authorities and in terms of an independent role in enforcing environmental laws. Of course, criminal law actions need the active involvement of the public prosecutors and, ultimately, the courts before which any cases are heard.

The active involvement of two separate and independent sets of authorities in the enforcement process creates its own problems: perhaps most importantly with respect to the choice which has to be made between administrative and criminal law sanctions in cases where different possibilities regarding appropriate actions are present. Both have their own policy considerations in this connection, and in practice the problem is often 'solved' by taking a wait-and-see position: let the administrative authorities try their luck first; if that does not work, then criminal prosecution can be initiated if the circumstances warrant it. Second, the investigatory apparatus under the direction of the public prosecutor's office is itself made up of a number of different elements: regular police, special investigative services, and regular inspection officials armed with special investigative powers. This also raises a number of questions regarding effective co-ordination of different activities.

What we have, then, is a situation in which a variety of administrative and justice agencies, officials and services ultimately determine the effectiveness of environmental policy in general and enforcement as a special part thereof. The picture is one of a large number of different actors who can, in principle, be involved in or have influence on the enforcement decision-making process. In the case of the Nuisance Act, for example, those who can exercise influence directly on the decision process include the city magistrate and municipal administrative officials and, in the case of criminal law actions, the public prosecutor's office, the police and special investigative officials (as well as the inspectors with investigative powers). There are, of course, a number of other actors from the general (and special) public(s) and other institutions that can be involved in a given instance of enforcement.

Under these conditions effective enforcement depends, in the last analysis, on adequate co-ordination along three dimensions: vertically, between levels of government; horizontally, between the inspection activities dealing with different sectors of the environment (or between the various regulations and permit conditions applying to one and the same firm); and between administrative and criminal justice authorities (in particular, police and the public prosecutor). Not surprisingly, adequately co-ordinated enforcement action is not always forthcoming.

Co-operative enforcement as co-production

In the late 1970s and early 1980s it became increasingly evident that the implementation of environmental legislation in the Netherlands was not proceeding as well as it should. For example, a study of the enforcement of the Nuisance Act (the most important and oldest environmental law applicable at the municipal level) indicated that an overwhelmingly large number of activities requiring a permit under this law did not have one; moreover, many of the permits that had been issued were inadequate. It was however, a number of scandals involving the disposal of chemical waste and the report (in 1983) of the government commission investigating these incidents that drew both public and political attention to alleged shortcomings in enforcement efforts.

These recent experiences with what is perceived to be inadequate enforcement of environmental policy have led the central government in the Netherlands to give a high priority to the 'intensification' of activities in this area. Specifically, a large number of critics argue that a larger role should be played by formal enforcement action, and that a failure to use the sanctions already available is itself an indication of a serious 'enforcement gap'. At the same time, despite various enumerations of different kinds of problems, there is little hard evidence that environmental laws are being inadequately enforced. The fact of the matter is that the authorities in the Netherlands (as elsewhere) rarely resort to formal actions (under either administrative or criminal law) in enforcing compliance with environmental regulations. For example, a recent inventory carried out in one Dutch province showed that in 1987 only 6 per cent of all registered violations of a number of environmental laws led to the issuing of formal citations.

However, even if we grant that few violations ever lead to formal citations and prosecution, can the small number of formal enforcement actions (the imposition of either administrative or criminal sanctions on violators) itself be taken as proof of inadequate enforcement? Or does it rather reflect the reality of the enforcement process in that, given the conditions under which inspectors seek compliance with the law, strict enforcement and punishment of offenders would be counterproductive for the (ultimate) realisation of the environmental quality objectives to which compliance with the specific regulations or permit conditions is supposed to contribute? Viewed in this way, it can be argued that enforcement officials have an instrumental view of the role of law in securing programme objectives, and consequently define their role in terms of facilitating compliance rather than punishing violations.

This suggests that, rather than interpreting the paucity of formal enforcement actions as an indication of an enforcement gap, we should be asking why officials approach the job of law enforcement in this way and what difference it makes for the level of compliance actually secured that they define their role in this way.

Obviously, whether we find enforcement problems will, in large part, depend on the way in which we conceive of the enforcement process (and the factors determining its effectiveness) in the first place. Neither rule making nor rule enforcement consists of unilateral actions by regulatory agencies wielding the various legal instruments formally at their disposal. On the contrary, such regulatory actions more often than not tend to be the result of negotiations between the parties directly affected: that is, in the first instance, the enforcement officials and, in the case of industrial pollution, the individual firms being regulated (Downing, 1983). Critics of traditional schemes of direct regulation have, of course, long been aware of this. Indeed, they have considered this bargaining between target group and governmental agencies to be one of the principal shortcomings of the traditional approach to regulation.

There have been two general types of reaction to this situation. On the one hand, it has been argued that rules and regulations must be formulated more precisely so as to reduce the amount of discretion available to enforcement officials in order to limit the 'interpretative space' within which they work. In this way both the need and opportunity for bargaining could be reduced, and consequently an important cause of the deflection of policy from its original intent could be controlled if not removed completely. Other critics have pushed for replacing traditional instruments of direct regulation with arrangements that would force polluters to internalise, via some kind of market-like incentives (such as effluent charges), the environmental costs of their activities into their production and investment decisions.

However, if complex bargaining processes are considered to be endemic to all interactions between regulatory authorities and members of the specific target group, irrespective of the policy instrument used (Downing, 1983, pp. 581–4), it will not be possible to do away with them, either within the current regulatory context or under the economic incentive approach called for by environmental economists. While such market-like instruments may indeed change the conditions under which such bargaining takes place, it will remain the dominant mode of interaction through which the individualisation sought by the targets of regulation themselves is realised. As actors interested more in their own long-term utilities than in general social efficiency, these firms will seek to bend any instrument (once it has been introduced) to their own ends. Indeed, as Majone (1989, pp. 95–115) has convincingly argued, they will invest resources – either individually or jointly – in attempting to influence the kind of instruments selected in the first place.

This conclusion is clearly at odds with the assumptions underlying much writing on the general features of the process of direct regulation. On the one hand, it is assumed that in carrying out these programmes the responsible government authorities will deal with all firms even-handedly and make full use of the formal possibilities of the law, On the other hand, it is expected that the regulated firms will then willingly (meekly) comply with the imposed conditions and modify their processes, materials and products accordingly. Such reasoning quickly leads to a picture of a regulatory process in which the main role is played by a powerful and arrogant agency enforcing bureaucratic rules on defenceless regulatory targets, irrespective of costs and consequences.

It is clear from the remarks above that this caricature does not correspond to the realities of regulation. In point of fact, both the costs that are ultimately borne by the regulated firms and the degree of effective control of polluting activities that is realised by the government agency are less than could be predicted or expected on the basis of a model of a sovereign control agency, representing the public interest, that confronts a dutifully complying firm. To be sure, if we look more closely at the firms, it does appear at first sight that the regulatory costs are indeed imposed from outside; that they are perceived as constraints emanating from the regulatory agency, as something to which the firm must react in making its investment and operating decisions. But this view neglects the important element of interaction between the firm and the agency.

Regulatory policy can be conceived of as a set of parameters – or 'enforcement variables' – that are intended to establish effective boundaries or constraints to the permissible behaviour of industrial emitters. Taken as a whole, in their mutual interrelationships these variables constitute the 'enforcement strategy' of the regulatory agency, selected so as most effectively to achieve the objectives of the policy being implemented.

It is assumed that a cost-minimising firm will react to a particular enforcement strategy by producing different amounts of pollution depending on its internal calculations with regard to the relative costs of compliance and non-compliance. In this sense, it would be true that the cost of complying with different levels of control depends on the enforcement strategy employed by the control agency. The reaction on the part of the firm in a concrete case would depend on the actions of the government agency in as far as these actions, in turn, affected factors or considerations of consequence for the firm's decisions regarding its environmentally relevant behaviour. For its part, the enforcement authority itself (or the officials through which it acts) has a range of possibilities in selecting the enforcement options it will use. For example, it must decide how violations will be defined, in what way compliance with permit conditions will be controlled and violations detected, and what will be done, in cases of violations, to bring the firm back in line. (See also Diver, 1980; Richardson *et al.*, 1982; Hawkins, 1984.)

Given the constraints under which enforcement officials operate, it is in their interest to strike a balance or seek an optimum trade-off between attempting to achieve strict enforcement against strong and effective opposition from companies running factories, and obtaining co-operation from such companies, but with the possibility that by so doing they have to compromise on specification standards. In addition to the costs resulting from possible resistance by companies, inspectors also face resource constraints within their own agency: the limited resources devoted to enforcement means that agencies (and individual officials) must constantly consider how they can achieve as much of their objective as efficiently as possible. It is important that we keep in mind that cost decisions cannot be omitted from consideration in deciding how far to go when enforcing regulations. Given this situation, these officials have to decide how much (or little) compliance they are prepared to allow at a cost acceptable to them (Peacock, 1984, p. 132).

In various countries research has confirmed that a system of negotiated compliance rather than strict enforcement is characteristic of the relationship between regulatory authorities and firms. There is strong evidence for a predictable pattern in the enforcement/compliance process that seems to transcend national boundaries. First, a policy of negotiated compliance is resorted to. If this fails, administrative measures may be taken: that is, the national equivalents of improvement and prohibition notices. Finally, formal administrative sanctions, even criminal law prosecutions, may be resorted to in the event that compliance cannot be secured along these more informal lines. Yet such formal sanctions are rare and prosecution, in particular, is the measure of last resort that signals the failure of bargaining over compliance. A strongly preferred strategy is the use of bargaining and problem solving to create mutually acceptable conditions for compliance. This means that the bulk of the inspectors' work will be concerned with inducing compliance, even to the extent of providing extensive information and advice to firms.

Clearly, how regulations in fact are applied – the values that are selected for these enforcement variables – and what, therefore, is ultimately demanded of a firm in terms of compliance are important factors in the decisions of the firm regarding its production and investment activities. However, while the actual costs of regulation for the firm will, to a large extent, depend on what the responsible government agency does or does not do in a particular case, the actions of the enforcement officials themselves will also be influenced by the actions of the firm – or the expectations that the agency has regarding the likely behaviour of the firm, acting alone or together with other interested parties *vis-à-vis* the enforcement agency itself or *vis-à-vis* other actors in the political process. These actions by the firm, and/or its allies, can be aimed at influencing the concrete enforcement output at issue in a given case, the parameters within which regulation as such is carried out, or the regulatory programme as a whole. In this sense, the costs of regulations for the firm will, in the last analysis, be a function of its ability to influence (directly or indirectly) the strictness with which the rules are defined and enforced in a given case.

Thus, in so far as the firm itself can be an important factor in determining or influencing the decisions of the regulatory agency regarding its (general) enforcement strategy and its application in specific cases, the enforcement variables to which it reacts cannot be seen as something imposed from outside (as an 'exogenous cost factor'). On the contrary, the firm is in a position to influence the course of the enforcement process, either through its own contacts with the enforcement agency or by political lobbying activities. At the same time, it can be realistically expected that the enforcement agency will be willing (or forced?) to 'trade off' enforcement costs with the individual firms in its area (Downing and Hanf, 1983, pp. 318–43).

It is in this sense that the target groups of regulatory policy can be treated as integral parts of the enforcement structure through which the effective level of compliance is determined. This conclusion with regard to environmental policy is but a special case of the general point made by other observers of business regulation: choices constraining market behaviour are not made exogenously by others than those whose behaviour is being regulated. Individual target firms have both the resources and the ability to influence the decisions regarding the severity or the structure of enforcement schemes.

At this juncture a concept may be introduced that is not normally applied to regulatory policy, but which nevertheless summarises nicely the above discussion. In connection with many human services programmes the concept of co-production is used to describe a situation in which 'the person being served [the client or consumer] is inevitably a part of the production process, if there is to be any production whatsoever' (Parks *et al.*, 1981, p. 1002; see also Kiser, 1984). In such cases, 'the resources, motivations and skills brought to bear by the consumer are . . . intimately connected with the level of achieved output' (quoted in Parks *et al.*, 1981, p. 1001). With the notion of co-production attention is directed to the important role of consumers, as co-producers of the service that they receive, under conditions where neither the 'regular producer' nor the 'consumer producer' (to use the terminology of Parks *et al.*) can provide the service alone and where, therefore, inputs from both are needed if anything at all is to be produced.

It is clear that this concept cannot be applied to the enforcement process with the same strictness as in the case of service programmes. Nevertheless, the idea of co-production is useful for underscoring the fact that the 'production of regulation' also depends, to a significant degree, on the combination of inputs from the 'producer' (the regulatory agency) and the 'consumer' (the industrial emitter) of the regulatory output. The application of this notion to regulatory policy (where it is assumed that regulations are enforced strictly and uniformly in like situations) may at first appear somewhat counter-intuitive. It does, however, enable us to emphasise the interactive character of environmental regulation, and to set our model of the enforcement process off from those perspectives that view regulatory outputs as being imposed on firms, or as having the character of given external costs to be dealt with by the firm on the basis of its own calculations as to the relative costs of compliance as opposed to the perceived benefits of non-compliance.

The social and organisational constraints on negotiated enforcement

Central to the argument presented here is the assumption that the position and behaviour of the inspectors and special investigative officials are crucial for determining the bottom line of environmental regulation. They are 'the hands and feet, eyes and ears' of enforcement. Both the administrative authority and the public prosecutor are, for a very large part, dependent on the activities of these officials, who interact directly with the 'offender', for the initiatives and information required if any administrative or criminal law actions are to be taken. Crucial for appreciating the central role they play in this process is the argument that 'it is not the law that determines what deviant behaviour is, but rather the inspectors and investigative officials who do so' (Hawkins, 1984: Diver, 1980). Violations and offences are 'created' by them in their interactions with the regulated firms, and with the bureaucratic organisations of which they are a part.

In order to appreciate the way in which this occurs, it is useful to conceive of the enforcement process as a whole in terms of a number of phases. Within each phase a number of decisions need to be taken by government officials which will determine what will happen in the subsequent phases of the process. The key question in connection with these decisions is which criteria or considerations form the basis for the determinations that these officials must make in the different phases of the enforcement process; under what conditions will a particular state of affairs be defined as a violation? What happens between the determination by an official (inspector, or even investigator) that something is amiss (in violation of the applicable law) and the initiation of a formal (administrative or criminal law) enforcement action? How do inspectors or investigative officials decide whether a strict interpretation of the regulations is appropriate, or whether a more conciliatory approach would be more effective?

An important factor shaping the behaviour of these officials as they perform their functions is the differences of perspectives and approaches that characterise individuals from different institutional backgrounds. Moreover, it is possible to find differences among officials coming from the same organisation. A further variation on this theme is the possible role conflicts between officials who combine the role of inspector and specially empowered investigator in one person. (They may also be pulled in different directions by the dual lines of supervision to which they are subjected: the administrative agency of which they are a part, and the public prosecutor in charge of criminal justice activities.) It appears that inspectors (even if invested with special investigative powers) will tend to be primarily concerned with bringing offenders around to the legally intended or desired state of affairs – putting things right. Police officials (along with members of special investigative units, themselves often ex-policemen), on the other hand, when confronted with a violation, will be inclined more quickly to define the situation as one requiring action to punish the violation. Indeed, they will be quicker in defining a situation as being 'in violation' to begin with. Thus, in the case of the environmental inspector we have an official who seeks compliance instead of deterrence – who is more concerned with convincing, advising and stimulating the firm to come into compliance than with the performance of his police-like role. Only seldom will use be made of the formal sanctioning procedures; such actions do not fit with the atmosphere of consultation and negotiating on the conditions under which compliance would be possible.

Under what conditions will an official (officials) opt for one or the other of these generic forms? In trying to answer this question, the concept of enforcement style draws attention to the process by which the reality of environmental enforcement is socially constructed in a multi-actor situation characterised by a high degree of mutual dependence. By means of an analysis of the typical modes of adaptation of enforcement agencies to this recurrent problem of the over-inclusiveness of protective regulation (i.e. the fact that regulatory schemes, in their attempt to be generally applicable, fail to differentiate among different kinds of firm and their motivations: that is, between 'good apples' and 'bad apples'), it should be possible to shed light on the circumstances under which officials consider one or the other strategy to be appropriate; the factors that determine their inclination to make use of these alternatives; and the reciprocal relationship between these styles, the behaviour of individual officials and the enforcement policy of the agency (Kagan, 1989, pp. 91–100).

Choices between these strategies are not made on the basis of the calculations of the individual enforcement officials alone. In seeking to understand what these officials do when they interpret the situation in which they find themselves and decide how to proceed in enforcing the legal rules, two points should be kept in mind. First of all, the coping strategies or rules for interpreting the type of situation that one confronts and the appropriate response to it are social rules. And second, the character of the rules developed by groups of enforcement officials will be affected by the larger organisational context as well as the general task and political environment within which the organisation and its constituent elements go about their business.

If, as we have noted above, it is true that 'pollution is not self-evident', then it does not define itself; enforcement agents do (Hawkins, 1984, p. 101). In this important sense the 'regulatory facts of life of pollution' - the existence of a violation; the nature of the case; the appropriate response – do not exist independently of the interpretative judgements which enforcement officials make about them. Consequently, as Hawkins argues, it is the routine behaviour of pollution control officers that constitutes the reality of pollution control law (Hawkins, 1984, p. 16). In other words, what legal rules in fact mean will be largely determined by the interpretations given them in practice by the field staff.

It is because of this than an understanding of how compliance is secured by enforcement agents requires that we appreciate how pollution comes to be defined, identified and raised as a matter requiring intervention: that is, under what conditions and on the basis of what considerations does 'dirty water' get transformed into a 'pollution' in the creation of a case on which some form of enforcement action must be taken? And in this regard it is important to note that, in responding to the various pressures and imperatives of the immediate work environment, it is not the individual enforcement officials alone who decide what is important in defining the situation in which they find themselves. In an attempt to create certainty and structure within the discretionary space within which street-level bureaucrats work, they create rules for interpreting situations in which they find themselves and for deciding how they will deal with a particular case when enforcing the material legal rules. These interpretive standards are developed within the group of officials and constitute in that sense social rules which function as a kind of self-regulation with regard to the exercise of their discretion (Aalders, 1987, pp. 13–33).

The accepted ways of doing the job are, therefore, broadly defined by some set of interpretive principles regarding how the organisation's legal mandate is supposed to be carried out, and are organised by the experience that officials acquire from their membership of an enforcement bureaucracy. Acquiring sound judgement is essentially a matter of absorbing a sense of the norms operating in the agency which guide discretion at the field level. Individual decisions are made within the context of what is 'normal' for 'cases of this kind'. New members – in the course of becoming socialised – learn how to categorise cases for purposes of decision making. The definition of the situation which emerges represents a social construction of reality, which is then institutionalised in certain routines and reaffirmed in repeated interactions both within the group and with relevant external others. It is these rules of interpretation that are then used to define the positions and perspectives from which these officials enter into the social process of applying the material legal rules.

By focusing our attention on enforcement control at the field (street) level where individual officials make important screening decisions regarding the existence of problems and the needs for remedies, we can examine the role these field officials play as 'gatekeepers' for the regulatory agency. At the same time, such an analysis must examine in what ways the behaviour of these street-level bureaucrats, both as individuals and as members of a social group, is shaped by fact that they are also members of a street-level *bureaucracy* and interact, both via this organisation and directly, with various aspects of their environment.

In his analysis of the process of developing and using such rules, Aalders points out that many treatments of this phenomenon pay too little attention to the influence of larger social structures on rule making within small (work) groups. He argues that these larger social units determine in crucial ways the actions of individuals and small groups (Aalders, 1987, p. 31). Not only the more general system of legal rules shapes these informal structures; influence is also exerted by both higher administrative levels such as ministries, political executives and courts and other judicial officials, and more general political structures such as interest groups, political parties and the general public. The reactions of these actors can lead to direct interventions in the work sphere of the enforcement officials or be fed back into the system of support and resources on which their individual and group futures depend. For this reason Aalders argues for a perspective that will incorporate the relations between interactions among members of the group, the forces that penetrate the group of officials from outside which influence the social rules and develop within the group, and the way in which these rules, once in place, are used in negotiating concrete cases in interaction with the regulated firms. (On this point, see also the discussion of the political environment of enforcement in Kagan (1989, pp. 105–12).

Although the perspective taken here is from the field level – the perceptions and experiences of officials at the bottom – it must be stressed at the same time that the mandate of these officials as well as their opportunities for action are refracted by organisational constraints and demands. Of particular importance for the search process with respect to rule application are the contacts which the groups of officials have with other groups, agencies and organs, both inside and outside the government apparatus.

These social rules are, then, a product of the interactions between the inspectors and their work group, these officials and the larger agency of which they are a part, and, in particular, the social relationships between inspectors and the firms they monitor. Once again we are reminded that the final enforcement product will be the result of interactions – bargaining – between officials and the activity being regulated. In this sense, enforcement is a social process linking actors from different sectors and levels of both government and society.

At the same time, by stressing the processes of social rule making we can see how street-level bureaucrats can be reintegrated into the broader social and organisational context. These officials function not as isolated individuals but as members of a work group, an organisational sub-unit, and, ultimately, as participants in a co-production process. We are, therefore, not talking about individual responses to these situations (although social processes work upon and are filtered through the personality and character of the individual actors). While it is true that not all officials will do the same thing in similar situations or that all members of the group are completely integrated into and motivated by group norms, these social rules do provide common points of reference around which this individual behaviour can be co-ordinated and integrated into a group product.

Concluding remarks

This chapter has attempted to present a framework for the examination of the behaviour of regulatory enforcement officials viewed as Lipskyian street-level bureaucrats. In particular, it is argued that the coping behaviours of this group of regulatory officials can best be understood as social constructs which serve as the basis from which individual officials engage with the targets of government regulations (and, in specific cases, with other interested parties) in the 'co-production' of regulatory outcomes. This is in contrast to Lipsky, who seems to suggest that such coping strategies are individual responses to a work situation characterised by substantial discretion, direct interaction with the public and uncertainty as to objectives and performance criteria. In Lipsky's analysis the social character of this behaviour is derived from the fact that these individuals have adapted in similar ways to a shared work environment. He does not examine the extent to which, and the structures through which, coping behaviour is a social product of the group of street-level bureaucrats itself within a broader organisational context.

This does not mean, of course, that the relations between different levels of management within an agency and between that agency and higher levels in the bureaucratic hierarchy are not without problems. Indeed, Lipsky does stress the tensions between agency leadership and the officials interacting directly with the public (Lipsky, 1980, pp. 16–25). Nonetheless, the attitudes and orientations of individual officials must be understood as the product of a number of individual, work group and organisational forces which provide points of reference for the interactions out of which decisions emerge in concrete enforcement situations. In any case, an analysis of enforcement style and the strategies which mediate the relationships between these officials and their task environment must include an examination of the mechanisms through which these different sets of actors impact upon the behaviour of street-level bureaucrats.

Street-level bureaucrats are subjected, both directly and indirectly, to a number of competing forces determining their use of discretion, by virtue of their position as the penultimate link in the implementation chain. In coping with the pressures and uncertainties resulting from their direct contact with the regulated public, there emerge over time shared frameworks of perception and evaluation that govern (and stabilise) the interactions between regulators and regulated. At the same time, this shared 'enforcement world' is regulated by the social rules generated within the work group to which individual officials belong. By acknowledging that the work situation of individual regulatory officials is shaped by both their interactions with the public and their membership of a larger group of similarly placed colleagues, the process of co-producing enforcement can be embedded in the social worlds within and outside the regulatory agency. And through them it can be linked to the broader political process through which environmental regulation is shaped.

References

Aalders, M. V. C. (1987) *Regeltoepassing in de ambtelijke praktijk. Hinderwet en Bouwtoezichtafdeling*, Groningen: Wolters-Nordhoff.

Diver, C. S. (1980) 'A theory of regulatory enforcement', *Public Policy* 28(3), pp. 257–99.

Downing, P. B. (1983) 'Bargaining in pollution control', *Policy Studies Journal*, 11(4), pp. 577–86.

Downing, P. B., and K. Hanf (1983) *International Comparisons in Implementing Pollution Laws*, Boston: Kluwer-Nijhoff.

Hawkins, K. (1984) *Environment and Enforcement: Regulation and the social definition of pollution*, Oxford: Clarendon Press.

Kagan, R. (1989) 'Editor's introduction: understanding regulatory enforcement', *Law and Society*, 11(2), pp. 89–119.

Kiser, L. (1984) 'Toward an institutional theory of citizen co-production', *Urban Affairs Quarterly*, 19 (4), pp. 485–510.

Lipsky, M. (1980). *Street-Level Bureaucracy: Dilemmas of the individual in public services*, New York: Russell Sage.

Majone, G. (1989) *Evidence, Argument, and Persuasion in the Policy Process*, New Haven, Conn.: Yale University Press.

Parks, R. B., P. C. Baker, L. Kiser, R. Oakerson, E. Ostrom, V. Ostrom, S. L. Percy, M. B. Vandivort, P. Whitaker and R. Wilson, (1981) 'Consumers as co-producers of public services: some economic and institutional considerations', *Policy Studies Journal* 9 (Summer), pp. 1001–11.

Peacock, A., (ed.) (1984) *The Regulation Game: How British and German companies bargain with government*, Oxford: Basil Blackwell.

Richardson, G., A. Ogus and P. Burrows (1982) *Policing Pollution: A study of regulation and enforcement*, Oxford: Clarendon Press.

CHAPTER 5

Delegating implementation problems: social security, housing and community care in Britain

Geoff Fimister and Michael Hill

Introduction

In his essay on local government finance in *Half a Century of Municipal Decline* (Loughlin *et al.*, 1985), Richard Jackman argues that the development, by the 1970s, of a crisis in local government expenditure derived largely from the increased tendency of central government to use 'local authorities as agents of its national policies for income redistribution, operating through various agencies of the welfare state' (p. 146). He goes on, in his conclusions, to argue:

> It is not the grant proportion but the redistributive nature of most of the services provided by local authorities that invites, or even necessitates, intervention by central government. That intervention is required to maintain reasonable uniformity of standards of services and of local taxes. If some areas, often already poor, have high spending and high taxes and others, already rich, low spending and low taxes, the migration of people and business will ensure that the rich areas get richer and the poor poorer. If local autonomy is to be revived, the extent of redistribution in local government would need to be reduced. (p. 167)

This argument, while perhaps overstating the issue of the migration of people and business, gets right to the heart of the problem about the development of autonomous social policies in local authorities. What Jackman might have gone on to say is that it is contradictory to argue that local autonomy can be revived if redistributional policies are reduced, when in fact it is redistributive concerns which have been of fundamental importance in injecting vitality into local politics. Arguments about redistribution have long been recognised as central to the democratic political debate, and it was the apparent possibility of participation in redistributive politics which drew many actors of the 'new urban left' into local politics in the 1970s and early 1980s (see Lansley *et al.*, 1989).

If *Half a Century of Municipal Decline* had been delayed to become instead 'Sixty Years of Municipal Decline', Jackman, instead of diagnosing welfare state policies as at the core of the problem about British local government, would have been able to record that central government had, in the 1980s, effectively made it impossible for redistributive goals to be pursued by local government. By 1985 central government had already undermined local government autonomy in housing policy, although the 1988 Housing Act and the 'ring-fencing' of housing revenue accounts embodied in the 1989 Local Government and Housing Act has taken this shift in policy very much further. In the field of education, it is the Education Reform Act of 1988 which undermines local government's capacity to operate redistributive policies. The central curb is governor control over school budgets within a structure superintended by central government, but the ultimate threat to an egalitarian local authority is the possibility of individual schools (likely to be the better-endowed ones serving better-endowed catchment populations) opting-out (see the discussion of this and other issues about the centralisation of policy control in Glennerster *et al.*, 1991). Above all, however, it is the reorganisation of local government finance with the imposition of strict central controls upon local revenue raising which has undermined the adoption of redistributive goals in local government.

There are, outside the policy areas of housing and education, two areas where local authorities seem to remain responsible for welfare services. One of these is the personal social services, the other is housing benefit. Interestingly, the latter is the one major area in which local government expenditure increased during the Thatcher era – housing benefit having become the modern approach to housing subsidy for low-income people. The former, personal social services, has been a policy area where local authorities have experienced strong pressures for increased expenditure in the general context of cuts – because of demographic trends and the consequences of other public policy changes (see Webb and Wistow, 1986). At the time of writing, social services are about to experience further change believed to involve resource enhancement, as the government introduces new policies for community and residential care. Developments of the 1980s in both housing benefit and community care policies recreate for local authorities an income maintenance role, which was abolished by legislative measures in the period 1934 to 1948 (principally the 1934 Unemployment Act and the 1948 National Assistance Act). This theme has been explored further elsewhere (Hill, 1989). Our concern here is to explore the way in which the delegation of such powers to local government, in a context of tight resource controls, creates a situation in which local implementers of central policies seem to have to take the blame for some of the individual consequences of those policies. This we contend is a central issue for central–local relations in the 1990s.

In Britain the absence of constitutional safeguards for local government makes it peculiarly subordinate to central government. Superordinate governments are likely to leave deliberately unresolved some key policy conflicts for lower-level actors. The examples we will explore – of conflict between social security policy and aspects of housing policy, and between a concern to extend community care and an unwillingness to pay the costs of that extension – are, we contend, typical examples. They offer striking case studies of situations in which Hogwood and Gunn's (1984) prescriptions for effective implementation, calling upon policy-makers to avoid embodying contradictions in their policies, are likely to be unheeded. One consequence of this is that lower-level implementers will be put into situations in which they have to try either to act consistently despite such contradictions, or will be likely to take the blame for them.

Housing benefit and rent levels

This part of the chapter updates a story which has already been examined elsewhere (Hill, 1989, 1990). In the 1960s, governments of both political colours encouraged local authorities to target housing subsidies upon low-income tenants by means of rebates or differential rent schemes. The Housing Finance Act of 1972 adopted a national scheme to do this. It also introduced a national rent allowances scheme for unfurnished private tenancies. This policy change left an area of anomaly, between local subsidy (albeit with partial central support) and central subsidy to tenants through the provisions for housing additions within the supplementary benefit scheme. Legislation in the 1980s – the Social Security and Housing Benefit Act of 1982 and the Social Security Act of 1986 – rationalised means-tested support for low-income tenants (and for low-income payers of local taxes) in the form of the housing benefit scheme, which was administered by local government but controlled and (almost fully) subsidised by central government.

Before this rationalisation occurred, a review of the supplementary benefit scheme had balked at it, making the following comment:

> any substantial changes to the existing arrangement could raise other problems, for example on coverage, entitlement, benefit levels and costs. Any form of integration would be likely to involve either an increase in costs which could not be accommodated within current expenditure plans without sacrificing other expenditure objectives or substantial problems of redistribution of current benefits. The familiar problem of the 'poverty trap' would also need to be taken into account . . . And, to extend, beyond the limits of the current supplementary benefit scheme, the number of those who would look to public funds to meet up to 100 per cent of their housing costs, while advantageous to ill-housed families of low paid workers, would raise wider social and economic issues. (Department of Health and Social Security, 1977, p. 58)

The government has opted to deal with this cost problem by ensuring that benefit tapers off sharply as income rises. Hence it has controlled the cost problem by intensifying the poverty trap, notwithstanding the fact that it appears to recognise the importance of the latter problem. It is indeed a significant one for British means tests, where the combined effects of withdrawal of one or more benefits and rising tax and insurance produce a 'tax' effect that often minimises the value of any pay increase achieved by a low-income worker. Furthermore, anything the government does to push up rent levels in general tends to increase the cost of the housing benefit scheme. In the early 1980s, therefore, we saw the Department of the Environment adjusting general subsidies to force local authority rent increases, and the Department of Health and Social Security responding to the 'knock-on' effect of this on housing benefit costs by steepening the tapers, complaining that the scheme was extending 'too far up the income distribution', a logical consequence of rent increases.

The local authorities had to cope with the practical consequences of these policies. Some local authorities, generally those under Labour control, tried at one stage to develop local policies which would partly resolve contradictions without harming low-income tenants. They sought ways of increasing those public-sector rents which would be wholly or largely subsidised by central government, while keeping other rents down. They were frustrated in that search by the inevitable readiness of the Department of Health and Social Security to amend the housing benefit regulations to close such 'loopholes'.

The position with regard to housing benefit support for private-sector rent payers was even more complex.

It can probably reasonably be said that there would be a consensus that if you have a benefit scheme which takes into account the level of an individual's rent, and which may, if income is low enough, meet that rent in full, you need rules to prevent landlords taking advantage of the scheme by charging exorbitant rents to benefit recipients. However, that consensus crumbles, at least in Britain, when consideration is given to the right way to do that. One way is to have a separate system of rent control, independent of the housing benefit scheme. That view is opposed by those, including the Conservative governments of the 1980s, who were quite happy to see the system of rent control crumble in the face of evasion and creeping deregulation. The consequence of that is, therefore, the need for a control system within the benefit scheme to 'protect public funds', since if benefit is available to pay any rent, market forces clearly do not provide any effective control.

The method used to provide this control within the housing benefit system is an elaborate regulation to be enforced by the local authorities. The regulation gives local authorities powers to limit housing benefit where they consider:

> that a claimant occupies a dwelling larger than is reasonably required by him and others who also occupy that dwelling (including any non-dependants of his and any person paying rent to him) having regard in particular to suitable alternative accommodation occupied by households of the same size; or . . . that the rent payable for his dwelling is unreasonably high by comparison with the rent payable in respect of suitable alternative accommodation elsewhere . . .

This power is qualified by regulations restraining its application where hardship would result from an enforced move, and also requiring authorities to delay its operation where the rent had been met without the aid of benefit in the past. It would not be appropriate to go into these qualifications in great detail here; what is important is that they appear to leave a considerable amount to the discretion or judgement of the local authority. One of the authors has done a considerable number of short courses designed to train local politicians in how to operate the Housing Benefit Review Board system, designed to deal with disputed decisions, for which they are responsible. The interpretation of the regulations related to high rent is always a central preoccupation of these events, and where authorities have made restrictions they have not surprisingly attracted requests for review. It is interesting to note the ideological dilemmas that the regulations pose for people at both ends of the political spectrum. Conservatives are worried about the conflict between their interest in supporting private landlords and their concern for public expenditure restraint. Labour members tend to want to curb 'profiteering' landlords, but are concerned about the impact of restrictions upon the welfare of tenants. Labour-controlled local authorities have probably been less zealous implementers of this form of eligible rent restriction than have been Conservative ones (Loveland, 1987, 1988). The tightening of the regulations in 1986 indicated that the government had been concerned about the under-use of restriction.

But the whole issue of restricting the level of rent to be met within the housing benefit scheme was brought into sharper focus by the government's deregulation of the private housing market. Already there were many loopholes in the rent regulation system, but the 1988 Housing Act determined that many tenancies should become what are termed 'assured tenancies' with 'rents freely negotiated between landlord and tenant'. However, the White Paper proposing the legislative change had this to say about the role of housing benefit:

> The housing benefit system will continue to provide help to those who need it. However, once rents are deregulated it will be necessary to ensure that landlords cannot increase the rents of benefit recipients to unreasonable levels at the expense of the taxpayer. Local authorities' discretion to restrict benefit on unreasonable rents is already being strengthened as part of the housing benefit changes to take effect in April 1988. The Government proposes in addition to require Rent Officers to scrutinise the level of rents which are being met by housing benefit. Where a rent is excessive, the subsidy to the local authority will be restricted to an appropriate market rent for the dwelling in question. Guidance to Rent Officers on the principles for assessing rent levels will be issued by the Secretary of State. The Government is prepared if necessary to place direct limits on housing benefit, rather than on subsidy. (HMSO, 1987, para 3, 18)

Various points in this quotation require further comment. The government obviously needed some local agents if it was to impose these measures. It initially developed a system of local rent ceilings. But recognising the rigidity of this approach, it then gave the task of determining housing benefit rent limits case by case to a group of public officials, independent of local authorities and accountable to central government: rent officers. These officials were in need of a new task if they were not to become largely redundant, as the Housing Act had taken many of their earlier rent-fixing powers away. However, the rent officers only determine appropriate rent levels to attract normal subsidy. Local authorities still have a duty to decide (a) whether applicants and their families belong within specific vulnerable groups whose rent must be met in full, and (b) whether suitable alternative accommodation is available and it is 'reasonable' to expect a move to it. The first of these tests involves an unambiguous judgement in most cases. The old, the sick and families with children are in the vulnerable groups. The second test is much more difficult to apply. It is significant that the word 'reasonable', which is used in so many regulations where discretion has to be exercised, appears here.

If authorities decide to meet the 'excess' rent, they will get roughly half the normal subsidy on that amount if the claimant is in a 'vulnerable' group, but otherwise no subsidy at all. Hence, in dealing with hardship cases under the 'rent stop' provisions, local authorities have to weigh a concern about the economical use of local resources against any concerns about the needs and circumstances of the applicant, using a complex regulation in which the government has expressed welfare concerns in a manner which readily obscures and undermines them.

Not surprisingly, it has been discovered that some authorities are more mindful of their own financial situations than those of benefit claimants. What then can claimants do in such situations? They cannot challenge the rent officer's determination; only the local authority is allowed to do this. They can, however, ask for a review by the Board, which the local authority is required to set up from its own elected councillors. There are obvious reasons for doubting the impartiality of such a board in a situation like this. However, exceptionally, the aggrieved claimant may take a case to the High Court to try to prove that a Review Board has misapplied the law. There have been such cases on this high-rent issue. However, the judge in the leading case so far was unprepared to accept that there was any contradiction between the two sets of regulations. He ruled, in a judgement that the Department of Social Security was obviously happy to report to local authorities in its Guidance Manual (1/90 revision) that 'a local authority was entitled . . . to take into account its own financial situation when exercising its discretion' (Queen's Bench Division, *Regina* v. *Brent London Borough Council, ex parte Connery,* 1989). The actual implications of this are still the subject of debate within local authorities.

The logic of the government's position on 'assured tenancies' and housing benefit is that it wants a free market to operate but has a problem that for some tenants the payment of benefit, hypothetically up to any rent level, means that they will not behave as a free 'bargainer' normally would. However, in Britain private renting is already a very bad deal, compared with buying, for most free agents in the market place. Hence, a high proportion of private renters are low-income people who rent because of a lack of resources to enable them to buy. They are, therefore, the very people most likely to be applicants for housing benefit. If rent officers prove to be zealous restricters of 'eligible rent' for housing benefit purposes and, as seems to be the case, local authorities are unwilling to bear the cost of overriding such decisions, and if the supply of housing to low-income people in the areas of housing pressure does not increase, what is likely to happen is that many people will remain in accommodation only partly subsidised through the benefit scheme, drawing on their other resources to bridge the gap between their officially allowed rent and the actual rent they have to pay. We are seeing the development of partial rent restriction by way of the housing benefit scheme, with many poor people paying premiums – and having their disposable incomes (after rent) reduced below the official poverty line.

To sum up, we have here a situation in which local authorities are largely passive implementers of a central government reform, but have, in exceptional circumstances, to take responsibility for, and bear most of the costs of, resolving a conflict between rents policy and social security policy. This is not the only situation in which local authorities can be put in a difficult position by housing benefit rules: other examples can occur in relation to late claims and to the operation of family assumptions in the means test. These create critical dilemmas for those local authorities which are concerned about the welfare of some of their poorest citizens.

Community care

The philosophy of community care – that frail elderly people and people with various illnesses and disabilities should wherever possible be supported in the community rather than enter institutions – is one with which it is easy to agree. Beneath the rhetoric, though, can be found a variety of different agendas: enhancing the dignity and quality of life of elderly people and people with disabilities is the chief motivating source for some; while limiting public spending on hospital and/or residential care is the main preoccupation of others. These objectives are not necessarily incompatible, if sufficient resources are diverted to care in the community. However, few policy-makers, managers and practitioners in the community care field are confident that this will be the case, and thus the flag of community care can be seen to flutter on the masts of ships sailing in very different directions.

This divergence of objectives can be found reflected in the

agendas of different central government departments. Those from the local government side who have been involved in consultations with central government over the introduction of new community care arrangements (now scheduled for April 1993) have noted how the apparently genuine good intentions of the Department of Health have collided with the ambitions of the Department of the Environment (DoE) to control and restrict local government spending (as well as the ever-present restrictive influence of the Treasury); how the DoE has seemed acutely uncomfortable with the notion that housing policy (for which it is responsible) is important to community care planning; and how the Department of Social Security has been preoccupied with divesting itself of responsibility for paying benefit in relation to private- and voluntary-sector residential care and nursing homes, while showing little interest in other benefit issues which impinge upon community care (Fimister, 1988, 1991).

It is indeed arguable that the question of social security spending on residential care and nursing homes has been the main factor driving the 'community care' changes. The restructuring of supplementary benefit which took place in 1980 was intended to permit more exact government control of spending and entitlements, by replacing a system which permitted considerable discretion to officers (albeit hedged about with voluminous administrative guidance) with one which was tightly defined by detailed regulations. As an apparently inadvertent side-effect of this process, access to supplementary benefit 'board and lodging' payments for people in private- and voluntary-sector residential care and nursing homes actually became more clearly established, creating a surge in claims and providing a stimulus to private provision in this area.

Although apparently unintentional, it would seem that this development was not entirely unwelcome to a government committed to the promotion of private provision. However, this attitude soon changed, as claims in this sector escalated rapidly. The government's 1989 White Paper on community care (Department of Health, 1989, para. 8.5) complained that the costs 'rose in cash terms from £10m. in December 1979 to over £1,000m. by May 1989'. By April 1991, the corresponding outlay had reached £1,625 million, the number of claimants having risen to 220,000, from a mere 12,000 in December 1979 (House of Commons Social Security Committee, 1991, para. 4). The government clamped down as early as November 1983, when locally determined maximum limits were fixed. From April 1985 these were replaced by a rigid system of national limits (varying by 'client group' and by type of care, with slightly higher limits in London after July 1986). While this gave the government some control over the pressure which homes' charges were exerting on benefit costs, it created a new social (and political) problem, in that the numbers began to grow of residents whose benefits would not meet the charges. This shortfall began to manifest itself in various undesirable ways, including financial pressure on residents and relatives; top-ups by increasingly alarmed charities; cross-subsidy by some homes from charges levied on other residents not dependent on benefit payments; some homes getting into financial difficulties as costs could not be met; some homes providing lower standards for those depending on benefits; some residents having to move home (see, for example, Age Concern, 1989; National Association of Citizens' Advice Bureaus, 1991; House of Commons Social Security Committee, 1991).

The government soon developed the view that this intractable problem needed to be removed from the social security system and placed elsewhere. This growing conviction was paralleled by the publication of some key reports which examined various aspects of community care policy and finance: an Audit Commission report (1986) which was highly critical of the unfocused nature of benefit spending in this area; the Firth Report (1987), reflecting the deliberations of a joint central–local government working party looking at the finance of residential care; the Wagner Report (1988) on overall residential care policy; and, above all, the Griffiths Report (1988), which the government hoped would produce ideologically acceptable proposals for change.

It should be stressed that it was not only a question of central government's need to be 'got off the hook': there was a strong professional view within the community care field, reflected also in the Audit Commission report, that benefit payments which did not rest on any assessment of need for this type of care represented an indiscriminate use of resources, and an incentive to the use of residential care where support in the community might be more appropriate.

In Britain, local authority social services departments (SSDs – an abbreviation which, for simplicity, we shall also use to embrace the corresponding 'social work departments' in Scotland) are responsible for providing a range of services, under various legislation, to vulnerable groups. Such services can include the direct provision of residential care accommodation, but (prior to April 1993) have not (with certain minor exceptions) included the assumption of financial responsibility for residential and nursing home care in private- and voluntary-sector establishments. Hence the (real if sometimes over-emphasised) financial incentive to local authorities to favour the use of such accommodation.

Griffiths' recommendation that SSDs should play the key role was not immediately welcome to central government. Although a certain amount of 'exporting' of community care problems (notably as regards supported lodgings and hostels – see below) had already taken place, the transfer of substantial additional resources to local government did not seem attractive, especially given that the strict central control which was possible in the case of the housing benefit scheme would not really be feasible here. However, no alternative could be devised and so, after a substantial delay, the White Paper appeared, confirming the lead role for SSDs. Griffiths' recommendation that the resources for community care should be substantially 'ring-fenced' was reluctantly accepted, a last minute response to pressure.

Before further examining the nature of the problem which was being passed to SSDs, some comment is required on the prior 'export' of other aspects of the finance of special needs accommodation. The finance of private- and voluntary-sector residential care and nursing home places was obviously a headache because of the cost and the difficulty in controlling it, but social security policy in the 1980s was also preoccupied with creating a system which was highly computerised, requiring fewer civil servants and individual assessments which were less detailed. 'Messy bits' which did not fit this scenario were to be purged, a theme which was a key feature of the major changes to means-tested benefits which took place in April 1988. Thus, although changes to the benefit position of 'non-straightforward' types of accommodation such as hostels and board and lodging were not made as part of the 1988 changes, they were nevertheless targeted for 'reform'.

The separate formula for board and lodging accommodation was abolished in April 1989, new claimants from that date needing to seek ordinary income support (as supplementary benefit was now known) plus housing benefit (Department of Health and Social Security, 1986). Board and lodging payments had been an increasing irritation to the Department: not only did they not readily fit into the new system of income support, but they had been highly controversial because of deficient upratings, harsh criteria for payment to young people, and various legal challenges to the regulations. However, the new proposals took no account of elements in the board and lodging situation which were not covered by ordinary income support or housing benefit, such as meals at commercial prices, or personal care costs. The latter were particularly significant as regards our present purposes: 'supported lodgings', where care costs are included as part of the charge, were not mentioned in the DHSS consultative paper, and the Department at first seemed unaware that they were a problem. Local authority associations, voluntary organisations and academic bodies were quick to point out that claimants could be left with little or no disposable income after paying charges, to the detriment of community care strategy. The DHSS then commissioned research on the subject (Young, 1988) which confirmed these apprehensions, but the change was implemented nevertheless. The Department was silent on the question of who was going to pay the care costs in such projects: it was clear at the time, and is even more so in retrospect, that the DHSS wanted SSDs to pick up this troublesome responsibility (as indeed, many already did), but could not say so while the government was still considering its response to the Griffiths Report. Finally, in November 1988, a minister came clean:

> Research shows that just over half of those local authorities which run schemes already fund them in whole or in part. They will continue to be able to fund them after next April. The consideration is entirely as it always has been – in the lap of local authorities. (Lord Skelmersdale, House of Lords *Hansard*, 1 November 1988, col. 146)

No offer of compensatory funds was made to local authorities.

The DHSS's desire to expunge care costs from the social security system had meanwhile become increasingly apparent elsewhere.

During 1987 the definition of a small unregistered residential care home was changed, so that a number of adult fostering-type schemes became treated as supported lodgings (at much lower rates of benefit), while residents of certain schemes sponsored by health authorities were designated as hospital patients for benefit purposes, thus having minimal entitlement.

In a follow-up exercise to the board and lodging proposals, the benefit position of people in hostels was also reviewed. In a striking parallel to the earlier process, research was commissioned (Berthoud and Casey, 1988) which again produced awkward findings – that care costs in hostels were substantial – but the changeover to ordinary income support plus housing benefit went ahead anyway (from October 1989). The potentially disastrous effects on the finances of a number of hostels led to widespread protest, including rumblings from within the Conservative Party. An elaborate system of 'transitional protection', both for claimants and for hostels, resulted, but the main change proceeded. From April 1991 the resources being spent on 'protection' were transferred to 'traditional sources of funding', mainly SSDs. This was hardly satisfactory, as it took no account of future developments in this field; ignored the position of those types of hostel, such as women's refuges, which were not 'traditionally' the province of SSDs; and distributed the funds via the revenue support grant 'standard spending assessment' system (see below) which bore no relationship to the distribution of hostels. However, it had enabled the (now) Department of Social Security (the health and social security sides of the DHSS had been split in 1988) to bound further free of the encumbrance of special needs accommodation.

Let us return now to the proposals for private- and voluntary-sector residential care and nursing homes. The government's intention is that, from April 1993, SSDs will have not only the role of assessing the needs of individuals for community care services, but also the financial responsibility for ensuring (subject to a means test) that such needs are met. (Originally, this system was intended to commence from April 1991, but it was postponed in July 1990, apparently because of political fears concerning the possible impact on poll tax levels).

Where residential care or a nursing home place in the private or voluntary sector is required, the usual procedure will be for the SSD to pay the proprietor the full charge, and then to recoup as much as possible by charging the resident. The charging formula to be applied to the resident will be statutorily determined, with very little discretion left to the SSD. The resident will receive ordinary social security benefits, including income support, and an income support 'residential allowance' paid at a standard level towards the housing costs component of the charge. (Income support payments are means tested, and so will depend on the level of the resident's other income). Originally, the housing costs component was to have been met through housing benefit, but there was a difference of opinion between central government departments (as well as between local authority associations) as to how this should be structured, and after a remarkable two-year delay, an announcement was made in March 1992 that an income support payment would be made instead. The whole of the residential allowance and most of the resident's other income will be paid over to the SSD by him or her. Any shortfall between the amount paid by the resident and the charge made by the home will have to be met by the SSD from its 'care budget'. (The above will apply to new cases: people resident at the point of change will remain within the old system.)

The level of the SSD's 'care budget' will therefore be crucial. We noted at the beginning of this chapter that the recent history of local government finance has been one of increasing central control. We have referred to the arrangements applying to education, housing and housing benefit. In the area of the personal social services, there is relatively little specific 'earmarking' of central government grant support for particular purposes: however, grant support is largely determined by the 'standard spending assessment' of what the central authorities think is an appropriate level of spending in this field for a given local authority. The ability to supplement this through local taxation is severely constrained, through central determination of 'business rates' and a system of central 'capping' of local tax levels.

The SSD's care budget will be made up partly of 'normal' grant aid for personal social services; partly of a transfer from social security funds to the local authority revenue support grant; partly of some minor specific grants; and partly of money recouped from charges. The making good of any deficiency will have to be financed from local taxation, with all the problems which that entails. The transfer from social security funds (to be made at national level and then distributed to SSDs through the revenue support grant mechanism) consists of the money which the Department of Social Security would have spent, had the old system continued. Estimating this, with appropriate demographic and inflation assumptions, while also tackling the issues of geographical distribution, is no easy task, and consultations between central and local government have been protracted and frequently controversial (Fimister and Robertson, 1992). For various reasons, there is a growing apprehension on the local authority side (and elsewhere in the community care field) that the whole system will be underresourced. One of those reasons is central to the theme of this chapter: the shortfall between the charges levied by homes and the level of social security payments made towards them.

The problem of this shortfall, described earlier in this chapter, is already serious and is likely to get worse. The Association of Metropolitan Authorities' provisional estimate of the shortfall in the first year, in terms of the new cases which SSDs will have to finance, is around £120 million (for England). This figure refers to the deficit between resources transferred to SSDs from the Department of Social Security and the cost of places in homes: for the DSS does *not* intend to transfer an estimated amount for the shortfall – the whole point of the transfer is that it is intended to represent the amount which the DSS *would otherwise have spent*. Local authority sources are very concerned that the picture could be much worse even than this, as there are undoubtedly substantial suppressed price rises in the system. SSDs will have the statutory responsibility to meet charges for necessary places, which the DSS did not. Many proprietors will expect to be able to increase charges, and an unknown number of people currently unable to afford to enter residential care will seek a place once the benefit barrier has gone.

One of the authors of this chapter has been involved from the outset in the consultations between central and local government, and has been at pains to tease out from civil servants why the government thinks that the shortfall will not be a problem. Three answers have been given: first, that SSDs will be able to use their local bargaining power to exert downward pressure on charges; second, that a proportion of people who might have gone into residential care will be maintained in the community at (usually) lower cost; and finally, that extra funds can be bid for as part of the 'normal' grant aid settlement. The strength of the first argument will clearly vary from place to place depending on the state of the market: that is, the degree to which proprietors are dependent upon SSD-sponsored residents. (The first argument is also inconsistent both with the rhetoric concerning the freedom of residents to choose a home, as any such bargaining will in reality be in the context of blocks of places, and with the aim of raising standards in homes.) The second argument is no doubt true to a degree, but there has been no official estimate placed on the proportion for which this is true. The third argument contains more hope than conviction that such funds would be forthcoming in adequate measure. The suggestion that the shortfall will be substantially offset by the above three factors is obviously an act of faith rather than a financial calculation, and appears to be given little credence outside of central government.

Whether or not one believes that ministers were sincere in their view that the transfer of these financial responsibilities to SSDs would enable the problems better to be solved, it is clear that the DSS will consider itself well rid of them. In shedding this financial commitment, moreover, central government will be sure to distance itself politically from the consequences of under-resourcing at the local level. Although a late decision was taken that resources would be temporarily 'ring-fenced' – specifically earmarked – for community care, apparent deficiences will be brushed aside. As far as the new system is concerned, ministers will claim that local authorities have been given adequate resources, and that any problems must be due to 'mismanagement', or 'overspending' on other areas.

Conclusion

As the new urban left began to win control of many London boroughs and of other cities, it sought opportunities to develop redistributive policies. It also sought, through welfare rights activities and more general anti-poverty strategies, to steer resources from centrally determined programmes to deprived areas. In its counter-moves against the urban left, Conservative governments have enormously limited local authority control over local expenditure. But in the area of social security policies a superficial glance seems to suggest a counter-trend. Through housing benefit, and through community care policies, local government seems to have acquired new powers in relation to the meeting of need at the local level. This chapter has argued that a closer scrutiny of what has been going on throws a very different light upon this apparent contradiction.

As far as housing benefit is concerned, local authorities have found that their freedom to manipulate policy has been severely restricted. Where there is some discretionary freedom, this occurs in a way which imposes costs on local exchequers, and probably brings discredit upon local government as the hapless arbitrator between conflicting central policies. It is a weak position from which to try to enhance welfare.

In the case of community care, local authority discretionary freedom is inevitably greater, inasmuch as what is involved is decisions about individual needs for care in the light of complex infirmities and enormously varied personal support systems. Our context here is a system where the stance of government is that subsidised care should be a scarce alternative, available when most of the resources for personal care have been exhausted (in more senses than one, since in many cases it is family and neighbour carers who can cope no more). An individualised rationing system is thus central. What we have then described is the way in which central government, driven on by a social security resource control problem, is delegating decisions to local government while firmly limiting the resources it transfers for that purpose. In this case local government is forced to ration care, drawing upon a limited resource pool whose size is determined by central government.

In both cases local government is cast in a difficult implementation role structured by central policies determined in an atmosphere in which the imposition of a particular conception of the welfare state is the preoccupation rather than the determination of an appropriate set of responses to need. The 'co-production' which Hupe describes in Chapter 6 of this book as characterising social assistance in the Netherlands certainly occurs in discussions between housing benefit applicants and local authorities about the rent levels to be met. It is already present in SSDs where social workers seek to put together care arrangements for their clients, and will become of even more importance under the new policies. What this chapter has sought to show is that central government has used its financial control powers to ensure that British local authorities will be constrained to drive a very hard bargain in any co-production negotiations.

It is suggested, therefore, that, in a context in which local government has been largely neutered as a redistributive agent, it has nevertheless acquired new duties as administrator of the more complex parts of income maintenance policy. This has posed policy problems at the local level, and has enhanced the tendency for implementers to be left to try to cope with the dilemmas built into the policy itself.

References

Age Concern (1989) *Moving the Goalposts: Changing policies for long-stay health and social care of elderly people,* briefing, London: Age Concern England.

Audit Commission (1986) *Making a Reality of Community Care,* London: HMSO

Berthoud, R., and B. Casey (1988) *The Cost of Care in Hostels,* London: Policy Studies Institute.

Department of Health (1989) *Caring for People: Community care in the next decade and beyond,* Cm. 849, London: HMSO.

Department of Health and Social Security (1977), *Social Assistance,* London: DHSS.

Department of Health and Social Security (1986) *Help with Board and Lodging Charges for People on Low Incomes: Proposals for change,* London: DHSS.

Department of Social Security (1992) *Housing Benefits Guidance Manual,* London: HMSO.

Fimister, G. (1988) 'Leaving hospital after a long stay: the role and limitations of social security', in S. Baldwin, G. Parker and R. Walker (eds), *Social Security and Community Care,* Aldershot: Avebury.

Fimister, G. (1991) 'Care in the community: the social security issues', in P. Carter, T. Jeffs and M. K. Smith (eds), *Social Work and Social Welfare Yearbook 3,* Milton Keynes: Open University Press.

Fimister, G., and G. Robertson (1992) 'Adding up and taking away', *Social Work Today,* 23 (38), pp. 16–18.

Firth, J. (Chair) (1987) *Public Support for Residential Care: Report of a joint central and local government working party,* London: DHSS.

Glennerster, H., A. Power and T. Travers (1991) 'A new era for social policy: a new enlightenment or a new Leviathan?', *Journal of Social Policy,* 20(3), pp. 389–414.

Griffiths, R. (1988) *Community Care: Agenda for action,* London: HMSO.

Hill, M. (1989) 'Income maintenance and local government: implementing central control?', *Critical Social Policy* (25), pp. 18–36.

Hill, M. (1990) *Social Security Policy in Britain,* Cheltenham: Edward Elgar.

HMSO (1987) *Housing: The government's proposals,* Cm. 214, London: HMSO.

Hogwood, B. W., and L. A. Gunn (1984) *Policy Analysis for the Real World,* Oxford: Oxford University Press.

House of Commons Social Security Committee (1991) *The Financing of Private Residential and Nursing Home Fees,* Session 1990/1: Fourth Report, London: HMSO.

Lansley, S., S. Goss and C. Wolmar (1989) *Councils in Conflict: The rise and fall of the municipal left,* London: Macmillan.

Loughlin, M., D. Gelfand and K. Young, (eds) (1985) *Half a Century of Municipal Decline,* London: Allen and Unwin.

Loveland, I. (1987) 'Politics, organisation and the environment: influences on the exercise of administrative discretion within the housing benefit scheme, *Journal of Social Welfare Law,* pp. 216–36.

Loveland, I. (1988) 'Housing benefit: administrative law and administrative practice', *Public Administration*, 66(1), pp. 57–75.

National Association of Citizens' Advice Bureaux (1991) *Beyond the Limit: Income support for elderly people in residential care and nursing homes,* London: NACAB.

Wagner, Lady (Chair) (1988) *Residential Care: A positive choice – report of the independent review of residential care,* London: HMSO/National Institute of Social Work.

Webb, A., and G. Wistow (1986) *Planning, Need and Scarcity: Essays on the personal social services,* London: Allen and Unwin.

Young, P. (1988) *The Provision of Care in Supported Lodgings and Unregistered Homes,* London: Office of Population Censuses and Surveys.

CHAPTER 6

The politics of implementation: individual, organisational and political co-production in social services delivery

Peter Hupe

Introduction

When the belief in rational actors was still wide spread in social science, in theory things were relatively simple. Policy was made at the top and implemented at the bottom. Since phenomena like policy discretion and street-level bureaucracy have been discovered, the number of problems seems to have increased. On the individual level there is the problem for street-level bureaucrats about how to cope with policy discretion, given their workload. On the organisational level there are problems about how to control and manage what these street-level bureaucrats are doing. On the political level there are problems of political accountability and responsibility. If policy outcomes appear to be different to policy intentions, how – given the constraints of democracy, organisational efficiency and labour conditions of civil servants – can the implementation of public policy be managed? That is the basic question underlying this chapter. The question is asked in the context of the Dutch 'Verzorgingsstaat', particularly in the field of public assistance in the Netherlands. Some structural characteristics, social developments and politico-cultural trends, like the application in the public sector of business-like notions of 'client orientation' and 'service centres', appear to make the Dutch case apt for applying and extending the theoretical notion of 'co-production'. Then our operational question becomes the following: to what extent and in what way can business-like notions of client orientation and service centres contribute to the solution of problems of accountability and the management of implementation in social services delivery?

This essay will be organised as follows. First some structural characteristics of the Dutch situation are mentioned. In the next section remarks are made about social security in the Netherlands. After that the National Assistance Act, developments in social security and some politico-cultural trends are sketched. Then the tasks of the municipal social services departments are considered. Following this the problems of implementation and accountability are analysed. As an answer to these problems the notion of co-production is extended and applied to the Dutch situation. Finally, the extent to which this extended notion of co-production appears to provide a possible direction for solution of the problems mentioned above is examined.

The Dutch political system

The Dutch system of intergovernmental relations is characterised by three layers: those of the national, provincial and local governments. National government at the moment consists of 'fourteen un-united ministries', headed by members of coalition cabinets. At the time of writing we have a Christian-Democratic (CDA) and Social-Democratic (PvdA) coalition. It is the third cabinet of Prime Minister Lubbers (CDA). The Prime Minister does not have 'his' or 'her' members of the cabinet as in Great Britain, but is *primus inter pares*. The municipalities in the system of intergovernmental relations can be seen as co-governments. They have certain exclusive tasks, for instance in the implementation of the National Assistance Act. Entangled with the public administration via sectoral policy networks there is what is called the 'societal middlefield' or 'private initiative'. In this intermediary 'field' between government and individual the 'pillarised' character of Dutch society is expressed (Lijphart, 1968).

Since the establishment of the independent state there have been different groups with different coherent religious, political and social orientations. They can indeed be called 'pillars' because one pillar may include several levels of income or education. There is the Christian-Democratic pillar, formerly consisting of three different pillars: a Catholic and two Calvinist ones. Their party is the Christian-Democratic Appeal (CDA).

Then there is the Social-Democratic pillar. It is called 'the Red Family', referring to the Labour political party (Partij van de Arbeid or PvdA in short), labour unions, public broadcasting company and other institutions. Furthermore, there is the liberal pillar. This used to be the meeting place for both conservatives and libertarians. Since the 1960s these two have split into a more traditional liberal pillar with the VVD as a political party and with a public broadcasting company, and next to that a 'new' liberal-progressive pillar with D66 as a political party and two public broadcasting companies expressing a 'contemporary lifestyle'. Characteristic of this lifestyle is that the affiliation with something like a 'pillar' is very loose. Nevertheless – or because of that – this latter 'pillar' seems to express the modern or, better, post-modern *Zeitgeist* of many younger people. The pragmatic political party D66 also attracts voters with a higher education who reject the traditional ideologies of the other pillars. Formed in 1966, Democrats '66 at the moment is one of the three largest parties in the country, even larger than the more traditional liberal party, the VVD.

The 1950s was the flourishing time of the pillarised system. While at the bottom there were strict social boundaries, at the top the élites of the various pillars met and in a somewhat paternalistic way ruled the country. The system of pillarisation is said to have eroded since then (Lijphart, 1968). Surely its importance has been influenced by processes of democratisation. In any case, 'pillarisation' still remains a peculiarity of Dutch society.

Social security in the Netherlands

The Dutch 'Verzorgingsstaat' (*zorg* = care) is the product of extensive public policy in the fields of education, housing, health care, employment and social security. In these fields, government and private organisations belonging to different pillars, have been working together; although in different forms. This Dutch type of the welfare state is called 'Verzorgingsstaat' because it takes care of its citizens 'from the cradle to the grave' – as it is called. In the Dutch social security system there are three types of law: employee insurance schemes, national insurance schemes and welfare provisions. The first two types of regulations provide for insurance schemes, the third for social services (see Van Vliet, 1988). The employee insurance schemes are meant for people employed by a private employer. These insurance schemes are compulsory for every employee. They insure them against unemployment, illness or incapacity for work. Employees and employers pay premiums for these insurances. Most of the benefits received from employee insurance schemes – for example unemployment benefits – are temporary. The national insurance schemes are meant for all Dutch citizens. Allowances are paid out of the premiums that every citizen aged 15 to 65 has to pay out of his or her income. On the basis of the national insurance schemes you can get an old-age pension, a widow and orphans allowance, allowances for exceptional medical expenses, family allowances or general disability benefits. The third kind of regulations are the welfare provisions. The National Assistance Act (Algemene Bijstandswet – ABW) is the most important of the welfare provisions. National assistance benefits are paid to all those who have no income or too little income. These welfare facilities are financed by taxes.

The three types of law are based on different principles. The employee insurance schemes are based on the principal of equivalence: the more you earn, the more premiums you pay, and the more you get. The national insurance schemes and the welfare facilities are governed by the principle of 'solidarity'. People pay higher premiums or taxes if their income is higher. For people in the same circumstances, benefits are the same. For instance, all people who have reached the age of 65 can apply for an old-age pension. Then the 'circumstance' is age (Van Vliet, 1988).

The National Assistance Act

The National Assistance Act (ABW) is a basic provision, financed by government and implemented by the municipal social services departments (Gemeentelijke Sociale Diensten – GSDs). It was put into operation in 1965 and replaced the Law for the Poor (Armenwet) of 1912. The ABW is the key-stone of the social security system in the Netherlands and is, in fact, the essence of the Dutch Verzorgingsstaat. When one is entitled to no or insufficient benefit under the two insurance schemes, one can claim a benefit under the ABW. The aim of the National Assistance Act is to give financial support to any resident in the Netherlands who is either totally or partly unable to meet his or her needs. The assistance is intended to enable the individual to meet necessary day-to-day expenses and, where possible, to earn their own living again. The Act is based on the principle that every citizen has a responsibility to provide for him or herself and any dependants. The state on the other hand has a duty to provide anyone with assistance who is unable, or no longer able, to meet the cost of providing the necessities of life.

National assistance is both individual and supplementary. It is individual, in the sense that, while based on flat rates, it may be adjusted from case to case according to the personal circumstances of the claimant and his or her dependants. The amount of the benefit therefore is not the same for everyone. It is also supplementary in the sense that a person with an insufficient income from work or from social security will be granted assistance to bring his or her income up to the level required to meet his or her needs. This means – and it is essential – that the legislator deliberately leaves a certain freedom to the implementer as far as the level of an ABW benefit for a specific individual is concerned. Of course, the standard rates are fixed every year. Nevertheless, there are opportunities for choice. First, there is 'special assistance' (Bijzondere Bijstand), with which the GSD implementers in particular circumstances may complement the standard rates. Second, the discretion is even greater, where the Dutch social security system is very complex and consists of many different laws. In some cases, making a claim for a benefit according to both Act X and Act Y would be justifiable. Then a more or less arbitrary decision may be made about the type of benefit that is applicable. This decision is thus the result of a process in which the client as well as the implementer defends their interests. Third, essential for the level of a benefit is the claimed marital status of the client or, rather, the nature of his or her household. It is obvious, for instance, that the ABW norm amount for a single person living alone is higher than the half of the benefit for a married or unmarried couple. Thus also the determination of how a person lives his or her life, may be an object of deliberation and checks between claimant and civil servant.

In general there are four groups of people who claim benefits under the National Assitance Act: *long-term unemployed*, who no longer have any right to receive a benefit from the Unemployment Act (one of the employee insurance schemes); *married women*, who have left their husbands or been left by their husbands; *school-leavers*: people who have left school and cannot get a job (because they have never had a job before, they cannot claim a benefit on the basis of the Unemployment Act); and finally, *shopkeepers*, whose private enterprises are no longer profitable. People without any income receive the standard amount for their situation. If someone or their partner has an income, such as (other) social security benefits, a pension or alimony, these are deducted from the benefit payments. Any capital or owned property is also taken into account. To give an indication: as of 1 January 1992, the net amount of the standard rates of the ABW per month for single persons over 23 living alone is Fl. 1200; for single parent families Fl. 1543; for persons over 23 sharing the same accommodation Fl. 1019; while couples receive Fl. 1714. Couples may refer to married or unmarried persons and may also refer to two women or men sharing a household. Lower rates apply for young single persons aged less than 23. For those aged 18 to 20, rates will also vary according to whether they live with their parents or not (Ministry of Social Affairs and Employment, 1992).

Categorisation and other social developments

In his book *In Care of the State*, De Swaan sketches the process of collectivisation in western countries like the Netherlands (1988). Not ideology, but pragmatism and an eye to constructive possibilities dominated the building of the Dutch Verzorgingsstaat. After the Second World War for some years the construction of an extensive social security system had priority in the Netherlands. The ministries involved designed many laws and regulations. The process of collectivisation was paralleled by a process of 'categorisation': for almost any category of citizens special rules and regulations were designed. Citizens became school-leavers, recipients of rent subsidies, claimants on national assistance and the like. People began to behave in conformity with these categories. In the 1970s and 1980s the basis was created for the phenomenon of the 'calculating citizen': the assertive individual who takes the fruits of the Verzorgingsstaat for granted and knows his or her rights. To be able to implement policies for the different categories, criteria are needed – criteria that often are not provided for by the legislator.

Apart from this process of categorisation Van Vliet points to two other developments that have affected the National Assistance Act and the tasks and functioning of the organisations that implement this Act. These are the increase in unemployment and the process of cultural individualism (Van Vliet, 1988). During the last decade there has been a strong increase in unemployment. This is due not only to decreasing employment but also and particularly to the increasing supply of labour. More women are participating in the labour market. The number of women who keep their jobs after their marriage is also increasing, and the same goes for the number of women who start working again after having children. Another factor causing the increasing supply of labour is a demographic one. The baby-boom children, born in the 1950s have entered the labour-market.

A consequence of these factors is that more long-term unemployed people and more school-leavers are claiming benefits under the National Assistance Act. The increasing unemployment and financial claims on social security as a consequence of that have contributed to the political wish to control and cut government expenditures in this field. These resulted not only in effects on the level of benefits, but also in cuts of the personnel and organisation costs of the GSD.

A third social development influencing the Dutch social security system is called 'cultural individualism'. With that term Van Vliet refers to a process in which the independence of the individual increases and the dependence on others, such as the Church, the community or the family, decreases. Since the 1950s drastic changes have taken place in people's views of marriage, family, number of children and independence. Also changes have taken place in actual practice. The number of households that deviate from the traditional family has grown. By the early 1980s the number of divorces had risen to a point where one out of every three marriages resulted in divorce.

In the last few years many discriminating elements have

disappeared from the Dutch employee insurance schemes. Men and women have acquired individual rights. The family no longer forms the only basis of legislation. However, in the National Assistance Act the principle of one benefit per household is still operating, which implies that no individual rights are acknowledged (see Smit, 1987). The definition of a household used to be simple, for only two kinds of household existed: families and single persons living alone. Now, however, as a result of the process of cultural individualism, the law makes a distinction between four types of household: single persons living alone; single parent families; persons sharing the same premises; and couples married and unmarried. To which category someone belongs is important because the level of his or her income depends on it. It is the task of the GSD civil servant to decide whether someone belongs to one or to another category. This task is complicated, because the law is vague at this point (Van Vliet, 1988).

Politico-cultural trends

In the previous section some social developments influencing the substance of social security laws were outlined. Accompanying them are a few politico-cultural or administrative trends that have an effect on the way laws are implemented. First, in the Netherlands there is a general trend of applying business-like and managerial notions in the public sector. Civil servants are seen as 'public managers'. They have to act in a business-like way. They should act that way, because the size of the budgets they receive depends on the outputs of their organisation, measured according to 'indicators' and agreed upon in 'contracts'. Local governments see themselves as 'entrepreneurs'. They compete with other local governments for the favour of big, if possible glamorous, multi-national companies, the settlement of which means municipal income and employment, but especially entrepreneurial prestige. Public service delivery organisations discover the citizen as 'client'. These organisations should be client-friendly and arrange their activities in such a way that costs and client satisfaction are in balance. Overall, managerialism in the public sector is taboo no longer. It is propagated at all levels of public service, irrespective of party affiliations. The traditional Liberals want a government that costs as little as possible. Therefore it must be run like a company. The Social-Democrats want a government that is primarily effective, but they also have an eye on value for money. The Christian-Democrats as well as the progressive liberals underline both arguments, while the latter make an issue of a client-oriented government for reasons of democracy. The only ones that have a somewhat more critical view are people affiliated with the Green Left. But they, too, think that government should interact with citizens in a proper way.

The Municipal Social Services Departments

The social developments and administrative trends mentioned above form the contextual framework for the development of the tasks of the municipal social services departments. At the end of the 1960s and the beginning of the 1970s the GSDs had to deal with a limited number of broadly categorised welfare provisions. In those years the GSDs developed into what we elsewhere called a welfare institution (Coenen *et al*, 1989 and 1991). The central task of guiding the assistance client was seen in terms of social aid. The style of rule application could be called political: GSD civil servants were aware of the fact that their authority was a delegated one, but at the same time they tried to maximise their autonomy in relation to the central authorities. The external orientation – that is the character and intensity of the relationship with the client – was that of a social work institution with a core of professional social workers.

At the end of the 1970s and in the first half of the 1980s the situation altered. There was an explosion of categorising policies. Fed by such political objectives as justice and solidarity and, later, by the necessity of making financial cuts, in these years governments intervened in society by increasing categorising policies. In the domain of social services all kinds of new categories were 'discovered': 'school-leavers', 'minima', 'real minima', 'long-term real minima', 'partially disabled unemployed employees', 'old aged and partially disabled shopkeepers' etc. Gradually the GSDs acquired the traits of what may be called a 'plain implementation organisation'. What this means is that priority was now given to the primary activity of processing benefit applications. The style of rule application became bureaucratic. The ideal was a well-functioning, bureaucratic organisation with clear hierarchical lines of competence and responsibility. The external orientation became an administrative one. The aim was to relate to the client in as formal and indirect a way as possible.

This development of the GSDs can be seen as a reaction to the complex problems raised as a consequence of the developments of categorisation, more unemployed and less money, and cultural individualism. These developments sharpened the problems of managing the implementation of a social security law like the National Assistance Act. In fact, these problems have manifested themselves at three levels. On the individual level there is the problem for the street-level bureaucrat of the GSDs of how to cope with policy discretion in the context of his or her large workload. On the organisational level there are problems about how to control and manage what these street-level bureaucrats are doing. On the political level there are problems of political accountability and responsibility. These problems are considered more fully in the next section.

Implementation and accountability

According to Lipsky's theory of street-level bureaucracy, social welfare workers, as well as teachers, police officers and other public employees who interact with citizens, behave in ways that are unsanctioned, sometimes even contradicting official policy, because the structure of their jobs makes it impossible fully to achieve the expectations of their work. Resources (primarily of time, money, human resources and skills) are inadequate to the tasks they are expected to perform. Goals and objectives may be conflicting or ambiguous. Job performance is extremely difficult to assess in the areas that matter most. Moreover, work with clients is often particularly stressful because of the high volume and the complexity of the task, and the need to interact with a client population that can be highly reactive to that intervention. When confronted with these conditions employees will try to protect their jobs by developing routines that promote fulfilment of at least a part of what is expected of them, as well as their own sense of well-being. They will try to perform in at least a partially acceptable fashion, but will also deviate from official expectations in the process. These individual solutions to work pressures, Lipsky argues, add up effectively to form public policy (Lipsky, 1989, p. 4). In fact, the aggregation of the separate discretionary and unsanctioned behaviours of the individual civil servants adds up to patterned agency behaviour overall. That is why you can say: policies are made on the street-level. They get their final form and substance in the interaction with clients.

In this interaction GSD civil servants are confronted with troublesome clients, some of whom practice fraud or are aggressive and who, in any case, are numerous. Policy discretion is on the one hand too narrow and on the other hand too broad. Of course, GSD civil servants have developed strategies to cope with this. Coping with the complexity of top-down given rules, they practise different styles of rule application (Knegt, 1986). Coping with their greater workload, they use different kinds of coping strategy in a narrow sense, as analysed by Lipsky (1980). As far as their professional standard is concerned, social services officers show cynicism and adapt their norms to their possibilities (Hudson, 1989). Confronted with clients they stereotype them (Knegt, 1986). However, all of these are 'solutions' on an *individual* level. It almost seems as if private solutions to private problems are involved. But public concerns are at stake. Street-level bureaucrats are expected to implements the laws: that is the task of the public organisations they belong to. Nevertheless, even for their direct supervisors it is difficult to open the black box of street-level bureaucratic interaction with clients – if they would like to do so (see Ringeling, 1978). *Bureaucratic unaccountability*, then, is a problem. Indeed, the unaccountability of the street-level organisation as a whole is problematic. How can local administration, responsible for the implementation of the National Assistance Act, administer law, if it does not have adequate insight into the factors leading to decisions about the provision of benefits to clients? This means that there is also a degree of what I would like to call *organisational unaccountability*. Moreover, there is a *political unaccountability*. Local government is responsible for the implementation of the ABW, but it cannot make this responsibility effective: either when it is confronted with policy makers in The Hague, or when it is challenged by client citizens complaining about what they have been given.

However, there are theoretical approaches that can throw light on certain new phenomena in Dutch social reality, while both theory and practice can show possible directions for solving these problems of accountability and the management of implementation.

Co-production as interaction with clients

In the field of commercial service delivery analysts have paid attention for years to the productive activities of consumers. When services are produced, 'the person being served (the client or consumer) is inevitably part of the production process, if there is to be *any* production whatsoever. Therefore, the resources, motivations, and skills brought to bear by the client or consumer are much more intimately connected with the *level* of achieved output than in the case of goods production. The output is always a jointly produced output' (Garn *et al.*, 1976, pp. 14–15). Parks and others have translated the notion of co-production to public service delivery (Parks et al., 1981). They make a distinction between 'regular producers' of goods and services and 'consumer-' or 'client-producers'. In a situation where neither the regular producer nor the client-producer *alone* can take care of the production of a service, incentives from both are necessary to produce the service. Despite the dissimilarities, this obviously is the case in social service delivery. It makes it justified to look at social service delivery in terms of co-production.

The client of a GSD is a Dutch resident, a citizen/voter and co-citizen of GSD civil servants. Besides that he or she is a client like all clients. That means that he or she is a consumer and source of market knowledge. Social services are co-produced in the interaction with clients. Negotiation and anticipation are, in fact, influencing social service delivery: particularly given the Dutch situation of public assistance, but also more in general (see Hanf in Chapter 4 of this book). At the moment in order to obtain an ABW benefit two people having some kind of relationship with each other may present themselves in the following ways: (a) each of them as a single person with a separate household; (b) each of them as a single person having a living apart together (LAT) relationship; (c) each of them as a single person being a co-parent;

(d) one of the two as a boarder, the other one as a landlord; (e) one of the two as a subtenant, the other one as an underleaser; (f) both as single persons sharing a dwelling; (g) as two persons sharing a household; and (h) as a married couple. Obviously, the entitlement to a benefit and, with that, the amount to be received differ according to this list. The difference in amount of money may be hundreds of guilders per month. It cannot be surprising, then, that the way one presents oneself helps to determine the financial result. Nor is it surprising that in the interaction with clients negotiation takes place.

These phenomena, however, do not fit in with the accepted top-down view of implementation. As far as they become visible (fraud), the reaction is sought in the direction of stricter criteria or better checks on the information the client provides. Nevertheless, it remains difficult to know what is happening in the interaction between street-level bureaucrats and clients. Therefore it can be fruitful to look at clients of the GSDs as co-producers of public assistance and consider the contribution that clients can make to the delivery of public assistance and, with that, to the actual problems of municipal social services departments in the Netherlands. How can we acquire the knowledge and compliance of clients in a way that acknowledges client participation and at the same time contributes to the task performance of the public organisations involved? For an answer to this question the individualistic notion of co-production must be extended and complemented with two different variants: those of organisational and political co-production.

Organisational co-production

Earlier it was stated that at the end of the 1970s and in the first half of the 1980s many GSDs could be characterised as 'plain implementation organisations'. Since then, however, a new type has appeared. Several GSDs have changed their role conception into one that can be typified as that of a 'service centre'. In the GSD as service centre an accurate execution of social security laws is no longer enough. Re-entry to the labour market and other 'secondary' objectives, like debt aid (*schuldsanering*), are aimed for. The style of rule application becomes more pragmatic: primarily workable solutions are sought. Rules exist to be followed, but in the words of Knegt, 'their meaning gets form not earlier than in the process of application in the complicated practice of public assistance' (1986, p. 166). Rule application becomes tailor-made. The external orientation involves rather more of a service delivery approach. Different from the GSDs as 'welfare institutions' the relation with the client is direct and businesslike rather than personal. A report of a project group of the association of GSD directors formulates this as follows:

> What the GSD can do for the client is largely determined by The Hague's rules and regulations, but a service delivery organisation will look, with the client, for possibilities to ensure that he or she is well informed and understands the policy, will use accessible language and will also in other ways try to ensure that the mode of operation fits as much as possible with the client's interests.

The service-directed external orientation of the GSDs as 'service centres' primarily means a business-like approach in the sense that much attention is given to processes of supply and demand. The supply must be clear to the client. This means proper information (passive and active), adequate guidance, clear decisions and forms, explicit and accessible complaint procedures (see McCarthy *et al.*, 1992), the development of a locally appropriate implementation policy and the selective activation of external networks. On the demand side a client-oriented GSD as service centre explores and knows its market (target group, district), knows how its clients live and takes care of client service. A variety of ways to do this is already being practised in the Netherlands. In Capelle aan den IJssel, for instance, a development was started towards creating a service centre comprising the fields of social security and well-being. In several municipalities there are service centres on the level of the entire local administration, for instance in Naaldwijk (see Van Engelen, 1992). The Ministry of the Interior intends to go even further to stimulate a development towards local public counters for integrated information and perhaps reception facilities for *all* government services, regardless of whether these are provided at the national, provincial or municipal level. Soon, the ministry will select a few municipalities for an experiment of this kind. These will be chosen from municipalities already active in the field of integrated service delivery. The cities of The Hague,

Task package	Internal orientation	External orientation	GSD type
Social work	Political	Social aid	Welfare institution
Execution of social security laws	Bureaucratic	Administrative	Implementation organisation
Debt aid	Pragmatic	Service	Service centre

Figure 6.1 The municipal social services department (GSD). *Source:* Coenen *et al.* (1989).

Groningen and Arnhem are among the candidates for such an experiment (*Binnenlands Bestuur*, 1992).

It is remarkable that the development toward 'civic service centres' can be traced in different European countries. In Great Britain the service centre has been called a 'one-stop-shop' or 'neighbourhood office', in Germany an '*Offenes Rathaus*' and in Denmark a '*Kvikskranken*' (Visser, 1991). Obviously there are many differences. What these phenomena have in common, however, is a central point that a client of public services can deal with. The first experiences with the civic service centres in the different European countries show a substantial increase in efficiency with a saving of money. Besides, the organisational culture changes. Any civil servant engaged in implementation must be(come) multi-skilled. Therefore continuous training is needed. Furthermore, since the ticket windows have been replaced by central counters and/or ordinary desks, aggression by clients has diminished (Visser, 1991).

Several municipalities do more than just present their 'products' in as integrated a way as possible. They also practice 'product testing'. This may involve using a city panel survey, in which a fixed group of inhabitants during a certain period are asked their opinion on the public service delivery in their municipality (for instance Delft). Rotterdam uses a variant of a 'quality panel' for social-cultural services. It consists of representatives of 22 civic organisations of lodgers, elderly people, women on public assistance and other specific groups. The findings of their research on, for instance, waiting periods at local agencies, are made public. Furthermore, the panel members discuss the results with the agencies with bad scores and suggest improvements (Kooke, 1992).

In many municipalities GSDs already consult their own clients. Here, too, this takes various different forms. There are client platforms (Haarlemmermeer) next to client councils (for instance, in Eindhoven, Arnhem, Delft and Alphen aan den Rijn). Thinking in terms of supply and demand implies service delivery on a contract basis, clarity of rights and duties and making arrangements about these with representatives of clients. In a fully developed situation the political and bureaucratic management of a GSD makes appointments with the civil servants of the organisation and also makes arrangements with clients. In the city of The Hague the GSD has introduced so-called benefit agreements between the GSD and individual clients in which rights and duties are described, these are eventually complemented with individual appointments (*Binnenlands Bestuur*, 1991). In the municipality of Capelle aan den IJssel the system is described as 'service on contract'. These all may be described as the formalisation of interaction with individual clients into a form of co-production. Capelle aan den IJssel provides an example of organisational co-production in the following form. The GSD produced a policy white paper on special assistance that was first discussed with representatives from the local network, before the mayor and aldermen presented it in the municipality council. Thus organisational accountability is enlarged. The GSD thus takes a role as 'co-producer' of public policy in a network of local service delivery.

In the co-production conception the problem of the ambiguity of rules and the often insufficient support that the GSD street-level bureaucrats receive from above is put in a different perspective. Cooperation and teamwork within the organisation become more important. The same goes for delegation and partnership at the level of the local service delivery network. The responsiveness of implementation can be increased: laws and regulations remain an essential source of rule application, but so do local circumstances, represented by the organised or in any case participating client and by local normsetting, for instance by means of a 'municipal implementation policy' formulated by local government using the freedom deliberately left by the legislator. With this we have arrived at the third form of co-production: that of political co-production.

Political co-production

Of course the development of GSDs as service centres and the greater involvement of clients are not panaceas for intrinsic policy deficiencies. For instance, one of the major problems, financial cuts, expressed in fewer personnel and in the reduction in the levels of benefits, can not be undone by them. Neither will they change the number of clients. They may even contribute to an increase in demands and a raising of expectations. Besides that, there are serious differences of interest and even in power between the various parties involved in the co-production process. A GSD civil servant, for instance, being a professional, will always have an advantage over an individual client as far as knowledge of the law and so on is concerned. Nevertheless, the notion of co-production, if extended into a public and collective form, can offer an approach to the solution of problems of accountability and the management of implementation.

The 'service on contract' notion implies attention to the context of the organisation and to the client, but also attention to the civil servant and the organisation of the internal process. Local government and the GSDs as public organisations become more important in this conception. Using actual policy instruments such as contract management and self-government, the local politicians are able to make arrangements with the management and staff at the GSDs. This happens in relation to the above-mentioned arrangements made with clients to set priorities on the basis

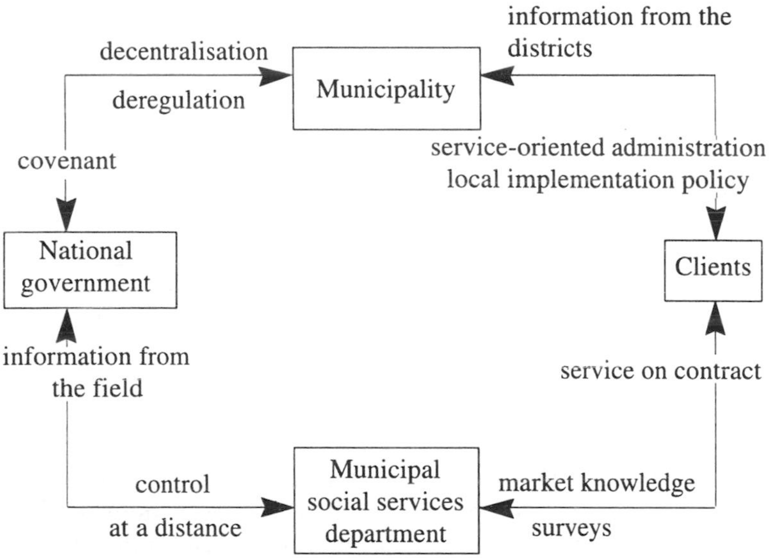

Figure 6.2 Social services delivery as organisational and political co-production. *Source:* Coenen *et al.* (1991).

of, for instance, a client's panel or a periodical survey in the specific local situation. The relation between national government and municipality is laid down in a covenant. In that covenant principles for assistance delivery can be arranged and in this way political accountability is increased. Local government therefore takes a political responsibility for the 'co-production' of public policy, indeed it acts as a co-government (see Hupe and Toonen, 1991). In this conception the GSD is no longer at the bottom of a hierarchical system, but is part of a multi-level co-production network. Thus one can speak of three forms of co-production. The original, individual form is complemented by an organisational and a political variant.

Co-production and checks and balances

The extension of the concept of social service delivery as co-production with an organisational and political dimension transposes some of the assumed 'individual' problems of the GSDs and their civil servants to the level where they belong: that is the level of public assistance as a public concern. It may be clear that in a system of co-production as policy making, lines and substance of accountability get a different character. Accountability is to be practised not only from the bottom to the top, to the director of the GSD, to The Hague, Westminister or Whitehall, but also horizontally: to client groups, to panels of users, to consumer councils. This accounting, and being held to account for, then takes place on several levels: between the individual civil servant and the individual client; between implementation organisation and community; between local administration and local politicians and between local government and national government. Implementation and the management of it no longer exclusively take place from the top down, but on levels necessary to have the public tasks involved carried out as responsively as possible. The local level is crucial then. Where *vertical* steering capacity shows deficits, the co-production aspect of social service delivery can be acknowledged and extended with an organisational and political dimension. It can contribute to public policy making by creating *horizontal* checks and balances.

Private problems, public solutions

The operational question of this chapter was: to what extent and in what way can business-like notions of client orientation and service centres contribute to solving problems of accountability and the management of implementation in social services delivery? We saw that these notions do play a role in the practice of Dutch social services delivery. The problems of accountability and the management of implementation were examined from the perspective of an extended concept of co-production. If applied also at a more collective and public level, the notion of co-production can solve some of the day-to-day problems that street-level bureaucrats have to cope with.

Provided with an organisational and political dimension and thus being organised, co-production is no longer just a general characteristic of service delivery, but it appears to offer a possibility to increase the accountability and responsiveness of public organisations and the civil servants working in them. Clients of social services can then be seen no longer merely as calculating citizens, but rather as integral parts of the implementation structure of public policy. The municipality, the municipal social services department, its civil servants and clients in fact all do play a role in the implementation of national assistance laws. These factual roles have to be reflected, acknowledged and shaped in a way that serves public objectives. It then appears to be possible to turn what seemed to be almost 'private' problems of civil servants into public solutions.

References

Binnenlands Bestuur (1991) 'More clarity on the rights and duties of benefit claimants. The Hague introduces "benefit agreement"', 6 December, p. 14 (in Dutch).

Binnenlands Bestuur (1992) 'Selection of municipalities for experimental service centres', 4 April, p. 2 (in Dutch).

Coenen, L., P. L. Hupe, P. Platen and M. Veenswijk (1989) *From Implementation Organisation to Service Centre*, Rotterdam: Municipal Social Services Department, Capelle aan den IJssel (in Dutch).

Coenen, L., P. L. Hupe, P. Platen and M. Veenswijk (1991) 'Innovations at the municipal social services department', *Sociaal Bestek*, 53(3), pp. 9–12 (in Dutch).

Engelen, G. Van (1992) 'As first municipality Naaldwijk has a "central counter": a result of client oriented thinking', *Binnenlands Bestuur*, 15 May, pp. 20–1 (in Dutch).

Garn, H., M. Flax, M. Springer and J. Taylor (1976) 'Models for indicator development: a framework for policy analysis', *Urban Institute Paper* 1206–17, Washington, DC: The Urban Institute.

Hudson, B. (1989) 'Michael Lipsky and street-level bureaucracy: a neglected perspective', in L. Barton (ed.), *Disability and Dependency*, Lewes: Falmer.

Hupe, P. L., and Th. A. J. Toonen (1991) 'The municipality as co-state: decentralisation in the Netherlands', in B. Blanke (ed.), *Staat und Stadt*: *Systematische, vergleichende und problemorientierte Analysen dezentraler Politik, Politische Vierteljahresschrift*, Sonderheft, pp. 337–54 (in German).

Knegt, R. (1986) *Rules and Reasonability in Public Assistance: Participating observation with a social services department*, Groningen: Wolters–Noordhof (in Dutch).

Kooke, S. (1992) 'An exercise in patience: quality panels measure waiting periods at local agencies', *Binnenlands Bestuur*, 27 March, pp. 18–19 (in Dutch).

Lijphart, A. (1968) *The Politics of Accomodation: Pluralism and democracy in the Netherlands*, Berkeley, Calif.: University of California Press.

Lipsky, M. (1980) *Street-Level Bureaucracy: Dilemmas of the individual in public services*, New York: Russell Sage.

Lipsky, M. (1989) 'The paradox of managing discretionary workers in social welfare policy', paper prepared for the seminar on the 'Sociology of Social Security', University of Edinburgh, 1989.

McCarthy, P., R. Simpson, M. Hill, J. A. Walker and J. Corlyon (1992) *Grievances, Complaints and Local Government*, Aldershot: Avebury.

Ministry of Social Affairs and Employment (1992) *A Short Survey of Social Security: Contributions payable as from 1 January 1992*, The Hague: Ministry of Social Affairs and Employment.

Parks, R. B., P. C. Baker, G. Kiser, R. Oakerson, E. Ostrom, V. Ostrom S. L. Percy, M. B. Vandivort, G. P. Whitaker and R. Wilson (1981) 'Consumers as co-producers of public services: some economic and institutional considerations', *Policy Studies Journal*, 9 (Summer), pp. 1001–11.

Ringeling, A. B., (1978) *Policy Discretion of Civil Servants: The 'spijtoptanten-probleem' as illustration of civil servants' activities with policy implementation*, Alphen aan den Rijn,: Samson.

Smit, O. (1987) *The Principle of Individualisation in the National Assistance Act*, The Hague: Staatsuitgever (in Dutch).

Swaan, A. de (1988) *In Care of the State: Health care, education and welfare in Europe and the USA in the modern era*, Cambridge: Polity Press.

Visser, C. (1991) 'Public friendly municipal service centres must save citizens the long road through local bureaucracy', *Binnenlands Bestuur*, 7 June, pp. 22–3 (in Dutch).

Vliet, I. Van (1988) *The Dutch Social Security System, Some Social Developments and Their Effects on the National Assistance Act*, The Hague: Municipal Social Services Department (in Dutch).

CHAPTER 7

Theory and methodology in the analysis of the policy process: a case study of the Warnock Committee on Human Fertilisation and Embryology

Erica Haimes

Introduction

This chapter is based on a piece of research (Haimes, 1990b) which I conducted into the British Government Committee of Inquiry into Human Fertilisation and Embryology (the 'Warnock Committee'). The Committee was established in 1982 to examine the social, ethical and legal implications of the new reproductive technologies, such as in vitro fertilisation. It reported in 1984 and many of its recommendations formed the basis of the Human Fertilisation and Embryology Act, 1990. My particular study used the work of the Committee and its report to explore one of the major social consequences of the deployment of these new technologies: the creation of families in which the adults and 'children' are not genetically related to each other. Since it is assumed that, in most families, the 'children' and parents *are* genetically related, the absence of such a connection can be socially problematic for all the parties involved, and decisions have to be made, by parents, by professionals and by policy-makers, on the best way to manage this form of deviance. In particular, should the 'children' themselves (either when they actually are children, or when fully adult) be told the circumstances of their conception and, if so, should they be told any details about the third party (the gamete donor or the surrogate) who contributed to that conception?

In this study I wanted to see how the Committee grappled with the problem of managing information about origins and reasoned its way towards a particular resolution. I surmised that by uncovering the repertoire of concerns which informed their final decisions we would discover more not only about this apparently narrow topic, but also about the social significance of genetic and biological ties to the broader topic of 'family' and 'family-ness'. We would also find out how such a complex issue is handled in the context of the requirement to make recommendations for government policy. I therefore approached this piece of policy analysis with three different types of interest: the substantive, in terms of how policy is made on a topic which challenges so profoundly our ideas about the role of biology in constituting family life; the methodological, in terms of deciding how to gain access to data which would shed at least some light on those substantive interests; and, third, the theoretical, in terms of how best to connect these issues to wider questions concerning the links between social action and social structure. On this last point, the social and political sciences have traditionally been very poor at making these connections (see Silverman, 1985, pp. 70–92), but increasingly researchers are being made aware of the limitations of studies which fail to consider such links. It is difficult, though, to discuss how the links might be made in abstract, partly because of the tendency to fail to consider all three dimensions of substance, theory and methodology, and partly because the nature of the links to be made has to be tied to the particulars of the topic being analysed.

Thus, this particular piece of work contributes to the development of a new agenda in the study of the policy process in two ways: first, by adding to the rich diversity of empirical case studies an area of study which has featured little in previous discussions of the policy process; and second, by making explicit a concern which tends to remain implicit in most case studies – that is, how to link the actions and beliefs of individuals in the policy-making process to explanations of that process which derive from broader structural theories of society. The following case study is therefore just as concerned with questions of theory and overall research design as it is with presenting substantive findings, but I would argue that this is necessary if we are to exploit fully the contributions of case studies in general to the analysis of the policy process. These issues will be examined in more detail in the discussion section after the case study.

Case study: the Warnock Committee

As I describe my study of the work of the Warnock Committee I shall try to convey how it became clear, as the study progressed, that links needed to be made between notions of agency and structure, in substantive, methodological and theoretical terms. I shall do this by showing how the background to the study shaped my research strategies, and then by considering how I tried to link the levels of analysis together.

The research strategies

My research strategy had three main steps, which were arrived at by trying to follow the prescriptions of an earlier study while remaining alert to the specifics of the current subject. This earlier study had examined adult adoptees who wanted to find out information about their origins by making use of the (then) new provision under S. 26 of the Children Act, 1975, giving them access to their original birth records (Haimes and Timms, 1983, 1985). Such people were, and still are, often characterised as suffering from an 'identity crisis', even by those responsible for making and implementing such policies. However, our study showed clearly that the notion of an 'identity crisis' is a highly individualistic concept which obscures more than it explains: in particular, it obscures the historical role of the policy-making and implementation structures in creating the secrecy surrounding adoption in the first place. In a later analysis (Haimes, 1988) I suggested that these policies reflected a wider cultural uncertainty about using adoption to create non-biologically related families. Therefore in the current research I was concerned to examine issues about genetic origins from the perspective of the policy-makers, to test the accuracy of such a claim and thus to put the question of genetic origins in its wider social and political context. Three main steps were necessary to achieve this: first, situating the work of the Committee on the origins issue in the context of earlier attempts to resolve these difficulties; second, analysing in depth the report from the Committee in order to try to explain why it made the particular recommendations that it did; and third, investigating these issues in even greater depth by conducting detailed, semi-structured interviews with the Committee members themselves. In this paper I shall give only brief details of that first step and concentrate instead on explaining why it was necessary to supplement the analysis of the Committee's report with interviews with the Committee members, and how I then tried to link those two steps to a broader, theoretical analysis.

The review of earlier attempts to resolve the origins issue in the reproductive technologies confirmed the parallel with adoption: that concern with information about origins is not simply confined to individuals and their 'identity crisis', but is also expressed, defined and redefined at the level of the institutional, and thus the social, through state interest (the relevant reports are listed on pp. 172–3). From the review it was possible to identify three competing strategies for the management of origins information which emerged and gained currency in the 1980s.

The first recommends telling no one about the 'child's' origins, particularly not the 'child' him/herself, on the grounds that there are no obvious benefits to be derived from this and in fact, to the contrary, there is some risk of damaging the 'child'. The second strategy involves telling the 'child' about the means of his/her conception, on the grounds that s/he would suffer from the effects in the family of that information being kept secret. However, what the 'child' can be told is limited by the principle of anonymity between all parties, since it is not clear to the proponents of this view what benefits s/he could derive from knowing the name of the third party, when at the same time the policy of releasing that information could lead to a fall in donor numbers. The third strategy recommends telling the 'child' as much as possible about both the donation and the donor, including the donor's name, on the grounds that s/he will need this to develop a full sense of identity.

The Warnock Report recommended the middle strategy. This is a particularly interesting strategy since it seems, paradoxically, to be both a radical change from the prevailing practice of secrecy, and at the same time a position of safety compared to the third possible strategy. This was enough to suggest that the report warranted further analysis. The details of this analysis are available elsewhere (Haimes, 1990a, 1990b), but in brief, it would appear that the case put forward for maintaining donor anonymity was tied to other more general features of the report, most notably its stated concern with the 'setting up of families' (1984, p. 2) and 'the process of family formation' (1984, p. 5). Given the range of technologies being considered by the Committee (gamete donation, in vitro fertilisation, surrogacy), the creation of a variety of family forms was possible, not all of which were acceptable to the Committee. With varying degrees of explicitness, the report presented the following requirements for founding an acceptable family:

(a) The potential parents should place value on the *idea* of a family.
(b) The potential parents should be motivated by love rather than by money, jealousy, pride, anxiety or any other 'negative' emotions.
(c) The family should have a stable environment.
(d) The family should have two heterosexual parents.
(e) There should be a genetic link between parent and child.
(f) The mother should experience pregnancy and childbirth.

These could be summarised as the ideological (a and b), the structural (or organisational, c and d) and the biological (e and f) dimensions of family life. The ideological components rest upon assumptions about the structural and biological constitution of the family but can, at the same time, override inconsistencies in the structural and biological elements, if those inconsistencies can be contained in some way. This appears to be the way in which the Warnock Report was able to find families created by gamete donation acceptable. The strategy of combining openness about the conception with anonymity between all parties means that the motivation to parent is reinforced by the willingness of the parents to disclose the conception process to the child (thus demonstrating the love and honesty within the family), while at the same time the non-conforming structural (a third parent) and biological (a non-genetically related nurturing parent) features are rendered invisible, to outsiders at least, and contained in terms of their impact by the anonymity of the donor.

Thus, the prescription to be open about the 'child's' conception reinforces dominant ideological notions of family life, while the anonymity of the donor contains the impact of the structural and biological non-conformity. Anonymity of the donor symbolically reinforces the legal provisions attaching the 'child' to the nurturing parents and also detaches the 'child' from the third party.

However, my research could not stop here since there is a problem with this explanation in so far as it depends on attributing certain intentions and ideologies to the Committee members, while, at the same time, glossing over the detailed reasoning through which they reached their decisions and produced the report. There is a danger, therefore, that such a neatly packaged explanation disguises rather than reveals the repertoire of concerns deemed to be relevant to this issue by the Committee members themselves. Therefore, I decided to investigate the validity of my analysis further, by conducting a series of in-depth, semi-structured interviews with the members of the Committee to try to gain a sense of how they worked their way through the puzzles they discovered when trying to make policy recommendations.

This, of course, posits a distinction between the report itself, as a document, and the social processes and individuals' beliefs and actions which lay behind its production. However, to ignore the latter or to deny their relevance would be tantamount to advocating a 'black box' theory of knowledge, being concerned with 'input' (e.g. the Committee membership) and 'output' (e.g. the Report), but with little regard for what happens in between. By contrast, conducting interviews with the members subjected the analysis of the report to a more rigorous examination on three levels: the methodological, the substantive and the theoretical. On a methodological level the interviews made it possible to detect the extent to which I imposed an 'outsider's' explanation on a situation which may be more complex than at first appears when explained by the 'insiders' on the Committee; on the substantive level they provided clarification of those aspects of the explanations (both my own and those within the report) which remained unclear; and finally on the theoretical level they provided further insight into how members conceptualised the links between their beliefs and their view of broader organising structures of social life, such as the notions of 'family' or of 'biology' or, of course, of 'policy'.

In a sense these interviews represented an attempt to peel back another layer from the Warnock Report to try to get closer to the ways in which members of the Committee perceived the issues they were discussing. Reports to governments from committees such as this require a degree of certainty and coherence which might not adequately convey how members experienced the process of reaching the views expressed in the report. Part of the purpose of the interviews was to get away from the tidy language of the report to gain a sense of how members thought about these issues in 'commonsense' terms, how they struggled with them and how they expressed them in everyday language. Therefore, this type of analysis makes extensive use of verbatim quotations from the interviews to convey members' expression of their conceptual depiction of these issues, when reflecting on their own and other members' reasoning.

A brief reference was made in the report to a difference of opinion, as well as to changes and modifications of views during the life course of the Committee (1984, p. 1), though little detail was given other than in the formal expressions of dissent. Therefore, the interviews were useful, too, in showing at least some of that diversity of opinion, as well as conveying the strength with which some of those views were held. Overall, the interviews provided further insight into how these complex issues were discussed, argued over, explained, justified, defended and elaborated by members as they went about their task of making policy recommendations to government.

It was not my intention, however, to use the interview data to undermine the contents of the report, since both must be understood in terms of the context in which each was produced (Silverman, 1985, p. 21); rather, my aim was to add to our understanding of the report. For similar reasons I regarded the interviews as simply another stage in the analysis embarked on in this study, not its culmination. Further questions and theories were likely to arise from the interviews, just as the interviews themselves arose to try to answer earlier questions and theories. In that sense the interviews, like the rest of the study, can be regarded as an example of grounded theorising (Glaser and Strauss, 1967). At the same time, it is important to emphasise that my interests in conducting these interviews were still fairly narrow, in so far as I concentrated on trying to clarify members' views on the new reproductive technologies and the management of information about the 'child's' origins: I was not conducting a committee study in perhaps the conventional policy analysis sense.

I am referring here to studies such as Phoebe Hall's *Reforming the Welfare* (1976), as well as more general analyses of the role of government inquiries and committees, such as those provided by Beattie (1965), Bulmer (1980), Cartwright (1975), Chapman (1973), Plowden (1971) and Rhodes (1975). The difference between Hall's study and mine is not just in terms of scope, but also in epistemology. Hall takes the ontological status of the social world as given and directs her analysis to discovering how sections of that world interlock in the policy-making process. In my study the analysis derived from an interpretivist epistemology in sociology, which sees the world as contingent and emergent, and, therefore, as constructed through the interaction, particularly linguistic, between individuals. Hence the need to see how members' constructions of the key concepts compared with my own in the analysis of the report: this is, essentially, a reflexive exercise (Hammersley and Atkinson, 1983, p. 14). In its concern with policy-makers' subjective understandings it has some features in common with Raab (1987).

Therefore, while I asked members for background information on how the Committee worked and how they regarded their task, this was very much a scene-setting exercise, rather than an attempt to conduct a detailed analysis of, for example, Committee procedures. It was at points such as this where my approach to the study of policy making was somewhat different from that of conventional policy analysis, such as in the studies mentioned above. At the point at which I turned my analysis to the even more micro-level examination of members' meanings, others might have turned to examine the *structures* of the Committee, such as the characteristics of its members, in terms of gender, class, profession, race, religion, age and the interests they might each have been presumed to represent.

I designed the interview around five main areas, but my intention in keeping with interpretivist methodology was to allow the Committee members to discuss these topics in a manner and an order they deemed appropriate. The five areas were as folows: first, members' current involvement in the new reproductive technologies; second, the interviewees' views on making public policy on these topics, and more specifically how they saw their own involvement; third, Committee procedures; fourth, infertility and treatment; and fifth, anonymity, genetic links and identity. It was in the fourth and the fifth sections that I was most sensitised by the concepts and speculation embodied in my previous analysis of the report. I hoped to explore with members their views on the different treatments to gain an idea of the connections they drew between the issues, what they defined as being problematic, what they viewed as resolutions: in short, to see how they constructed and expressed their understanding of these issues.

As with all qualitative data from semi-structured interviews, those from my interviews, being verbatim extracts, take a great deal of space to present. It is tempting to try to extract for the purpose of this paper some data, such as what members had to say about the family, to display the richness and complexity of their thoughts. Though I have done that in other papers, I decided that here it would be counter-productive since I want to follow on with what was learnt from the interviews as a whole, much of which depends on the interweaving of various strands: to present one strand would be misleading. It is better, therefore, to refer the reader to the source of the full analysis (Haimes, 1990b) and to present here instead a summary of what the interviews added to the analysis of the report.

My analysis of the report had attributed an almost conspiratorial clear-sightedness to the Committee members, of the goals they had in mind and a coherence of understanding to enable them to achieve those goals: such a claim required further investigation. The interviews with the Committee members indicated that, though they were very clear on some issues, they were also unclear and consequently inconsistent on others.

These inconsistencies can be found in what the members said on both the range of technologies and more specifically on the family, anonymity and origins. They include, for example, expressions of unhappiness (which did not appear in the report) about donor insemination, while at the same time using it as a model to justify other donative practices; views which argued for regarding semen and egg donation as the 'same' while in fact drawing explicit distinctions between them in terms of donor motivation; arguments that the desire to perpetuate one's genes is entirely natural and justifies the assistance given to infertile people, while suggesting that it is an entirely inappropriate motivation for donating gametes; regarding support for the view that the parental concern to have a genetic link with a 'child' is important, while questioning the importance of the genetic link from the 'child's' perspective; contradictory positions on the relative importance of the genetic and the carrying relationship in discussions on embryo donation and surrogacy; arguments for prioritising the needs of the 'child', as an individual, when discussing certain family set-ups, while presuming the balancing of interests of 'child' and family in other family set-ups; distancing the donor by keeping him/her anonymous while at the same time accepting third party conceptions; claiming not to hold conservative notions of the family while regarding certain family set-ups as deviations from an unstated norm.

These inconsistencies indicate exactly that which I conducted the interviews to discover: that is, how the members grappled with these issues in everyday commonsense terms. These inconsistencies and the detailed data from which they were derived emphasise just how difficult members perceived these problems to be. What is perhaps even more important in terms of my analysis of the report, is that they clearly had no readily available formula, such as 'the dominant ideology', of the family or anything else with which to solve these difficulties: in fact there was evidence to suggest that some members actively resisted too strong a statement of support for traditional notions of the family. What we find instead is that they grappled with these issues and resolved them through a series of largely unconnected pragmatic decisions. There is, therefore, a marked contrast between the apparent clarity of the Committee's position in the report and the evident confusions expressed by members in their interviews. The nature of that contrast merits further discussion.

In the interviews, members were able to make the larger, cruder distinctions between those foundations for a family life which they considered acceptable (assisted reproduction for couples using their own gametes) and those which were unacceptable (applicants for treatment who are homosexuals, or single people) without much hesitation. Only one voice challenged this. Where they had more difficulty, however, was when these unarticulated notions of the family were challenged at a point which required much finer distinctions to be made, such as at the level of the significance of genetic relationships, for example, in the case of semen and egg donation. Most members were unable either to articulate the nature of the challenge that these procedures embodied for their ideas of what the family should be like, or to explain the nature of the response they wished to make to those challenges.

This was even more noticeable when yet finer distinctions were demanded of them, in the case of the relative importance of the genetic and carrying relationships in embryo donation and surrogacy.

It is curious to note, therefore, that while we might expect the notion of the family to collapse under these challenges and have no more value in helping the Committee members to resolve their difficulties, this in fact did not happen. Although members' notions of the family were vague, they were not weak. This can be heard in their responses when they said, for instance, 'I simply don't know' about a topic on which they had nonetheless come to a conclusion; or, similarly, when they resorted to explanations based on their 'gut feelings'. Such responses acknowledge both a challenge to their views and an inability to articulate a clearer response to that challenge, but a feeling nonetheless that the challenge has not completely undermined their position, even though they cannot say why.

It was just such a (strong) version of the family which informed members' reasoning on the best way to handle origins information: that is, a desire to protect what is seen as the most valuable aspect of the donation procedures, the family unit. Not just the nurturing family unit, but also the donor's family unit. This, in spite of the fact that the very existence of third party conceptions might be just one of many challenges to the notion of the family upon which the value attached to the family unit is based.

Linking members' meanings and family policy

We can derive two conclusions from examining the report and analysing the interviews. The first is that the view of the *report* as invoking a dominant ideology of the family (an ideology of familialism, to use the phrase from Barrett and McIntosh (1982)) was basically correct. However, it would also be fair to claim that I was correct to doubt the neatness of that analysis, since it is evident from the *interview* data that the members' reasoning about the family, particularly in addressing the nature of the relationship (biological and social) between parents and 'children', is much more complex than simply applying a formula derived from a 'dominant ideology'. It is clear that we have to engage with that complexity, rather than just ignore it.

This can be done by pursuing several lines of inquiry, but for the purpose of this chapter I shall just present one: how best to characterise the link between what we know from the interviews and what we know from the analysis of the report. This will indicate how theoretically and methodologically the data from the interviews and the analysis of the report link with the macro issues of family and of policy.

It might be tempting to suggest that the final report from the Warnock Committee was simply a compromise between irreconcilable differences, but this would imply a negotiation between at least two clearly articulated positions, both of which move to a third clearly defined position. However, neither the interviews nor the report bear this out. I would argue that, if anything, the report represents a suspension of difficulties, based on members' reasoning about the relationship between their own views and the appropriate way to produce recommendations for policy. They would not be alone in this. Morgan, for example, suggests:

> persons involved in the framing and enacting of legislation both draw upon conventionally held notions of familial relationships (or more complicatedly, upon notions of what these conventional notions are . . .) and, in so doing, reinforce these notions through their public pronouncements or through their deployment in law and judgement. (1985, p. 72)

And indeed there is some support for this from Mary Warnock herself:

> When we are faced with such massively difficult calculations, where the unknown factors are literally innumerable, the principle of utility (the principle that we should so act as to maximise benefit and minimise harm) offers little or no practical guidance. Does it follow, then, that where public policy, policy for a whole society, is in question, utilitarianism should be abandoned? Should we instead seek a kind of consensus, derived from what people vaguely feel about their origins, their roots, their commitments to their own children . . . ? Are we simply to try to think what sort of society we would feel it tolerable or intolerable to live in? I suggest that in the end this is what we must do. (1985b, p. 152)

A similar view was expressed by one of the members during the interview:

> 'I think if you don't understand the English way of life, you don't understand these kinds of committees. I mean, it was a very English thing . . . The idea was that you bring in a group of people with different kinds of expertise who are nevertheless there not to sell their own expertise or sell particular ideologies, in any concerted way, but there to perform a public service, of looking at this phenomenon from the point of view of expertise and from the point of view of common sense. And then thereafter to do what they were asked to do, which of course was mainly, as a lot of people failed to remember when they read Warnock, they were asked to present material with a view to legislation which of course . . . modifies the way you deal with things and the kinds of conclusions which you reach. We weren't simply there to make a series of moral or social judgements about the issues under concern, you were there to see how these could be put into legal form. Nothing was allowed to go through without some consideration, though not all of that is going to appear in the Final Report. So I think I have a sort of slightly old-fashioned English view that it isn't such a bad way of doing things after all.'

Bernardes suggests that everyday actors hold at least two notions of family life: that based on their personal experience and that based on a culturally dominant 'family ideology' (1985, pp. 203–6). From the interviews it is evident that the Committee members were working with at least this one contrast and perhaps others too. This does not mean, though, that their efforts should be condemned for this, as if it indicated some sort of inadequacy on their part; rather it is the responsibility of the researcher, having recognised this, to inquire further into what it can tell us. In particular, the researcher has to investigate how everyday actors *work with* their awareness of the 'dominant ideology' of the family, rather than accept too easily the idea that such actors, especially policy-makers, simply echo the ideas of that ideology. This is what the interviews show.

In terms of the report, however, Bernardes suggests that we should not be too surprised if policy statements do not fully reflect the complexities of dealing with family matters:

> One (and only one) of the reasons that dominant groups and institutions have fiercely resisted any public move away from the notion of 'the family', is not only because of the strength of family ideology, but also because of enormously wide-ranging (and astonishingly complex) policy reformulations that would be

> required if social policy attempted to deal with family 'reality' rather than attempt to corral all families into behaviour and lifestyles conforming to the image enshrined in family ideology. (1985, p. 206)

Thus, the Committee members made recommendations for practical policy. Though they were able to contemplate a range of family forms, they found the complexities of evaluating those forms were made easier by reference to one particular form, which then became the basis of their recommendations in the report: the two-parent, heterosexual family. (This point can be developed further using the suggestion from Bernardes (1985) that everyday actors work with a version of lay functionalism when thinking of the family: see Haimes (1990b).)

In sum, without the interview data, the report would be seen as 'just another' statement of dominant values; with the interview data we learn more about the difficulties of talking about the family; with the two together we learn about how those difficulties become transformed into that statement – that is, we learn a little bit more about the policy-making process.

Discussion

We need now to consider whether this case study helps us to answer the question I raised at the beginning of the chapter: how do we link the actions and beliefs of individuals in the policy-making process to explanations of that process which derive from broader, structural theories of society? As a case study I would suggest that it does help us at least to make a start on forming such connections, though as Flynn (this volume, Chapter 3) points out, most endeavours will only be partial at the best of times. However, we can go beyond this particular case study to start to draw out more general ideas about how we might develop this form of analysis. To do that, though, we need to return to two more fundamental questions: why are such links necessary; and how, in any particular study, might they be established?

In order to understand why we need to make these links we also need to understand how prevalent the lack of such links has been in social science in general. Silverman, referring to the division between individual actions and structural theories of society as the micro-macro division, says that this has been both fundamental, but also limiting, to the discipline of sociology; instead he argues: 'While research data are often mainly gathered at either a structural or at an interactional level, sound analysis and intelligent conceptualisation requires that *both* levels (and their relations) should be addressed' (1985, p. 70). Giddens has developed structuration theory for exactly this purpose. Bryant and Jary refer to it as: 'an approach to social science that avoids the dualisms of subject and object, agency and structure and structure and process, which have so bedevilled other social theories' (1991, p. 2).

It is only appropriate that public policy analysis should also benefit from such attempts: indeed, Small (1989) makes a point similar to Silverman's with reference to the study of policy making in health. Such an attempt opens up the possibility of asking a greater number of questions about the policy-making process coupled with the possibility of discovering a greater number of ways of answering them. This in turn allows for a more comprehensive analysis of the policy-making process. In the context of this particular collection such an imperative encourages us to follow Ham and Hill's entreaty to stand back and ask 'the bigger questions' about, for example, the role of the state (1984, p. 17), but to *combine* this with Lipsky's endeavours to 'search for the place of the individual' (1980, p. xi). In this collection the limitations of just dealing with large-scale theory or just dealing with individuals' actions have been noted. Both Hanf and Hupe (this volume, Chapters 4 and 6), while appreciating the analytical power of the concept of street-level bureaucrats, express concern that such workers could be seen as isolated individuals; both suggest ways in which, going beyond Lipsky, such individuals could be placed in their social contexts.

I share similar concerns to those expressed by Hanf and Hupe, though I would express them in slightly different ways, both substantively and methodologically. It is possible to see from my case study that Lipsky's concern with the individual can be applied to aspects of the policy-making process other than just that of implementation at the street level. The task at the 'top' end of the policy-making chain can clearly be just as complex and ambiguous and just as difficult to resolve. As my case study shows, it is possible to make policy at the 'top' without resolving those ambiguities and complexities: indeed, it is questionable whether such a resolution would be desirable, particularly in the area of family and reproductive policies. The case study also gives a clue to the types of problem which those further down the chain might experience, as well as indicating that in such a complex area where multiple interpretations are possible it is quite likely that different problems might arise.

This substantive observation just serves to reinforce the following methodological point, however: that in claiming to place the individual in his/her social context we need to be more precise and more explicit about exactly how we have achieved that task. This takes us from the first question of *why* we need to make the links between the individual and structural theory, to *how* we make those links.

The answer to this question necessitates that attention be paid to methodology: that area of analysis which is concerned with the links between theory and data, an area of particular concern to any case study. Hill and Bramley (1986, p. 20) note the need to attend to such issues, but this is generally a neglected area in political science. In terms of linking individuals' beliefs and actions to broader, structural theories, the connections between theory and data have to be grounded in detailed, empirical material which demonstrates just what those beliefs and actions are, to account for and display sufficiently the ability of individuals to create for themselves a meaningful context of action. Then, and only then, can these meanings be linked to an explanation which allows for the possibility of such beliefs and actions occurring in the first place. These data have to be elicited from individuals participating in the situation under study, usually through the means of participant observation and/or detailed semi-structured interviews.

Such methods, despite the fine examples of Bulmer (1986), Finch (1986) and Walker (1985) appear to be under-used in the field of public policy and political science. Through these methods, however, it is possible to elicit actors' beliefs not just about the substantive topic under analysis but also, in the case of policy-making studies, about *their* views of their location in both the policy-making structures and the wider structures in society. This is why it is not sufficient to *presume* that the 'structural' characteristics of individuals (for example, their gender, religion, ethnicity, age, occupation) are a strong predictor of their views and role in the policy-making process, without at least reference to how those individuals make use of and evaluate those characteristics themselves. Reference to such characteristics is not irrelevant to understanding the policy-making process, but it is certainly not sufficient. The participants' own views on these structures are, of course, not the only legitimate view, but in so far as such views might guide their actions they have some relevance to the ways in which social theorists might wish to characterise those structures. Subsequent reference to all-embracing theories about power or the state, and so on, then have to refer back to the views of those individuals who, in specific contexts, comprise the state or exercise the power.

However, such prescriptions to make these connections carry little force unless tied to specific studies. Indeed, it is one of the central claims of structuration theory that 'structures are produced and reproduced in specific contexts' (Bryant and Jary, 1991, p. 13), so to claim that we can link individual actions to a structural explanation requires the exposition of such links to be tied to an empirical example. With reference to particular studies it becomes possible to identify where the links have been carefully pieced together and where, indeed, gaps still remain.

This is why in my case study I have devoted so much space to explaining the reasoning behind each research strategy, even though this results in a chapter which is perhaps somewhat different in tone and content to many of the others in this collection. I tried to link individuals' actions and beliefs to structural concepts of 'ideology', 'family', 'policy' and 'history' by going to and fro between the levels of analysis and identifying, and attending to, questions which remained to be answered from each level. That is, I went from historical analysis of policy, to the analysis of the report in terms of structural variables, to the analysis of interviews with the members, back to the analysis of the text, to the analysis of ideas of the family (in light of the analysis of both the report and the interviews), back to the analysis of how the policy was formulated in the report.

Quite how adequately this was done is another matter, but it was important to show that such an attempt was made. Perhaps even more important is the fact that my grounds for claiming that such links had been made were also made as explicit as possible. This, perhaps, is one of the main weaknesses of the committee studies I cited earlier: that they are not sufficiently explicit about how they arrive at their own interpretations of their data. Tomlinson (1987) expresses a similar concern when, in a review of policy case studies, he claims 'interpretation is lost' and therefore the reader has no way of assessing how the conclusions have been reached.

It could be argued that a concern with actors' understanding of the key concepts is particularly important in studies of policy in areas such as the family where there are multiple definitions and meanings. We need to see that policy-makers struggle conceptually as much as anyone else, and, as Silverman argues, we need also to resist the temptation to reduce those struggles to a single logic like 'dominant ideology' or 'the role of the state' (1985, p. 71). However, it is only by engaging, in depth, with the detail of what these actors actually say, that we can appreciate its complexity and can thus offset the temptations of a more simplistic analysis.

Silverman recommends Foucault's approach to linking agency and structure through detailed empirical analysis and to avoiding simple explanations: 'For instance, although relations between men and women, and within families, work and educational institutions, do make it possible for the state to function, they are not projections of the state's power. Each has its own pattern and relative autonomy' (1985, p. 90). Foucault argues: 'Fathers, husbands, employers, teachers do not simply "represent" a state power which itself "represents" the interests of a class . . .' (cited in Silverman, 1985, p. 90). This is perhaps the problem of an overdependence on externally formulated rational models of the policy-making process (Bulmer, 1986, p. xviii): they show neither the actors' interpretations of that process, nor the researchers' interpretations, nor the links between them. The need to tie such discussions to actual empirical studies raises questions about the influence of the particular substantive topic on the sorts of connection which it is possible to make between individuals' actions and macro-level structures.

The temptation in policy analysis is to overlay the topic with one or other of the 'standard' theories of, for example, Marxism or pluralism. However, as Hill discusses in the Introduction to this collection, there is a question about how useful such theories are for fully explaining empirical reality. For my study I could, for example, have drawn upon an élitist or a pluralist or a Lukes model of decision making as presented by Ham and Hill (1993, chapter 4). However, it is not clear what these models actually 'look like' when manifested at the micro level, though it is perhaps possible, having studied the micro level, *then* to characterise the decision making in terms of one of these three (or any other) models.

Certainly such theories experience a severe challenge from topics like those raised in my case study, to do not just with 'family', but also with 'biology' and 'culture'. While there are Marxist analyses of these issues, the extent to which they could provide an adequate account of members' struggles is questionable because even when the appropriate micro-level data are collected, for example by certain neo-Marxist researchers, those data then tend to be subjected to a macro-level, theoretical analysis, often without a clear exposition of the links between the two. Similarly, even a feminist analysis, which has topics such as these at its centre, has been shown to be not wholly adequate. For example, it would have been tempting to stay with the feminist analysis of the report which represented the Committee as straightforwardly advocating a patriarchal nuclear family, but instead I developed an interpretivist analysis of members' accounts to test this out. Then, rather than stopping there, I tried to locate those accounts in Bernardes' theories of lay functionalism, in order to understand how these accounts help us to understand the nature–culture divide.

While such an analysis revealed inconsistencies in members' perceptions and reasoning, we can return to Lipsky's analysis and argue that these are the result not of personal failure but of the constraints experienced by the individuals. However, what is important about the interviews in my case study is that we can actually see/hear what individuals perceived those constraints to be, rather than having to surmise what they might be. The members were constrained not so much by the interests they were perhaps supposed by others to represent, nor by the more dominant interests of other members, but by their culture: that is, they were constrained by the limited cultural possibilities for making conceptual sense out of the role of biological factors in constituting family relationships. They experienced these constraints directly because the technologies they were dealing with pushed them to these limits. In addition, because they had the task of making recommendations for policy, they were not able, as is often the case with conceptually complex cultural meanings, to allow the issue simply to remain unresolved. This does not mean that they actually resolved the issue without ambiguity (hence the questions raised by their strategy of anonymity), but they did nevertheless reach a position which they at least deemed to be a resolution.

It might be suggested that members of the Committee experienced certain difficulties because issues about family, biology and indeed reproduction in general are essentially private issues, and therefore the difficulties lie in the attempt at making public policy on personal issues. While that is certainly *part* of the dilemma, it would be a mistake to see it as a complete explanation, for a number of reasons. First, even if this topic were regarded as unproblematically private, it would still be necessary to analyse exactly why and how that presents problems for policy-makers. Second, such issues are not, in fact, unproblematically private, since, as C. Wright Mills (1970) would argue, the notion of the personal or the private is still very much a social notion because it only acquires the meaning of being private within a particular set of social arrangements. Third, all social policy issues have a private dimension, and indeed Lipsky refers to this in terms of how street-level bureaucrats think through the difficulties of their tasks (1980, p. xiv). Therefore, the designation of certain issues as private and others as public, though relative, reveals something about cultural values, but values, like structures, are created and recreated by actors as they conduct their everyday lives. This again returns us to the necessity of studying the links between the individual and the structural.

Having established why such links need to be made and in suggesting *how* they might be made (in part at least), it is nonetheless important to add a final caution. It is important to see the world as socially constructed, albeit within complex cultural values, but this should not result in reducing structural perspectives to interpretivist perspectives or vice versa. In this case study I tended to use structuralist theory to address 'why' questions (why did the report advocate a particular family type? why did this particular type of policy emerge? and so on) and interpretivist theory to address 'how' questions (how did members characterise the importance of genetic links? how can we hear, in what they say, a defence of a certain family formation? and so on).

However, in claiming to make these links I hope not to present the naive view which wants to take the best of each theory and combine them, while conveniently forgetting the incompatibility of the epistemological base of each. Instead, I would follow

Bhaskar (cited in Silverman, 1985, pp. 77–9) in arguing that we cannot understand social structures without realising that they are produced through interaction, but that this interaction has to occur within society and the structural forms which shape that society. Thus, within my case study I found that interviews with the Committee members showed how they structured their understanding of these issues in terms of the family (and its biological and social base), in terms of the report and in terms of their policy task. Therefore, notions of the family and of policy were reproduced by what was said in the interviews, but were also added to, changed and developed by how they talked about them. That is, the members were not constrained by particular notions of the family, even though reference to the family was the only way in which they could sensibly talk about these issues. Hence, constraint and creativity occur side by side.

Conclusion

Linking action to structure has been a central concern for sociology even though it has not been achieved on many occasions. It has not been so central to political science, but by opening up this area via a case study of policy making the importance of such issues to the analysis of the policy process may be established. A willingness to engage with methodological issues helps us to follow Hill's encouragement, in the Introduction to this volume, to sharpen the tools of policy analysis.

Note

I should like to thank Michael Hill, Robin Williams and Peter Selman for their assistance with various aspects of this chapter.

Reports

For clarity and ease of reference I have listed here the main reports which provide the historical and contemporary policy context for the Warnock Report.

American Fertility Society (1986) 'Ethical considerations of the new reproductive technologies', *Fertility and Sterility*, 46(3), Supplement 1.

Artificial Human Insemination: The report of a commission appointed by His Grace the Archbishop of Canterbury, Society for the Propagation of Christian Knowledge, 1948.

British Medical Association, *Annual Report of the Council. Appendix V: Report of the Panel on Human Artificial Insemination* (Chairman: Sir John Peel). *British Medical Journal Supplement*, 1973, 7 April, Vol II: 3–5 ('The Peel Report').

Department of Health and Social Security, *Report of the Committee of Inquiry into Human Fertilisation and Embryology* (Chairman: Dame Mary Warnock), HMSO, 1984 (Cmnd. 9314) ('The Warnock Report').

Department of Health and Social Security, *Legislation on Human Infertility Services and Embryo Research. A Consultation Paper*, HMSO, 1986 (Cm 46).

Department of Health and Social Security, *Human Fertilisation and Embryology: A Framework for Legislation*, HMSO, 1987 (Cm 259) ('The White Paper').

Department of Health, Education and Welfare, USA, *Report of the Ethics Advisory Board on Human in Vitro Fertilisation*, May 1979 (in Grobstein, 1981).

Glover, J. (1989) *Fertility and the Family*, report on reproductive technologies to the European Commission, London: Fourth Estate ('The Glover Report').

Home Office and Scottish Home Department, *Report of the Departmental Committee on Human Artificial Insemination* (Chairman: The Earl of Feversham), HMSO, 1960 (Cmnd. 1105) ('The Feversham Report').

House of Lords, *Human Fertilisation and Embryology Bill*, HMSO, 1989.

House of Lords, *Human Fertilisation and Embryology Act*, 1990.

Statens offentliga utredningar, Sweden (1983: 42) *Children Conceived by Artificial Insemination*.

Statens offentliga utredningar, Sweden (1985: 5) *Barn genom befruktning utanfor kroppen*.

Victoria Government, Australia, Committee to consider the social, ethical and legal issues arising from in vitro fertilisation (Chairman: Sir Louis Waller): (a) *Interim Report*, 1982; (b) *Report on Donor Gametes in IVF*, 1983; (c) *Report on the Disposition of Embryos Produced by IVF*, 1984 ('The Waller Report').

References

Barrett, M., and M. McIntosh (1982) *The Anti-Social Family*, London: Verso/NLB.

Beattie, A. (1965) 'Commissions, committees and competence'. *New Society*, 19 July, pp. 10–12.

Bernardes, J. (1985) 'Do we really know what "the family" is?' in P. Close and R. Collins (eds), *Family and Economy in Modern Society*, London: Macmillan.
Bryant, C., and O. Jary (1991) *Giddens' Theory of Structuration*, London: Routledge.
Bulmer, M. (ed.) (1980) *Social Research and Royal Commission*), London: Allen and Unwin.
Bulmer, M. (1986) *Social Science and Social Policy*, London: Allen and Unwin.
Cartwright, T. J. (1975) *Royal Commissions and Department Committees in Britain*, London: Hodder and Stoughton.
Chapman, R. A. (ed.) (1973) *The Role of Commissions in Policy Making*, London: Allen and Unwin.
Finch, J. (1986) *Research and Policy*, Lewes, Sussex: Falmer.
Glaser, B., and A. Strauss (1967) *The Discovery of Grounded Theory*, Chicago, Ill.: Aldine.
Grobstein, C. (1981) *From Chance to Purpose*, Reading, Mass: Addison-Wesley.
Haimes, E. (1988) 'Secrecy: what can artificial reproduction learn from adoption?' *International Journal of Law and the Family*, 2, pp. 46–61.
Haimes, E. (1990a) 'Recreating the family? Policy considerations of the "new" reproductive technologies', in M. McNeil *et al.*, (eds) *The New Reproductive Technologies*, London: Macmillan/British Sociological Association.
Haimes, E. (1990b) 'Family connections: the management of biological origins in the new reproductive technologies', doctoral thesis, Department of Social Policy, University of Newcastle upon Tyne.
Haimes, E., and N. Timms (1983) *Access to Birth Records and Counselling of Adopted Persons under Section 26 of the Children Act, 1975*, Final Report to the Department of Health and Social Security.
Haimes, E., and N. Timms (1985) *Adoption, Identity and Social Policy*, Aldershot: Gower.
Hall, P. (1976) *Reforming the Welfare*, London: Heinemann.
Ham, C., and M. Hill (1993) *The Policy Process in the Modern Capitalist State* (2nd edn), Hemel Hempstead: Harvester Wheatsheaf.
Hammersley, M., and P. Atkinson (1983) *Ethnography: Principles in practice*, London: Tavistock.
Hill, M., and G. Bramley (1986) *Analysing Social Policy*, Oxford: Basil Blackwell.
Lipsky, M. (1980) *Street Level Bureaucracy*, New York: Russell Sage.
Mills, C. Wright (1970) *The Sociological Imagination*, London: Penguin.
Morgan, D. H. J. (1985) *The Family, Politics and Social Theory*, London: Routledge and Kegan Paul.

Plowden, W. (1971) 'An anatomy of commissions'. *New Society*, 15 July, pp. 104–7.

Raab, C. (1987) 'Oral history as an instrument of research into Scottish educational policy-making', in G. Moyser and M. Wagstaffe (eds), *Research Methods for Elite Studies*, London: Allen and Unwin.

Rhodes, G. (1975) *Committees of Inquiry*, London: Allen and Unwin/ Royal Institute of Public Administration.

Silverman, D. (1985) *Qualitative Methodology and Sociology*, Aldershot: Gower.

Small, N. (1989) *Politics and Planning in the NHS*, Milton Keynes: Open University Press.

Tomlinson, D. (1987) 'Social policy and epistemology: recapturing the lost world of interpretation in case studies of community care', paper presented at the Annual Conference of the British Sociological Association, Leeds, UK.

Walker, R. (ed.) (1985) *Applied Qualitative Research*, Aldershot: Gower.

Warnock, M. (1985) 'The artificial family' in M. Lockwood (ed.), *Moral Dilemmas in Modern Medicine*, Oxford: Oxford University Press.

CHAPTER 8

Public policy transformation: regional development policy in Sweden

Bjorn Beckman

Introduction

A great number of actors participate in formulating, authorising and implementing public policy. They represent organisations in the public sector but also organisations in the private sector. Modern descriptions of public policy decision making and implementation in welfare states use such concepts as networks, complexity, decentralisation, overload, bargaining and vague control. A clear-cut division of roles and responsibilities between public and private organisations has in many cases been difficult to find (Hjern, 1985). Moreover, the traditional political-bureaucratic hierarchy is hardly discernable. The absence of hierarchies and role division seems to be more evident in some policy areas than in others. Such policy areas often include ones where private organisations are strategic actors. Regional development policy is one such area, and provides a good example of the mixed economy in the modern welfare state.

This chapter deals with changing relations between the centre and the periphery in regional development policy in Sweden. The aim is to present the change that has occurred from a basically 'top-down' policy to a policy characterised by a 'bottom-up' approach. This will be done by analysing the shift in relations in three aspects: policy instruments, policy initiation and decision situation. Some implications of the decentralisation efforts or the bottom-up policy will also be discussed. One topic is the feasibility of central control or steering of the periphery. Another is the extent to which public-sector decisions and management processes can be seen as distinctively different from private-sector ones.

Regional development policy

Regional development policy in Sweden is a policy based on discretion and on compensation. Geographical areas are given different forms of assistance because of their regional problems. These problems are characteristically slow growth in the economy, high unemployment and a low level of technical knowledge in the workforce. Moreover, these regions are sparsely populated. Regional development policy is partly an issue regarding economic efficiency, where political intervention should correct the inefficiencies of the market both at the periphery and at the centre. But the basic value in regional development policy is an ideological commitment to social cohesion. This social cohesion or the principle of equality is conceived particularly in geographical terms. Variations between living conditions for people in different regions have been considered too great to be accepted. Therefore a regional development policy has been established to compensate regions, counties or cities in policy areas considered important for regional development. The aim is to achieve regional balance.

'Regional balance' is the essence of intentions in Swedish regional development policy. In the early 1970s regional balance was interpreted as requiring a policy involving measures to adapt regions to the changes brought about by industrialisation and modernisation. In the early 1980s, however, regional balance was looked upon as needing a policy intended to keep a stable share of the population in each region. Public measures were expected to be taken if the regional distribution of the population changed. In the early 1990s, however, regional balance is once again seen as not necessarily being undermined if such changes occur. Instead regional balance is thought to require a policy for economic growth and adaptation to a post-industrial society, in a European context. Policy measures have to be authorised in order to keep a fair geographical distribution of welfare regarding employment, services, environment and individual choice in housing. Thus the meaning of regional balance has changed over the last twenty years.

The reason for focusing upon these different phases in order to analyse the evolution of a policy is to illuminate the typical character of the policy in each phase. The changes in the policy should be viewed not as great changes but rather as adjustments of the policy to new problems and new situations. New policy instruments have been added to existing ones. Thus in each phase the policy consists of a number of instruments combined to constitute a policy, but the different instruments were brought into regional development policy at different times with varying backgrounds, ideas and functions.

In Sweden regional development policy has gone through three phases from the late 1960s to the early 1990s. They have been called industrialisation, mobilisation and technical diffusion (Back and Eriksson, 1988; Beckman and Carling, 1989).

Regional development policy involves central government in trying to influence other actors by the choice of (steering) instruments. Examples of such instruments are mandates and grant-in-aids, where the authority of the state is used (Bacharach and Lawler, 1980). But the state can also influence in other ways: for example, by the use of information (Andersson *et al.*, 1977). By the dissemination of information the state influences the knowledge, values, perceptions and informational content of decision making. Thus actors may be influenced to change their behaviour. As an instrument for influencing other actors, however, information seems to be weak. By contrast mandates and grants are perceived as strong steering instruments (Beckman, 1987; Elmore, 1987). Mandates usually prescribe a certain behaviour for actors. In Sweden, for example, firms are mandated to supply a very detailed set of information when applying for a location grant. The location grant, on the other hand, is an economic incentive, influencing the conditions for a decision-maker in order to have a direct influence on his or her behaviour.

Thus mandates, economic incentives and information are used in regional development policy to influence private actors as well as public actors such as local authorities. In most situations policy-makers use combinations of policy instruments in order to achieve their intentions. These combinations and their transformation during the last twenty years will be dealt with below.

Before we analyse the three phases in regional development policy we have to make some more comments on policy instruments. One concerns where the policy initiative lies. There are differences in the design of instruments. Instruments may require a reaction from public organisations. The location grant is an example. The proper authority reacts to applications from firms. The authority makes an examination of the application to see if it fits the mandates. After such an examination the grant will be given or refused. The initiative to start the decision-making procedure is in the hands of the would-be recipient. But instruments might also be designed in a way that gives the public authority the policy initiative. The authority then starts the process in an active way: for example, in a planning procedure. This type of instrument is called 'proactive'.

A second comment concerns the decision-making situation. Regional development policy is a selective policy in at least two ways: the geographical designation of regional assistance areas; and the selection of the lines of business and classes of employees which are eligible for regional assistance. The decision making is also discretionary with a case-to-case procedure. The precision of the mandates is important when dealing with each case. A very precise mandate will give a very limited discretionary possibility in decision making, while imprecise mandates will increase the scope for discretion. In the latter case a bargaining situation might arise.

We have a situation where the public authority needs information from the firm in order to make the decision on a location grant. At the same time the authority tries to influence the project either by influencing the contents of the project or, for example, by limiting the grant. The firm might threaten to reconsider its project or to move the project outside the regional assistance area. Thus there may be a bilateral decision situation. Regarding other policy instruments there are multilateral decision situations, such as in planning or in the decisions on the establishment of organisations for technical diffusion (Magnusson, 1980; Johansson, 1992).

Phases in regional development policy

Industrialisation

The period frequently characterised by the term 'industrialisation' is the period when regional development policy came into existence.

The policy started in 1965 as a means of influencing the location of industrial investment (prop 1964: 185). Later it grew into a planning regime in order to build up an urban system, and a large number of economic incentives were introduced (prop 1970:75; 1972:111).

During the industrialisation phase the centre – that is, central government or a national agency – took the decisions regarding regional assistance to firms. Regional authorities were involved in a consultative procedure, but did not otherwise influence the decisions. The policy can be characterised as a reactive policy, the public authorities reacting to applications from enterprises which wanted to expand or locate their activities inside the regional assistance area (SOU, 1980, 6).

During this period the system of investment funds was also used. When private companies made profits part of these were required to be transferred into investment funds. Companies then had to secure government permission to use the money for new projects in the future. In order to influence development in northern parts of Sweden, the government included in its permission for the use of investment funds the obligation to invest in the north. Thus the government reacted to applications from firms to use their investment funds.

Regional assistance for investment was supplemented by a planning system. Regional development planning, however, took place in all regions. The planning process focused on co-ordination of public organisation activities, and was linked to the implementation of the amalgamation of local authorities (Beckman, 1977; Magnusson, 1980).

Industrialisation of the areas with regional problems was the main feature of regional development policy in the beginning. By supporting growth in industry in the designated assistance areas, the level of employment and subsequently the out-migration of the population could be influenced. Within a macro policy of modernisation and economic growth in the nation as a whole, the aim was to accelerate the modernisation process in the areas where industry was weak.

In the regional assistance areas a number of towns were supposed to function as growth centres, and relocation of economic activity, and thus employment, from the southern and central parts of Sweden to these growth centres was a central feature of the policy. Thus regional development policy basically consisted of economic incentives (subventions) to firms in industry so that they would locate their activities in certain growth centres, or expand their activities in the regional assistance areas. This idea was the foundation of regional development policy and its main instrument.

At the beginning of the 1970s regional development policy was broadened, becoming seen as an element in an urban system policy. The policy instruments used were specific targets for public investment to support the establishment of urban systems in certain specific regional centres.

The establishment of this urban system was further strengthened by the decision to relocate central agencies to a number of primary centres in central and northern Sweden. Regional development aspects were more thoroughly discussed, and influenced governmental and parliamentary decisions regarding the location of regiments and regional colleges, the fares on railway and air transport, as well as telecommunications.

Further regional assistance instruments – transport assistance, vocational training grants and employment grants – were added to the location grants. Moreover, the definition of 'investment' was expanded to include premises or equipment for industrial service and activities related to industry.

Information as an instrument for influencing actors was also introduced. When companies wanted to expand or locate their activity in areas around the three big cities of Sweden, they had to be informed of other location possibilities.

But the most important regional development instrument turned out to be the expansion in the public service sector. This was partly due to incentives given to local and regional authorities by central government. Specific grants and equalisation grants to local authorities were very important in this respect.

By the end of the industrialisation phase the planning system had evolved to the point where regions used it to try to put pressure on the centre in order to get resources to solve their regional problems, and to claim that their primary centre was an excellent location for national agencies to move to from Stockholm or for new regional colleges.

At the beginning of 1970s regional development policy broadened its emphasis. The policy consisted of compensating private firms for their added costs due to geographical location (in the north), and, at the same time, of building up good infrastructural conditions in order to support the expansion of industry. The latter part of the policy was the task of a growing public sector.

The decisions on assistance to firms were made at the centre, either by a central agency with close relations to the ministry responsible or by the government. The decisions were discretionary to facilitate the selection of cost-effective investment and to try to ensure that the choice of technology resulted in an expansion of employment. Thus the state played a role based upon a Keynesian view of the economy, using intervention in order to fine-tune the economy (Bogason *et al.*, 1991).

The planning dimension of regional development policy was characterised by the ambition that economic growth could be achieved by planned public investments. This reached its peak with a programme in which all local authorities were classified according to their roles in the urban system (prop 1972:111). Gradually this involved an increased role for public organisations other than central government, such as municipalities and county councils. Their role, however, was connected to the next phase in regional development policy.

Mobilisation

The mobilisation phase in regional development policy was closely connected to the effects of the oil crisis in Sweden. Between 1976 and 1984 important efforts were made by the state to solve the resultant crises in Swedish industry. These measures had a much larger scope than regional development policy and have had important effects on regional development. But their effects were much more important in areas outside the designated regional assistance area than inside. Efforts were made in order to solve the problem of unemployment; but in contrast to the earlier phase, unemployment now increased dramatically in densely populated areas and a process of industrial restructuring took place. Moreover, the national growth in the economy slowed down. The strategy of industrialisation was still the main part of regional development policy, but mobilisation increased in importance.

The policy instruments for industrialisation changed slightly, with broader definitions of eligible activities within private firms.

These included investments in marketing, education and so on, examples of what are called 'soft' investments. To a small degree the decision-making system was decentralised when the county administrative boards were given some decision-making power regarding location grants. In an effort to influence the big industrial companies in Sweden, a new information system was introduced. The government established a regional policy council where the government discussed regional policy questions with representatives from the big companies (prop 1975/76:211).

At the same time the planning system in regional development policy reached the peak of its importance. A most ambitious scheme was authorised, combining a five-year plan with a planning report each year. Thus every year regional development issues were routinely and repetitively discussed among the organisations in the counties. The intention with the yearly report was to combine development planning with the public budget process, and thereby to co-ordinate the different parts of the public sector. Moreover, in the first two years of this period, special reports had to be presented. The issues were formulated nationally, but the actual organisation, procedure and data were to be decided by each county. The reports dealt with such issues as a programme for the development of industry, especially the small and medium-sized firms, vocational education and strengthening the equality between the sexes in the labour market. The special reports were to be presented to the government and forced the organisations in the counties to collaborate in new combinations and on new issues. A learning process in the counties was set in motion by the national government.

Other efforts to mobilise and co-ordinate regional actors were also tried. Procedures regarding the location grant involved the County Administrative Board, the County Development Fund, the County Labour Exchange Board, local authorities, county council and interested organisations. The government also established a number of implementation groups connected to decisions on regional packages (see below).

When the non-socialist government came to power in 1976 special measures for sparsely populated areas were established as a third branch in regional development policy. These included such things as grants to modernise the equipment in country shops and support to small-scale work projects in peripheral areas. The decision-making powers were granted to the County Administrative Board in co-operation with the County Agriculture Board and the municipalities. As sparsely populated areas were defined by county the attention was in some respects turned to problems inside each county.

In order to understand the policy transformation, the concept of external co-ordination may be used (Scharpf, 1978). In this context external co-ordination means that superior authorities influence structural factors in the county: for example, a change in the mandates. Central government forced organisations in the regions to co-operate on a number of different regional issues. They were required to make special reports in order to secure new resources. Within the regions it was perceived as important to come to an agreement. Repetition of this experience over several years taught the regions to co-operate. As the government linked the requirement of the production of special reports to the programme for regional development, this influenced collaboration on future projects (cf. Axelrod, 1984). These actions taken by the government also strengthened the legitimacy of the County Administrative Board.

The legitimacy of the County Administrative Board was also strengthened by the mandates for the public authorities in a county. Over time other organisations grew more dependent on the County Administrative Board. Regulations seen in the perspective of external co-ordination have been of great importance.

To start with, mobilisation was an issue in order to mobilise employment so as to guarantee the expansion of the public sector. An increase in employment in the public sector took place especially at county and local level. The other aspect of mobilisation is connected to mobilisation of jobs in the private sector. More precisely, this involved efforts to create new employment in areas where unemployment increased dramatically during the late 1970s and early 1980s because of the closure of industry in shipbuilding, wood products, mining and steel. In order to achieve full employment, regional assistance could be given all over the country, and employment effects came to be the most important factor regarding the level of subvention.

At the end of the mobilisation phase regional development policy was decided within implementation groups at county level where a number of regional actors bargained. During the late 1970s and early 1980s a great number of problems in firms appeared in all parts of Sweden, involving closures and threatening to increase unemployment. On such occasions a standard repertoire developed. The government supported the establishment of an *ad hoc* network in the region. This was to a large degree financed by specific economic resources in regional policy packages. In the network representatives from the County Administrative Board, the specific municipality, the County Development Fund, the County Labour Board, the unions and the firms met in order to try to 'solve the crisis' by developing initiatives.

Another aspect of mobilisation was the increase in the room for manoeuvre of regional actors that was given by further decentralisation of decision making. A decision-making system of three layers – county, central agency and the government – was established. A consequence of this was soon found to be that regional coalitions were built up to bargain with the central level in order to get a favourable decision for an enterprise in their own region (Henning, 1983). This occurred throughout the country as firms were eligible for regional development assistance almost independent of location.

The County Administrative Board in each county got a grant with no strings attached, that could be used according to the 'county's own priorities' in a new programme called regional development projects (prop 1978/79:112; Johansson, 1992). One of the intentions with this programme was also to strengthen regional co-operation and co-ordination. The programme can be seen as the institutionalisation of the special implementation groups for regional development mentioned above. In all counties regional development projects were expected to take place. Thus the county came to function as an important arena for decision making.

Central government was a dominant actor wherever big companies were involved. The structural problems in industry were dealt with by the government (Ministry of Industry) in a very centralised way. The government negotiated directly with the company, and regional and local interests were not involved very much (Berglund, 1987; Beckman and Carling, 1989).

In the early 1980s regional development policy changed to a very decentralised policy. Location grants, regional projects, support to new firms, new planning systems, almost all policy instruments, became decentralised to a large extent. The central level had a role only in economically large decisions (prop 1981/82:113).

Regarding location grants, eligibility was further expanded – for example, to infrastructure investment in support of tourism, conference centres and handicraft. Moreover, the criteria for decisions were less connected to efforts to increase employment than before.

A new type of incentive was also introduced, providing for a general and automatic subvention to industry in the northernmost part of Sweden. Industry obtained a subvention when the yield from social taxes on salaries decreased in that area.

Within the decentralised regional development policy, the central government influenced regional development by creating specially designed programmes for specific geographical areas. This involved geographically oriented efforts for a specific number of years with resources decided by Parliament, outside the regular regional development policy. This type of policy has in Sweden been labelled 'regional policy packages' and was heavily used during the first years of the 1980s. As these efforts were a response to the structural crisis in Swedish industry, much of the money was spent in areas outside the regional development assistance area. The government negotiated with firms, regional and local authorities in order to construct the package. Implementation of the package was often through a special implementation group.

The urban-system scheme established during the industrialisation phase was abolished in 1982. When regional development policy is actually decided at county level, national priorities cannot be upheld. Moreover, once regional development policy did not deal with the expansion of the public sector and the location of public investment, geographical priorities were not seen as a necessary instrument. The regional assistance area was redesigned in order to concentrate the efforts in the northern parts of the country.

Technical diffusion

In the mid-1980s a new logic dominated regional development policy. The central factor was technological knowledge (competence). Economic development was driven by changes in technology.

New technology was seen as the most important force in the modernisation process. Thus a new element, the development of technology and technological diffusion, was added to the existing policy instruments (prop 1984/85:115).

At the same time regional development policy returned to its original logic. This logic meant that business activities and industry were to be the driving forces in regional development, a condition that is also put forward in the theories on technology and innovation as a critical factor in industrial progress. Economic growth in the private sector, especially in industry, became seen as a key variable, and this growth is expected to take place in the market. Public measures such as planning and service provision were no longer a central concern. Regional development policy was seen as involving measures on the margin to influence actors in the business community.

The basic element in contemporary regional development policy is compensation (see above). Compensatory measures deal with technological knowledge and the use of technology in industry. The new direction of the policy is best symbolised by the large number of research and development organisations that have been brought into existence all over the country (Johansson, 1992). In close co-operation with universities, regional colleges and technical high schools, a large number of technical centres, resource centres and innovation centres have been created. The aim of these efforts is to develop a higher level of technical knowledge with the support of the resources in the different centres. But the organisations can also be seen as a result of a decentralised policy involving regional mobilisation.

Another aspect of this policy is the increasing tension between growth and compensation. Although the government to a large extent favours and supports the creation of centres in the regional assistance area, so far R & D organisations have been primarily beneficial to densely populated areas, those areas where economic growth has traditionally taken place.

Economic incentives were given when technological service and technological development were included in the location grants. But the importance of the logic of technology can best be seen in the decisions regarding regional policy packages. New regional colleges, new technical high schools and economic support to R & D centres became central elements in each regional policy package. The most important examples are the rapid expansion of the space research centre in Kiruna and the creation of a technical university in Bergslagen.

Technological diffusion is another measure to strengthen technological competence. Small and medium-sized enterprises were the targets for technological diffusion. The government asked the County Administrative Boards to present a number of special reports on technological issues (cf. planning above). The reports dealt with the diffusion of technology to small and medium-sized firms, including research and infrastructure for communication and regional development. In conjunction with this work many measures were taken at all levels of the decision-making system. But most efforts were made in a decentralised way with the counties creating programmes of their own. Moreover, assistance was given to support the creation and growth of technology-based companies.

The efforts to influence actors in regional development policy have been directed towards the private sector. In many of the technology-oriented measures the policy instruments have the character of initial support to innovations. The economic incentives can be found at both the central and the regional level. Most of the incentives were based on the assumption that public organisations should actively find firms with an interest in the programme – a proactive policy. Moreover, new funds were given in order to increase the economic resources for soft investments so that subventions could be given when new technology – for example, computerisation of a production line – was brought into a company.

With technological competence in focus in regional development policy, geographical areas lacking this competence are compensated by public policy. The policy measures consist largely of establishing an infrastructure that can support the development of technological competence and technological diffusion. Technical research and education are central policy instruments in such an endeavour.

These instruments have changed from reactive incentives to proactive incentives. Planning as a notion of co-ordinating policies has disappeared. Instead information and bargaining have increased in the decision-making system. Multilateral bargaining arenas make up the present decision-making system. This contrasts with the old system of location grants (in the industrialisation phase) where a company applied for regional assistance to a central authority.

One such decision-making arena is the programme for regional development projects, 'the grant with no strings attached' (see above). The participation in the programme for regional development projects in five counties is presented in Table 8.1 (based on Johansson, 1992).

As in many decentralised programmes, variation is the dominant feature illustrated by Table 8.1. The counties differ considerably in their pattern of participation. The decision-making network is a mixed-economy network with private firms heavily involved. In the Swedish debate on public–private relations the County Development Fund, which is a publicly funded organisation dealing with consultancy and the development of small and medium-sized firms, is usually seen as an organisation working with a private logic. With this in mind it is therefore often classified as a private organisation.

The organisations presented in Table 8.1 are the eight organisations that have the highest national index on participation. It is therefore difficult to say if the network is an open or a closed network. But a closer analysis shows the following. The County Administrative Board and the County Development Fund participate in most of the projects, though their share is diminishing. The third kind of organisation in the network is universities and colleges. The other organisations may be local authorities or enterprises, but the situation differs from project

Table 8.1 Participation in regional development projects in five counties, 1979–1986 (index)

	County				
	AC	*H*	*K*	*M*	*Y*
County Administrative Board	50	86	78	46	80
County Development Fund	57	41	42	22	47
University regional college	17	49	25	57	25
Local authorities	33	47	27	–	37
Firms	36	31	20	51	47
Other county authorities	24	29	32	42	19
National authorities	21	24	–	–	26
Specific development organisations	–	–	79	71	–

to project. On the whole the network is rather open but either the County Administrative Board or the Regional Development Fund is a key participant.

As the regulation authorises the County Administrative Boards to decide which projects to support and the boards have a duty to act on issues of regional development, the high level of participation by these organisations is not a surprise. The Regional Development Fund, on the other hand, has as its main task to support the development of small and medium-sized enterprises, a special target group in regional development policy. But the regulation says that the County Administrative Board and the Fund should co-operate in regional development. Their participation in the network may be seen as a regulated participation. The same can be said of the other organisations to a certain extent. For example, if projects deal with research-oriented activities, it is rather natural to include a university or college in the project if the competence can be found there. To sum up so far, the character of the network is to a certain extent the result of the mandates for regional development policy.

The discussion on regulation also gives some idea of power and dependence relations in the network. The consent of the County Administrative Board is needed in order to get access to economic resources in the programme. This consent gives the County Administrative Board a considerable power, but in order to achieve its policy the Board is dependent on other organisations. The power of the County Administrative Board depends on the level of its economic resources and its legitimacy for other actors.

The activities in regional development policy during 1979–86 have changed several actors' perception of dependency in the country. A study of twelve counties found that in only four counties most of the participants were negative about joint participation (Johansson, 1992). This change in 'climate' in the counties can to a large extent be explained by one fundamental aspect of dependence. During the 1980s the economic situation for public organisations in the counties has been characterised by cut-backs. In real value terms it has been a decade of retrenchment. On the other hand, one authority, the County Administrative Board, has been given expanded financial resources through the programme for regional development projects. Thus there is an opportunity to compensate losses by working together with the County Administrative Board. As the objectives for regional projects were extremely broad, almost all activities could be included in the programme. The problem was to get the idea accepted by the Regional Development Bureau of the board. As one person who was interviewed said: 'It is not a question of large sums of money, but on the margin they are very important.' Thus the perceived dependence on the County Administrative Board has increased among the other organisations in the county.

But on the other hand the County Administrative Board is dependent on the other actors to achieve regional development. This is especially the case regarding the private firms. The Board gives great consideration to the views presented by firms, and gradually as the economic situation improved in the mid-1980s the County Administrative Boards became very dependent on the firms.

To sum up, the dependencies in the networks are comparatively unilateral and connected to structural situations. Nonetheless one of the lessons from the oil crisis is that economic resources at the margin may be an important instrument in a decentralised policy. External support is a factor that may increase an organisation's importance in a decentralised network. Another lesson is that the structural situation in which policy instruments are used has to be taken into consideration.

It is also necessary to pay attention to the discretion in decision making in a county. Looking at Table 8.1 it can be found that, in contrast to the other regions, two regions were autonomous in the sense that national authorities were not participating in regional development projects. In one county (M) the participation of local authorities was very low and in another (H) very high. Two of the counties created specific *ad hoc* organisations for regional development. These were organisations where the relations between the public and the private developed in ways in which the distinctness of each actor could be discussed.

Implications of decentralisation: the public–private dimension

Regional development policy has been transformed to a decentralised policy, where actors in networks seem to be an important property of the policy. The mixed-economy character of the networks is an important fact. This section will deal with four aspects of the public–private dimension in regional development as a decentralised policy (cf. Beckman, 1987; Johansson, 1992).

The first aspect concerns the problem of control and steering. In studies of public policy we assume that political or public intentions are carried out through policies. But in many cases in regional development projects this assumption has been challenged. In a number of cases the interests representing the business community argued for activities or projects where the logic of the market was more pronounced. Discussions dealt with topics such as the organisation of the projects, criteria for success and the control of the project. If the business interests did not get their demands accepted, they did not participate. Their view was that regional development projects should support the market and be a contrast to traditional public planning. In most cases the public organisations accepted the private view in the discussions. Thus a number of projects took place where the activities were more or less commercial, and where a high proportion of the costs for the projects could, in the boom of the 1980s, be earned from marketed activities. In these cases the assumption that the County Administrative Boards were in control of regional development policy seems to be questionable. And as we found in the preceding section, the dependence relations varied according to structural conditions.

The second aspect to be dealt with regards the motivations for using mixed-economy networks or organisations as instruments in regional development policy. In which ways are the new types of organisation better equipped to solve regional development problems? The network organisations are considered to increase the contacts or information flow. The network gives a large supply of knowledge, experience and resources. By integrating knowledge and resources to an *ad hoc* organisation the legitimacy of its action is seen to be increased. Moreover, the mixture of experience has increased the capability of finding new solutions to regional problems.

A third aspect often mentioned is the possibility of stabilising networks as *ad hoc* organisations, if the activities are successful. Thus a large number of *ad hoc* organisations have developed from projects organised in networks. By this procedure regional development policy is seen to be more explicit than when the activities are run by the County Administrative Board, for example. To this might be added the fact that regional development policies can be identified by the *ad hoc* organisation, and this is seen as positive. Moreover, the issue of accountability within the market is more evident if *ad hoc* organisations are used.

Networks, however, are seen to be very flexible organisations. They are able to maintain autonomy in relation to other interests and are usually small (at least in comparison to most firms and public bureaucracies). Hence the decision-making procedure is perceived as rapid and efficient within a network. It is also easy to terminate activity in a network. Thus network organisations seem to be easy to build up and to close down.

Networks transformed into *ad hoc* organisations are classified as 'private organisations' in Sweden. As private organisations they can avoid many regulations regarding public access to information, decision-making procedures, the right to appeal and so on. These aspects have been very important for business community interests. The network organisations have to be run in the same way as firms or in a business-like manner. In that way it is possible to gain confidence and respect in business circles. In order to co-operate with firms they have to behave like firms.

A fourth aspect is symbolic. A new network or *ad hoc* organisation is a symbol of action and decision-making power. The authorities are trying to solve regional development problems by establishing a network where many actors participate. On many occasions the networks have their own names to help demonstrate their importance.

Networks organisations in regional development policy seem to have roles that in certain respects are in contrast to the image of a public bureaucracy. But the complex structures and dependency relationships within networks seem to facilitate evasion of the influence of government policy instruments.

The co-ordinator of the network is a key participant. Of course, the task of co-ordinator involves a traditional bureaucratic function. Minutes have to be written, motivations for decisions have to be recorded, contracts have to be drafted, economic control is necessary, etc. Over time it seems that this role increases the tendency to bureaucratise network policy.

Participation in negotiations or having the function of a broker and mediator seems to be one important role for the co-ordinator. There are many issues which are solved by negotiation: financial conditions in different projects and sub-projects run by the network, leasing contracts, consultancy contracts and most of all negotiating with other participants in the network in order to reach decisions.

Closely linked to the role as a negotiator is the task of representing the network either as a lobbyist or as a receiver of demands. In the latter case many network organisations deal with activities closely connected to technical diffusion and technical research. Innovators, consultancy firms and so on therefore try to get into the network organisation in order to gain access to its resources. It is often a difficult task to focus activities on a central idea. Many network organisations have failed as vehicles for regional development because of a spread in their activities. The co-ordinator is also a lobbyist in relation to other organisations. The role of the co-ordinator includes the task of influencing other organisations such as firms and national bureaucracies. There is also a task to present the network organisation as an important actor in regional development in the region, in the country and on the international field.

The co-ordinator role within networks in regional development policy varies considerably. In almost all cases there are no regulations that limit the action-space of the co-ordinator. The tasks are very general and no co-ordinator can be seen as a specialist in a field important for the project. The co-ordinators in a project or a network organisation are generalists with broad experience. It seems that special knowledge (expertise) is of no importance, but the capacity to work in many areas and in several roles at the same time is characteristic of a co-ordinator. The contrast to the traditional role of the public bureaucrat is evident.

Summary

The transformation in regional development policy in Sweden was studied through a number of phases, within which the rationales for the use of policy instruments differed. The central arguments in this chapter can be summarised as follows.

Regional development policy started with the aim of modernising sparsely populated areas by industrialisation. The logic was to build up growth centres where industry could get service from private actors and where the public sector guaranteed a number of welfare functions. The policy instruments used were subventions to industry, location grants and planning of the public sector. The decision-making situation was in most aspects a bilateral one where the central government had a dominating role.

By the end of the 1970s the situation had changed. The economy of Sweden was not growing any more. Regional development policy focused on the mobilisation of employment. This mobilisation took place in networks in an increasingly decentralised policy. Proactive information linked with economic incentives was used to change the logic of regional policy. Employment was supported regardless of geographical location. Decisions were taken by multilateral bargaining.

During the 1980s technical knowledge and technical diffusion have been added to regional development policy. Research and development efforts in support of private firms have grown into a distinct feature of regional development policy. A mixture of policy instruments have been used, and actors in regional networks have had crucial roles in formulating, deciding and implementing regional policy. The logic of public–private co-operation has changed roles, power relations and organisations in regional development policy. This has involved both a move away from the use of traditional bureaucratic modes of organisation, and the further advancement of decentralised decision making.

References

Andersson, S., A. Mellbourn and I. Skogö (1977) *Myndigheten i samhället*, Stockholm: Publica.

Axlerod, R. (1984) *The Evolution of Cooperation*, New York: Basic Books.

Bacharach, S., and E. Lawler (1980) *Power and Politics in Organizations*, San Francisco: Jossey-Bass.

Back, P.-E. and A. Eriksson (1988) 'Sumsk regionalpolitik 1965–1987' in *Regionalpolitiken som politikområde*, Helsinki: NordREFO.

Beckman, B. (1977) *Regional förvaltning och regional planering*, Lund: Department of Political Science.

Beckman, B. (1987) *Att bilda FoU-organ m.m.* ERU-rapport *51*, Stockholm.
Beckman, B., and A. Carling (1989) *Förhandlingsekonomin i regionalpolitiken*, Stockholm: Arbetsmarknadsdepartementet, Ds 1989:28.
Berglund, B. (1987) *Kampen om jobben*, Gothenburg: University of Gothenburg.
Bogason, P., N. Aarsaether, B. Beckman, L. Jensen, and S. Sjöblom (1991) *Statens ansvar för regionalpolitiken*, NordREFO 1991:3.
Elmore, R. (1987) 'Instruments and strategy in public policy', *Policy Studies Review*, 7 (1), pp. 195–210.
Henning, R. (1983) 'Regional policy: implementation through bargaining', *Scandinavian Political Studies*, 6, pp. 195–210.
Hjern, B. (1985) *Supportive Resources in Compulsory Education: Municipal implementation strategies in Sweden*, APSA Annual Meeting, New Orleans.
Johansson, J. (1992) *Offentligt och privat i regionalpolitiken*, Lund Political Studies 69, Lund.
Magnusson, H. (1980) *Kommunerna och den regionala planeringen*, Lund, Studentlitteratur.
Scharpf, F. (1978) 'Interorganizational policy studies: issues, concepts and perspectives', in K. Hanf and F. Scharpf (eds), *Interorganizational Policy-Making*, London: Sage.
SOU (1980:6) *Offentlig verksamhet och regional välfärd*, Stockholm.

Parliamentary records

prop 1964:185 Riktlinjer för en aktiv lokaliseringspolitik
prop 1970:75 Fortsatt regionalpolitisk stödverksamhet
prop 1972:111 Regionalpolitiskt handlingsprogram m.m
prop 1975/76:211 Samordnad sysselsättnings- och regionalpolitik
prop 1978/79:112 Regionalpolitik
prop 1981/82:113 Program för regional utveckling och resurshushållning
prop 1984/85:115 Regional utveckling och utjämning

CHAPTER 9

Implementation in the hands of senior managers: community care in Britain

Jaqi Nixon

Introduction

In November 1989 the British government published a White Paper, *Caring for People*, which was concerned with the development of a new policy of community care for people with social needs. In their foreword to the White Paper the ministers responsible for the policy noted: 'Helping people to lead as far as is possible full and independent lives is at the heart of the Government's approach to community care' (Department of Health, 1989).

The White Paper was translated into legislation in 1990 with the passing of the National Health Service and Community Care Act. The Act places a responsibility on local authority social services departments (SSDs) for co-ordinating the planning, assessment and delivery of community care. Initially, full implementation of the Act was intended by April 1991. At a later stage the central government department responsible for the legislation, the Department of Health (DoH), decided that implementation should be phased over a two-year period leading to completion by April 1993.

Community care and the policy–making context

During the 1980s the British government believed it had a mandate to introduce radical change. This was illustrated by the many new policies which were introduced. In the early part of the Thatcher years priority was given to fiscal, economic and labour policies, but it was inevitable that in due course the underlying changes in ideology and values which marked this period in British policy making would also affect social policies. Between 1987 and 1990 social welfare attracted the particular attention of the Thatcher government. Major legislation was either passed or brought into force which affected social security policy, school education, and services for children and their families. Community care policy was thus part of a larger political agenda which sought to reduce what government viewed as traditional and unacceptable expectations of the role of the state as the main provider of welfare (but see also Fimister and Hill, this volume, Chapter 5, for discussion of another motive for reform). As Plant has summed it up:

> The strategy seems to be to create an environment more favourable to market allocation in this sphere, in the hope that, over time, people will look to the state less and less for welfare, taking responsibility for their own lives. (in Drucker *et al.*, 1988, p. 12)

By 1990, while already sensitive to what the next election might require of them, the government had nevertheless invested a great deal of political and official time in fleshing out the principles which constitute the hard core of its community care policy. This core (which others, e.g. Whitmore (1984), might prefer to call the policy paradigm) included expanding private care within a more mixed-economy approach to service delivery, ensuring more effective control over community care expenditure, and identifying quality more in terms of consumers' than providers' interests, and in terms of outcomes rather than processes. As well as being required to adopt these new principles for community care, local authorities, and especially SSDs, were also called upon to develop new structures and new ways of working in order to put the policy principles into practice. Here then was a policy which had been sculpted by the centre for use by agencies at local level.

Having issued policy directives on community care, central government then proceeded to play fast and loose with local authorities concerning finances for the new policy. With no ring-fenced community care budget (until a late change of policy) and with the major flow of funding postponed from April 1991 until

1993, policy implementers at local level were unlikely to view positively their responsibility for putting community care into practice. Even if ultimately an extra tranche of a local authority budget is intended for community care, with stringent controls and penalties being separately imposed on local government expenditure, it seems unlikely that the new money would be anything like sufficient. This is discussed further by Fimister and Hill in Chapter 5. Was this not another example, then, of a central government off-loading major responsibilities on to local government, but at the same time not adequately resourcing the venture?

Certainly community care policy would seem to offer an excellent case study with which to illustrate the problems of translating national policy intentions into service or programme practice. It is a policy that places many new demands upon local authorities in Britain which are at present facing more general difficulties concerning the resourcing of services, additional legislative responsibilities, and uncertainties about their future role as democratically elected bodies accountable to a local constituency. Moreover, embodied in the policy core of community care is a general critique of professional social work which has always sought to be identified with the provision of 'quality' services in social care, and yet has been unable to demonstrate effectively enough that this has indeed happened. However, implementation of community care requires the setting of objective criteria by which standards can be judged and, as Pollitt has argued:

> An explicit standard is de-mystifying: it can be used as the basis for a more intelligible system of public accountability . . . No longer is it possible for professionals to concentrate mainly on technical aspects of the delivery process . . . to the exclusion of the actual experiences of those 'processed' . . . a close correspondence between professional autonomy and responsiveness to clients . . . is anything but automatic. (Pollitt, 1990b, p. 437)

Some may argue that social work is especially vulnerable in the face of this charge since, unlike certain other professions, it does not yet have its own self-regulating body.

Taken together, then, these features of the community care policy could appear to present a heavy and unwelcome burden for local authority SSDs, and to pose something of a threat to the social services professionals. And yet community care seems to have been converted into an opportunity, an acceptable challenge, and to have been taken up with enthusiasm by senior social services managers across the country, eager to demonstrate their prowess in meeting implementation deadlines and in getting the policy under way. As one director of a social services department explained: 'Full implementation of the Community Care Act will continue to create cash headaches for Social Services Departments. That said, we're committed to carrying on with the job and to fulfilling the other phases to 1993' (Mason, 1991, p. 7).

Another director was reported as knowing that, although 'it will be tough to implement the new order given current financial constraints . . . [it] must be seen as a major opportunity for social services' (Murray, 1990, p. 16). And another commentator noted: 'The funny thing is that most people in social service departments have grown strongly attached to the NHS and Community Care Act. It has clustered around itself a surprising political consensus and fostered some unlikely alliances' (Hatchett, 1990, p. 10).

Where attempts have been made to introduce 'bottom-up' community care plans, which are now required by the legislation, it has been noted that 'advocates are enthusiastic about the cultural and organisational changes wrought by their programmes . . . This may indicate a degree of commitment and dynamism which augurs well for their community care plans' (George, 1991, p. iii).

As recently as April 1992, when arguments about community care funds became quite fierce between local authorities and central government, directors of social services were still reported as 'relishing the challenge of the Children Act [implemented in 1989] and the community care changes' (Brindle, 1992, p. 26).

Why, then, is community care perceived as presenting more of an exciting opportunity, rather than an onerous duty, for those who are charged with the responsibility of making radical organisational and procedural changes so that the policy can be put into effect?

This chapter attempts to answer the question by exploring, in a number of ways, the relationship between professional communities at central and local government levels, and the needs, values and interests of the key senior managers in SSDs who are responsible for the implementation of the policy within their localities.

Creating a cornucopia or being handed a poisoned chalice?

It is important to note at the outset that even a centre-dominated policy is one that is shaped in a particular context. This context has its own fissures of interests, its own limitations in acting as either a co-ordinating or a policy-controlling body, and draws upon a range of experience in its relations with local authorities. Participants at central level include the professional members of the Social Services Inspectorate (SSI), as well as civil servants from different policy communities within the DoH, and the politicians and external policy advisers, all of whom have their own interests to serve and their different agendas to address. In addition, there are organisational limitations on the capacity of this diverse central group to monitor or influence the implementation of policy at the local level.

Nor should one overlook the fact that central government departments have their own distinctive cultures, particular interests and styles of working. While these may have undergone some change during the 1980s, there is nevertheless some continuity in a department or a policy section of a department on account of the relative permanence of the officials and professional civil servants responsible for servicing it. The section of the DoH concerned with social services policy could be described in general terms as more of an 'advocate' for spending on its policies than a 'guardian' of the Treasury purse (Rhodes, 1986a); as tender-minded rather than tough-minded.

There are a number of possible explanations for the general enthusiasm with which senior social service managers in local government have taken up the challenge of community care. The first is that they have no difficulty in recognising that there are elements of the policy which, professionally, are wholly desirable and which they would want to adopt. That issues of quality assurance should be dealt with more systematically within departments is one example, and that service users should be able to contribute to assessment decisions is another. In order to achieve consensus concerning the whole of the policy core, however, it may be argued that a policy community located at the centre had to include not only central government actors but also senior social services professionals from outside. A number of writers have noted the key role of professionals in decision making at the centre, playing their part in the construction of 'ideological corporatism' (Dunleavy, 1991). Thus the policy consensus is the result of 'a fusion of interests' (Whitmore, 1984).

While the general style of the Thatcher governments was to remove traditional ways of doing business with local government, and to develop a more *dirigiste* approach, it is important to recognise the continuing diversity in relationships between separate government departments and local authorities. It follows from what we noted above that DoH actors concerned with social services are more likely than other government personnel to give time to discussion of substantive policy and service issues as well as of budgetary matters.

So, in respect of community care, the government provided opportunities for positive policy inputs from key protagonists outside its own immediate territory. Participants included those who are traditionally identified as representing the interests of the main social services groups, such as the Social Services Inspectorate (SSI) (a group of professional social workers and other experienced personnel located within the Department of Health), members of national organisations representing the interests of social service workers or user groups, and, most important for the purpose of this discussion, the directors or other senior personnel from local authority social services departments (see Gaffney, 1990). According to Day and Klein (1990), the directors are the 'barons' of the social services community.

Thus senior managers themselves have part ownership of the policy, making it a matter of both belief and principle that they should implement community care as effectively as possible. They will in turn convey their commitment to the policy to both politicians and practitioners at local authority level. As Henkel (1991) has suggested, the Department of Health is prepared to consult with senior managers from local authorities in order to reduce the possibility of local councillors misshaping the policy by their own political input.

Alternatively, it could be argued that these contributors have been allowed to influence not so much the policy core of community care but rather the way in which 'what' has to be done by local authorities is to be translated into 'how' it is to be done. This is the language employed in practice guidance documents which have been produced by the SSI. The values which underpin the policy core remain those of the government, and these have been fairly unambiguously stated. They include the commitment to an extended private market in social care, the control and reduction of local authority public expenditure, checks on professional discretion and a clearer focus on individual, rather than collective, needs. Senior social service managers who are able to identify with these values, as well as those who, at least, feel satisfied that they have been able to make some difference to issues of 'how' it is to be done, were thus well placed to keep open the 'flows of ideological influence' (Whitmore, 1984) from the centre to the locality and so facilitate the implementation of community care.

Whichever of these alternative general explanations is more plausible, by participating in a policy community at the centre, the senior representatives of social services, together with representatives of non-statutory national agencies, have had some impact on the shape of the community care policy. While they have been willing to accept some parts of the hard core of the policy, they have also managed to negotiate about other elements and have dislodged these, as it were, from the core so as to make them more suitable for discretionary responses at local level. That central government may have been prepared to negotiate and to compromise, even on policy core issues, requires further and more specific analysis.

First, the DoH received professional advice from its SSI that certain aspects of the original community care policy were simply not feasible in practice: for example, that too strict an adherence by SSDs to a split between service purchase and service provision, a key element in the policy core, could not be sustained in some areas. Thus the SSI helped to identify potentially difficult areas for implementation. Since it will be the SSI's responsibility to ensure central government intentions are carried out, this was a sensible thing to do. Furthermore, as Day and Klein make clear, the inspectors are ultimately dependent upon the directors of social services for the delivery of the policy: 'The leverage of the SSI in dealing with recalcitrant authorities is limited . . . Even an overt inspectorial role, the SSI's experience makes plain, does not eliminate the need for nose-stroking and persuasion' (1990, pp. 22–8).

Secondly, somewhat suspicious of the advice offered by its own

Inspectorate, the DoH decided to make use of private consultants in order to obtain an independent and alternative perspective. Henkel has suggested that government use of consultants provides for its policy decisions 'credibility partly because they come from the private sector', bringing with them 'values and methods from industry and commerce' (Henkel, 1991, p. 126). The DoH had already benefited from the advice of one such consultant at an early stage of developing its community care policy (Griffiths, 1988), whose short report provided the necessary impetus for introducing 'values and methods' from commerce into this policy domain. Now, at this later stage of policy implementation, it might have been expected that the consultants' recommendations on the key 'market' principle of splitting purchasing of services from provision of services would differ from those of the SSI. Certainly they proposed a number of ways in which the purchaser/provider split could be achieved, depending upon the circumstances prevailing in different SSDs and the wider context in which they are operating. In addition, however, they also provided evidence of the potential problems of separating the two responsibilities in some areas. This opened the way for the Department to accept that some aspects of its community care core policy would require further consideration, and possibly warranted negotiation with other social services actors.

Thirdly, and separately, senior social services managers had themselves argued for the need to retain flexibility in policy implementation. They are likely to have argued that, while welcoming the main tenets of community care policy, such as the mixed economy of care, they would have difficulty selling this package to local politicians. They would need to be able to convey this principle in their own language in order to make it more palatable. Thus they wanted opportunities for both professional and political manoeuvring at local level. Senior managers would be able, therefore, to recommend to their own politicians the need to apply the brakes for some of the community care measures, and to modify other elements of the policy, prior to implementation.

In consequence, while some of the original policy core would remain intact, other parts, which were predicated on practical and political feasibility at local level, had yet to be determined. This very familiar situation of potential flexibility in implementation helps to lessen the burden and increase the discretionary influence of those responsible for carrying community care policy to the localities. Evidence from a pilot study of 24 local authority SSDs suggests, at least in the early stages of implementation, that authorities have indeed displayed a diversity in response. They have variously defined government 'policy intent in ways compatible with their values and interests' (Wistow *et al.*, 1992).

Small but beautiful?

A further general explanation for senior managers' support for community care policy may be that local authorities in Britain are now expected to start behaving more like central government departments, where, since 1990, large areas of executive responsibility have been decoupled from policy departments, and their respective ministers, to form independent agencies. This expanding initiative has been entitled the Next Steps and represents a major change in central government administration. It reflects the current philosophy of having 'professional managers at the top, with ministers in a strictly hands-off role' (Hood, 1991, p. 6).

According to Dunleavy, senior managers in central government departments, bereft of large areas of executive responsibility, will nevertheless continue to safeguard their job satisfaction by reducing, rather than expanding their budgets: 'the marginal benefits curve for senior officials will shift radically . . . Their incentives to advocate further programme budget increases are reduced' (1989, p. 268). Dunleavy later argued, contrary to 'public choice' perspectives of government bureaucracies, that 'there are multiple reasons why self-interested officials vary greatly in the extent to which they push up expenditures' in order to pursue their personal interests (1991, p. 197). With limited opportunities for obtaining personal financial gain, top bureaucrats will seek to enhance 'work-related utilities' and to 'pursue a bureau-shaping strategy' rather than a 'budget-maximising' one. This means that they will try to develop the agency more in line with 'staff' than 'line' functions, which in turn requires a high level of management discretion and a concern about broad policy issues rather than with detail. Thus the ultimate quest for the senior managers is to reshape the agency so that it takes on more of a small, central, élitist character and becomes less concerned about the size of either its operations or its budget (Dunleavy, 1991).

Dunleavy's important analysis is directed at central government agencies. It could be argued, therefore, that budget reductions are not yet viewed by local authority senior managers as a potent indicator of performance (indeed, they were promised major increases in community care budgets for 1993). Nevertheless the fundamental proposition that job satisfaction is to be secured in ways other than by service expansion is appropriate for senior managers responsible for the implementation of community care. Though still having much to do, they are less likely to have direct responsibility for the provision of services, partly because of devolved responsibilities within their own departments and partly because there will be some movement in the direction of privatising social care, taking provision of services out of the department altogether. In their report on initial changes in SSDs, as a consequence of community care policy, Wistow *et al.* (1992) noted that the most significant potential change was in establishing not-for-profit trusts for the provision of residential care, and that this did imply a substantial reduction in the SSD's role as a direct provider. In addition, general cuts in SSD public expenditure have been reported for 1992–3.

Thus as SSDs move along a continuum, identified by Dunleavy as stretching from a service delivery bureau to a regulating or control bureau, the senior managers will increasingly become removed from decision making in respect of the development or delivery of services, and so will be looking to enhance their job satisfaction through the adoption of 'bureau-shaping strategies'. These may well include off-loading traditional departmental functions which no longer appear compatible with the senior managers' vision of what status-conscious, slimline SSDs should look like. Already some local authority managers are considering whether to take advantage of the intended purchaser/provider split required for community care, to create two separate departments to replace the existing SSD. One department would carry responsibility for commissioning of services, not just for community care but for child care work also. The other department would retain responsibility for service provision. A further functional demarcation, already separate in principle, is that between quality assurance and service provision in SSDs. Some argue that areas of responsibility associated with inspection, registration and regulation of services will become a more high-status activity than service delivery (Challis, 1990).

Alternative career paths?

Given such changes in the character of SSDs, the career interests of some directors of social services may now best be served in a national forum rather than in a particular locality ('technocrats' not 'topocrats', Rhodes, 1986b). And once again, it can be argued that community care policy has helped to open up such opportunities by enabling representatives of the senior managers (ADSS), and of other social services organisations, to work more closely with central government. One director, for example, explained that 'some presidents have had the ear of the minister. More than ever before the ADSS has made inroads into Whitehall'. Another director suggested that 'with recent legislation the task was so enormous that the DoH required our help and [our president] seized the opportunity' (Sone, 1991).

Having made the most of such an opportunity, senior managers are well placed to continue to be active members of the national social services policy community. This community, like other policy communities, may be characterised by closely knit and relatively stable relationships between a small and select number of groups or individual participants, and will generally organise itself around a particular government department (Grant, 1989; Richardson and Jordan, 1979). Thus, having established themselves as effective members of this élite community which focuses itself upon the DoH, some senior managers could be well placed to move 'up' and away from their local authority department. Flight into the private sector, where their newly acquired entrepreneurial skills will be especially valued, is also becoming an attractive alternative path.

In addition there may be better career opportunities within other areas of the local government hierarchy, rather than at the national level. As Clarke and Stewart (1989) have suggested in respect of future 'enabling councils', local government departments will no longer be delineated according to traditional professional groupings. Moreover, the new departments will not necessarily be headed up by someone who shares with his or her staff a particular professional background or similar qualifications. Already there have been opportunities for accountants and librarians, for example, to take up senior management posts in SSDs. And in one recently restructured English local authority, which is described by its chief executive as streamlined and rationalised, and where 'the new culture is to challenge and question' previous policies and practices, architecture and quantity surveying, traditionally the responsibility of a chief architect and chief surveyor respectively in local authorities, have been transferred to the housing department.

In similar fashion, there would be more scope for directors of social services to move across traditional departmental boundaries, or for major services to be transferred from one director to another. According to Clarke and Stewart an 'enabling council' is also likely to give priority to collective local authority values rather than to professional values. This will mean that social services managers will on occasions also have to make decisions which support either the organisational values of the local authority or those of their profession. Reputations are more likely to be made if priority is given to the former.

Real managers?

A separate though related feature of community care policy is its management appeal. The introduction of a new public management (NPM) movement is one of a number of international 'megatrends' in public administration (Hood, 1991) in the past decade. While there has been unquestionably a political context in which NPM has been nurtured in Britain (and in the USA), it has also had a wider, apolitical appeal (Pollitt, 1990a). According to some critics of NPM it is 'a self-serving movement designed to promote the career interests of an élite group of new managerialists . . . rather than the mass of public service customers or low-level staff' (Hood, 1991, p. 9). The culture and set of values which have accompanied this movement have certainly become increasingly attractive to senior managers in social services. These might be thought of as representing one of the last strongholds of a professional service culture within the public welfare sector. However, as a group, senior managers are increasingly demonstrating a real enthusiasm for working within a management culture framework. They have come to relish the business of financial management, negotiating contracts with the private sector, developing information systems and producing performance measures, which enable them to distance themselves from the different type of decision making undertaken by professional staff at the user and client level.

More generally, too, these NPM 'values' support the development of new structures characterised, as we noted above, by decentralisation and fragmentation. Flynn refers specifically to the implications of these structural developments for public-sector managers, and suggests that it offers scope for 'real management', which is about control rather than about traditional notions of managing in the public sector, namely administering services and supervising staff. 'Real managers impose their will on their subordinates and on the trade unions' (Flynn, 1990, p. 178). This style of management is not necessarily one which appeals to all senior managers, and perhaps least of all to the small number of women managers in social services, who are well placed to recognise the incongruities between the new 'values' for public service managers and the gendered assumptions about caring roles built into community care policy (Hallett, 1989). Nevertheless the climate of NPM in which all managers operate does help to give legitimacy to the controlling approach. In addition 'real' managers are likely to be involved as much in negotiating deals with other public and private agencies as in handling internal affairs. This then creates a greater gulf between the top and bottom of a public agency.

Community care has certainly offered greater potential for directors who want to demonstrate the possibility of central control without direct intervention on their part, and who wish to spend more time away from the day-to-day activities of the department. And there is no reason to expect that directors of SSDs should not make more of these opportunities, which represent the emerging management norm.

Nor is it altogether surprising if directors are also now more prepared to identify themselves publicly as an élite group working in social services (Sone, 1991), thereby dissociating themselves from social workers in particular. As social work continues in its quest for greater professional credibility, currently by means of a

General Social Services Council, senior managers are meanwhile becoming increasingly remote from the generation of generically trained social workers. As one director explained, they do not possess 'the breadth of knowledge or involvement across the whole of a department's work' (Brindle, 1992). This in turn may help to explain why, for their part, social work practitioners are now more suspicious of senior managers' involvement in casework decisions.[1]

Taken together these developments suggest the possibility of an even wider gap opening up between people in local authority social services who engage in professional decision making and who are likely to be towards the bottom of the departmental hierarchy, and those whose decisions revolve around matters of structure, systems and strategies. Unlike senior members of the medical profession, senior social services staff, the majority of whom are still drawn from social work or related areas, do not practise their profession. Doctors who retain responsibility for the delivery of medical services may also retain higher status than their counterparts who divest themselves of this work and who devote themselves instead to the purchase of services. But in social services the opposite is likely to be true. Senior managers may wish to distance themselves from the legacy of their professional past in social work, where traditionally status has not been high in Britain. Added to this is the wider trend towards de-professionalisation at the top, and the replacement of specialist professionals by general managers, with a premium on experience rather than expertise. This trend has itself been encouraged by a government eager to control professional influence and authority, including that of the medical profession, in the public services.

Effective management is also identified with opportunities for autonomy. In considering effective implementation of radical changes in the NHS, for example, Ham *et al.* (1990) recommend that central government should give a lead about core values but should allow 'managers discretion on how to deliver on these values'. Apparently this 'loose–tight organisation . . . has found favour in business because it gets results' (p. 17). As we have noted above, community care policy fits this model well. Government has been explicit about its core values concerning effective use of financial resources, and has given directives that certain structures and processes which are central to policy delivery must be in place by a specific date. But in addition, the Department of Health has left 'scope for innovation and flexibility at local level' (Department of Health, 1989, ch. 1). This permitted space for local discretion becomes even more apparent when guidelines on practice are examined. One example is directly concerned with a core policy issue, namely the need to separate purchaser and provider functions in social services:

> Social Services Departments should *keep in mind* the distinction between purchaser and provider roles and *guard against* care managers fulfilling *too much* of a provider function.
>
> Achieving a clear-cut distinction between the purchaser and provider *will not be easy in practice* because there is an *inevitable overlap* between the two.
>
> SSDs must *take account of their own characteristics*. (DoH/SSI, 1991b, emphasis added)

In this same document the word 'evolving' also appears on more than one occasion.

As regards the 'basic principle', to bring decision making as near to the user as possible through individual care managers, there is further scope for local discretion: '*responsibility does not necessarily have to be devolved . . . it may be kept at team or district level, particularly in the early stages*' (DoH/SSI, 1991b, emphasis added). All this has led one commentator to conclude: 'If you get the feeling . . . that government doesn't really expect to see the whole thing up and running by the end of the decade, you could just be right' (*Insight*, 1991).

Thus community care policy offers a gift to SSD managers, who will gain credit for implementing what is essentially a centralist policy and, at the same time, will retain sufficient control of policy developments in their own domain to satisfy their need for independence. This devolved management is what Hoggett (1991) refers to as 'freedom within boundaries'.

So we find in community care policy a happy combination of elements acceptable to senior managers. As well as giving them scope to deal more effectively with certain professional matters, it makes legitimate the implementation of a demanding government policy, suitably tailored for local authority use, even without adequate resources. It also enhances further the management-dominated environment in which public-sector managers increasingly wish to operate. Community care policy, it can be argued, serves the interests of managers themselves. They may use it 'to promote a set of beliefs which highlight the special contribution of management and thereby justify management's special rights and powers' (Pollitt, 1990a, p. 9). And even if all else fails, senior managers will still have opportunities to secure job satisfaction or pursue career opportunities in other ways which are not available to lower-level workers (Dunleavy, 1991).

Community care policy at the bottom?

What remains less clear is the extent to which the management culture will percolate to, or rather capture, the lower reaches of decision making within SSDs, which are currently the repository for professional judgement and discretion. Decentralisation and separation of budgetary responsibilities from service delivery may help to convert the peripheries of a department to NPM values. For example, standardised procedures for assessment of need for community care are already being put into place, and decisions are increasingly being based upon quantitative data which can be handled more efficiently by improved technologies. Moreover, there is a sense of competition between local authority SSDs and those health authorities whose investment in information technology systems and personnel has outpaced their own. In general SSDs are likely to want to catch up. Do these developments suggest a radical reduction in professional discretion in social services, to the extent that there will be little scope for field workers either to enhance policy or, to use Lipsky's early notion of the street-level bureaucrat, to undermine or distort community care policy in implementation (Lipsky, 1980)?

While organisational procedures and processes may move towards greater standardisation both within and between social services agencies, there will nevertheless remain opportunities for discretion and flexibility at the lower levels of decision making. It is still the case that policy delivery remains dependent upon the commitment and good will of those operating at the next tier down. We noted above the recognised importance of autonomy for senior management responsible for community care. Similarly, for others at lower levels there continues to be a need for space and opportunity in which to be creative and innovative. This is likely to include scope for applying professional judgement. Thus it can be argued that the new management culture, while influencing all aspects of community care policy, will not necessarily achieve dominance at all levels. Professional discretion will remain, and professional values will not allow the core values of the NPM culture to go uncontested. There will be an attempt to stem the flow of the NPM culture, which is currently seeking out new channels through which it can reach all areas of the community care enterprise in SSDs.

An uncertain future?

The sum of the argument presented here is that community care, more than any other policy which is the concern of social services in Britain, has helped to bring SSDs within the fold of the dominant value paradigm for the public service in the 1990s. This paradigm encompasses new perspectives on social welfare and on the relationship between the state and the individual, new structures for public organisations and a new style for public-sector management. Without community care acting as the catalyst for change, local authority SSDs may still have been running against the tide in public services, seeking to hold fast to traditional public service and professional values about what services need to be provided and for whom, and to traditional ways of organising and managing their diverse responsibilities.

But implementing community care meant that government needed the active support of the senior managers of SSDs, and more particularly of the directors. By their general willingness to 'buy' community care and to promote it within their localities, directors have at the same time advanced the cause of new-style public agencies. They have played a crucial role in turning round SSDs to make sure they are in better shape for survival. There is a common view that many of the trends which have been outlined here, and which have paved the way for new model SSDs, are irreversible.

In turn, senior managers needed community care. It has helped to open up for them new opportunities for job satisfaction within their own departments. It has offered scope for a change in professional identity, from a professional social work specialist to a general manager, which may serve well those managers who want to remain within the local authority. And, finally, it provides a possibility for new openings at a national level for those managers who have gained experience of working within the policy community and whose reputations have been enhanced as a consequence.

There are, however, factors which make for an uncertain future both for community care policy and for SSDs more generally. Concerning the former, there is the all too evident contradiction between one part of the policy which seeks to emphasise user-led provision and another which requires a resource-led response. There is the possibility that the first of these will increase user expectation and so lead to greater demands being made upon social services. At the same time a closer intra-departmental scrutiny of budgets and a more systematic use of needs and performance indicators are likely to lead to reductions in supply for some groups of users. Such contradictions may result in conflicts between 'enabler' and user, rather than the desired partnership between the two. It is at this point of conflict, too, that the difference between the values of the private market – where no such contradiction exists, since greater consumer demand is equivalent to producer interests – and those of the dedicated professional in a public agency is most apparent. It will test to the limit the 'political sensitivity' skills of the professional turned senior manager of social services as he or she seeks to work effectively with local politicians in a new-style local government (Baddeley, 1989). Alternatively, senior managers may find themselves having to relinquish responsibility for the SSD altogether. A take over of social services responsibilities by health authorities or by Family Health Service Authorities is not to be ruled out. Supported by central government, their general managers already have considerable experience of operating a business-oriented service, and their information systems, identified as essential in implementing community care, are usually superior to those of local authorities.

Relations between the centre and social services may also become more confrontational rather than consensual, as at present. If additional funding from 1993 is still *inadequate* funding for effective or satisfactory community care, then it is hard to imagine any sustained enthusiasm on the part of senior managers for retaining

responsibility for its implementation. They may even come to the conclusion that they have indeed been handed a poisoned chalice which they would be prepared to pass on. Either way, senior social services managers who are now better equipped with appropriate and transferable management skills will be looking for career opportunities elsewhere. As individual self-interest takes over from collective self-interest, and as top managers move on, the quality of service for community care may, in turn, be systematically undermined.

Note

I am grateful to Barry Wilson, University of Brighton for this suggestion.

References

Baddeley, S. (1989) 'Political sensitivity in public managers', in *Local Government Studies*, March/April, pp. 47–66.

Brindle, D. (1992) 'Life on the edge of an elephant trap', *The Guardian*, April, p. 29.

Challis, L. (1990) *Organising Public Social Services*, Harlow: Longman.

Clarke, M., and J. Stewart (1989) *Challenging Old Assumptions: The 'enabling council' takes shape*, Luton: Local Government Training Board, August.

Day, P., and R. Klein (1990) *Inspecting the Inspectorates*, York: Joseph Rowntree Memorial Trust.

Department of Health (1989) *Caring for People. Community Care in the Next Decade and Beyond*, London: HMSO.

Department of Health (1990) *Community Care in the Next Decade and Beyond. Policy Guidance*, London: HMSO.

Department of Health/Social Services Inspectorate (1991a) *Inspecting fo Quality*, London: HMSO.

Department of Health/Social Services Inspectorate (1991b) *Purchase Service*, London: HMSO.

Drucker, H., P. Dunleavy, A. Gamble, and G. Peele (eds) (19 *Developments in British Politics 2*, Basingstoke: Macmillan.

Dunleavy, P. (1989) 'The Architecture of the British Central State', pt *Public Administration*, 67 (3).

Dunleavy, P. (1991) *Democracy, Bureaucracy and Public Choice*, He Hempstead: Harvester Wheatsheaf.

Flynn, N. (1990) *Public Sector Management*, New York: Harvester Wheatsheaf.

Gaffney, P. (1990) 'Business as usual?', *Community Care*, 15 February.

George, M. (1991) 'The initiation process', *Community Care*, 28 March.

Grant, W. (1989) *Pressure Groups, Politics and Democracy in Britain*, Hemel Hempstead: Philip Allan.

Griffiths, R. (1988) *Community Care: Agenda for action*, London: HMSO.

Hallett, C. (1989) *Women and Social Services Departments*, New York: Harvester Wheatsheaf.

Ham, C., J. Huntington, and G. Best (1990) *Managing with Authority*, Birmingham: National Association of Health Authorities.

Hatchett, W. (1990) 'Ready and waiting', *Community Care*, 26 July.

Henkel, M. (1991) 'The new evaluative state', *Public Administration*, 69 (Spring), pp. 121–36.

Hoggett, P. (1991) 'A new management in the public sector?', *Policy and Politics*, 19 (4), pp. 243–56.

Hood, C. (1991) 'A public management for all seasons?', *Public Administration*, 69 (Spring) pp. 3–19.

Insight (1991) 'Briefings', 10 October.

Lipsky, M. (1980) *Street Level Bureaucracy*, New York: Russell Sage.

Mason, P. (1991) 'What next for SSDs?', *Community Care*, 4 April.

Murray, N. (1990) 'Running on the spot', *Community Care*, 2 August.

Pollitt, C. (1990a) *Managerialism and the Public Services*, Oxford: Basil Blackwell.

Pollitt, C. (1990b) 'Doing business in the temple? Managers and quality assurance in the public service', *Public Administration*, 68 (Winter), pp. 435–52.

Rhodes, R. A. W. (1986a) in M. Goldsmith (ed.), *New Approaches to the Study of Central–Local Government Relations*, Aldershot: SSRC/Gower.

Rhodes, R. A. W. (1986b) *The National World of Local Government,* London: Allen and Unwin.

Richardson, J. J., and A. G. Jordan (1987) *Government and Pressure Groups in Britain*, Oxford: Clarendon Press.

Sone, K. (1991) 'Need an umbrella?', *Community Care*, 16 May.

Whitmore, R. (1984) 'Modelling the policy/implementation distinction: the case of child abuse', *Policy and Politics*, 12 (3), pp. 241–67.

Wistow, G., M. Knapp, B. Hardy, and C. Allen (1992) 'From providing to enabling local authorities and the mixed economy of social care', *Public Administration*, 70 (Spring), pp. 25–45.

CHAPTER 10

Headteachers as managers in Sweden and Britain

Mai-Brith Schartau

Introduction

This is based principally on a survey of headteachers in Sweden and partly on 'qualitative semistructured elite interviews' with 12 Swedish and 3 British headteachers and their superiors, subordinates, union representatives and representatives for client associations. The study was carried out between 1987 and 1991, and altogether about 50 people were interviewed (Schartau, 1992).

National economic problems in Sweden and Britain have turned expenditure growth to constraint or even decline. Change has in the past been achieved through growth; now it has to be achieved out of existing resources. 'Efficiency' and 'productivity' have become prestige words when talking about public-sector activities. Good management on all levels in the organisation has become an important tool to reach these goals. In both countries a nearly blind faith in leadership is to be found in different documents emanating from central government.

This chapter deals with one kind of public manager at the local level: the headteacher. In spite of different political systems, the prescriptions from central authorities are similar in both countries. There are, however, organisational differences, which make their working conditions different.

There is a lot of literature documenting the great importance of local educators in implementing or, more likely, resisting innovations and reforms from above (Boyd, 1987). The literature of educational politics points in incompatible directions: a top-down approach with command and control or a bottom-up approach involving local adoption of reform ideas. A kind of synthesis underlines the importance of management, of new and persuasive symbols and of reform and change as forms of organisational learning and resocialisation. It shows how, when and what kind of top-down strategies can be effective.

Studies have shown that adaptation to political direction in Sweden, as in most countries, varies between different schools. The steering of the school is not entirely effective. Decisions made at the central level are not always implemented at local level.

In the middle of the 1980s the interest in school management was growing considerably in Sweden. A stronger position for the headteacher was accentuated in a governmental proposition. He or she is seen as a key actor when political intentions are to be implemented, and because of this, the headteacher is to be given greater scope to exercise management. Demands for the renewal and development of the educational system result in demands for a better leadership in schools.

There are plans to improve educational quality and school effectiveness in Sweden as in other countries, and the headteacher is supposed to facilitate these improvements. New theories have been developed to accommodate the increased complexity of this management role. The theories assume that the problems the headteacher faces are more complex than before and that the decisions to be made are more difficult (Glasman and Nevo, 1988).

The Swedish school system is less well known than the British one. It consists of the nine-year compulsory school and the voluntary upper secondary school, both under a municipal mandate. The costs of these educational activities are shared between the municipalities and the state. Private schools are very few in number, and they receive certain state grants towards their activities.

Compulsory schooling is divided into three levels: junior, intermediate and senior, each of which comprises three school years. At the first two levels, all pupils take the same subjects, and the schools for these levels can be found in nearly every community. Senior-level grades are housed in larger schools.

In Sweden you do not choose which school you go to, which means that there is not the same competition between schools as in Britain. In a proposition dated 1988, however, it was mentioned that the wishes of children and parents in choosing a school 'shall be satisfied as long as it is economically and practically possible'.

Parental choice among schools, of the sort there is in Britain, may be needed to counterbalance the strong current thrusts toward managerial control (Boyd, 1989). Combined with school-based management, this can be an inspiration for increasing professionalism and engagement of teachers and headteachers, and for gaining the involvement and commitment of pupils and parents that are needed for a good school. But it can also bring about serious problems for the headteachers and their staff.

Management in theory

Management research has, through statistical analysis, tried to find a limited number of specially important dimensions. Management style means a collection of habitual patterns in meeting role demands (Barber, 1972). Those two most frequently found – 'initiating structure' and 'consideration' – were identified in the 1950s during widespread research programmes at the universities of Ohio and Michigan (Bryman, 1986; Bass, 1981).

'Initiating structure' involves the creation of a good structure – for instance, by organising, planning and developing rules for decisions and administrative routines and for improving the equipment and milieu. This partly builds on McGregor's Theory X: people are by nature indolent; they work as little as possible. They must be persuaded, rewarded, punished, controlled; their activities have to be directed (McGregor, 1960).

'Consideration' means awareness of the knowledge, capacity, feelings and goals of subordinates. This resembles McGregor's Theory Y: it is the responsibility of management to make it possible for people to recognise the human characteristics for themselves. The social and emotional needs of the group are emphasised here. For some management experts this kind of management is not only a means but also a goal in itself.

A third dimension developed more recently is 'degree of

delegation'. Subordinates should be given freedom and responsibility to work independently. This dimension can be compared with an older and more well-known one: the authoritarian–democratic dimension. An authoritarian style means that the manager determines the policy and directs the implementation in a way that limits the discretion of subordinates.

This top-down approach can be hard to realise in schools, where the subordinates, the street-level bureaucrats, have a professional status. On the whole, the conventional top-down approach to the implementation process has come under attack (Barrett and Hill, 1984). Researchers have been accused of using an unrealistic rational comprehensive model. In response to this, Elmore (1980) and others have developed the bottom-up or backward mapping view.

Many reasons have been given for the difficulties that lower-level managers in the public sector have in trying to direct street-level bureaucrats (Lipsky, 1980). Among them are requirements for fair judgements, problems with diffuse and sometimes contradictory goals, and the difficulty of controlling the work. New interests, which were not able to participate in the early stages of the policy process, may become involved. While the manager tries to achieve the goals of the organisation – that is, if he or she is able to and wants to follow what is prescribed from above and has clearly understood it (Lundquist, 1987) – the street-level bureaucrats occasionally want to work according to their own preferences. They want to enlarge their sphere of independence and they sometimes look upon the dictations of the manager as illegitimate.

This puts the headteacher in a typical middle manager's dilemma, between the local education authority and the teachers. From a top-down perspective, the middle manager is supposed to explain the intentions of the top downwards. From a bottom-up perspective, he or she is supplying the top managers with information about activities in the organisation (Billis, 1984). It is hard to balance conflicts between expectations, wishes and claims from top managers and subordinates. The head feels a role conflict (Katz and Kahn, 1978).

The management process is a very complex network consisting of different forces (Kellerman, 1984). In particular, management can be seen as a function of the organisation (Cole, 1986). Managerial work must therefore be adjusted to the demands of the situation, regarding both the quantitative balance between the different kinds of measurement taken and the quality of those measurements. To understand management fully, one must pay attention to the organisation. Important variables to study are task, structure, procedure, personnel and culture (Lundquist, 1987). 'Structure' here means the distribution of authority; the relationship between different positions or roles. By 'procedure' is meant the methods used to carry out the tasks of the organisation; working forms and rules. Structure, procedure and personnel together define the manager's freedom of action.

An organisation cannot be studied in isolation from its environment. Implementation of change is influenced by the situational and historical context in which reforms are taking place (Olsen, 1970). Different environmental conditions and types of relationship with outside parties will require different types of managerial action.

There are organisational differences, especially in tasks, structure and procedure, between schools in Britain and Sweden. But there are also some factors in the environment that can vary, as we shall now see.

Environmental factors

Environmental factors can both facilitate and obstruct the work of the headteacher. A factor which favours some managers may create obstacles to others.

Strong politicians in the local education board could be a source of security for the managers and a guide for their planning. Headteachers in Sweden emphasise that, with further decentralisation, it is of great importance to have strong local politicians who are able to maintain the rights of the school and feel responsible for it. In Britain, where local authorities are losing power, the situation is different.

A good relationship upwards is important to headteachers in both countries. To have good co-operation with a strong senior manager strengthens the position of the headteacher and helps with policy implementation. If the senior manager is weak, the headteacher feels less pressure from above, but on the other hand he or she has to solve all the problems alone. It is, of course, also helpful to have good co-operation with all the staff at the central education authority office in the municipality. Local staff can be a great support but also a source of irritation because of a tendency towards bureaucratisation.

There are great differences between the local authorities in both Britain and Sweden when it comes to the view they take of management. In some municipalities this issue is regarded as very important; in others it is hardly discussed. In those where the importance of management is stressed, the local authority makes a point of choosing suitable candidates for posts.

Usually there is no co-operation between Swedish headteachers within the same municipality. It is a lonely job, and headteachers often feel insecure without colleagues to lean on. In Britain different kinds of management team are usually built up. Headteachers from the same kinds of school or newly appointed heads see each other regularly. These groups can be a compensation for not having teams at school. Although there is competition between schools, the headteacher has people with whom ideas can be exchanged.

Socially troublesome pupils often create a unity among teachers, making them support each other. It may then be harder for the headteacher to influence them. Disturbed pupils can also demand so much energy that they take priority over other matters.

Earlier research has shown that a lack of resources at the local level does not affect the final results significantly (Boyd and Hartman, 1988), although with decreasing economic resources the headteacher's freedom of action is being reduced. However, good economic circumstances are not enough; somebody must also be able to see and utilise the possibilities.

In Britain the financial situation seems to be much worse than in Sweden. There will be great difficulties in the future if more cuts are imposed. Even when more children are entering a school, the extra money is given in arrears. Some schools are having a hard time economically and are dependent on parental good will. There is continual pressure to save money and become more effective. Small schools are being closed because they are too expensive. There are no economies of scale from concentrating resources in large schools, but in such schools it is easier to move money between different accounts.

In Swedish schools there are 'home and school associations' comparable with parent–teacher associations (PTAs) in Britain, but the Swedish associations are of very little importance to the headteacher. In Britain PTAs elect a committee which meets regularly and organises a variety of social and fund-raising activities throughout the year. Swedish parents do not support their schools in the same way.

Tasks

Here we are concerned with organisational tasks, not specific managerial ones. In Sweden large schools are seen as undesirable for the pupils, who experience anonymity and insecurity. To cope with this, the organisational recommendations under the new National Curriculum provide for school work to be reorganised in such a way that two or more classes, from the same or different grades, constitute a working unit. The staff of this unit are then expected to form a working team, and together to plan, carry out and follow up the work of the unit. Special working unit conferences should also be held. These organisational changes have not yet been fully implemented.

Every school in Sweden must have one or more local working plans, based on the National Curriculum as well as on local priorities. In Britain each school has a special curriculum, setting out its intentions for its pupils. This is a kind of overarching goal which is established by the headteacher and the governors. The National Curriculum in Britain has not given rise to changes in tasks and organisation in the same way as in Sweden.

Swedish pupils with learning difficulties are assisted in class by a remedial teacher. If problems are serious, a child can receive further assistance: he or she can attend special day schools or be given an adjusted course of studies, which differs from the ordinary curriculum. One of the aims is that pupils with difficulties should be enabled to work together with the class or, when this is not feasible, to return to the class as soon as possible and take part in ordinary lessons.

In Britain the development is the same. The 1981 Education Act introduced new concepts regarding special educational needs. Each Local Education Authority (LEA) has a duty to identify all children in the area who have special educational needs. For each of these children a special 'statement' is made, which describes the child's special needs and the ways in which those needs might be met. These children are educated in ordinary schools provided certain conditions can be met.

In Britain many schools now have to compete for pupils. The consequences of making tactical errors may be severe – the final penalty is closure of the school. The headteacher and the governors must learn how to estimate the likely nature and extent of the local pressure on admissions. If popularity is uncertain, problems will be great and will quickly worsen if they are not tackled at once. The immediate effect of a low intake will be a fall in the budget share of the school. In the long run this implies that teaching and support staff will have to be dismissed. In the short term a reduction in running expenses will be necessary. The lack of books and other materials will be felt directly by teachers and pupils and noticed by parents. It will be difficult to make the changes required to introduce the National Curriculum. No computers and other technology facilities will be bought and no specialist staff appointed. This will increase the likelihood of parents choosing other schools for their children. It is hard to plan in advance if you do not know how many children you will have, or how to make school development plans for three years ahead.

Schools are now run more like businesses in both countries. However, the difficulties which follow are much worse in Britain. While the Swedish headteacher is struggling with the implementation of the National Curriculum, his or her British colleague has to fight for the survival of his or her school.

Procedure

For many years, control of Swedish schools has been heavily centralised. Through legislation, regulations and curriculum, the state gives detailed instructions and rules for school activity. The government issues the Education Ordinance and lays down guidelines including general timetables for school work. For about twenty years, efforts have been made to decentralise decision-making powers concerning school activities to local education authorities, school management and school staff, acting in consultation with pupils and their parents.

In recent years the detailed regulation of schools has decreased appreciably. According to a proposition of 1988/89, the direction of schools shall in the future be a more local responsibility: this involves goal steering instead of order steering, a strengthened local school management, better information and more effective evaluation and superintending. Goals and guidelines will be given in national curricula, and these must be clear and distinct.

Most state grants in Sweden used to be distributed at junior level with reference to the number of teacher periods for every partial or complete unit of 25 pupils. The corresponding unit at intermediate and senior levels was 30 pupils. A special subsidy was centrally earmarked for helping pupils and schools with special needs. Within municipalities, the local education board defined the distributional rule best suited to the needs of the school.

These rules for state aid were seen as an obstacle to the local authorities in trying new forms of organisation or making rationalisations. A new system has been developed and came into force in July 1991. A special sector aid (state grant) is now given to the local authorities of a fixed sum per child per school. The headteacher is usually responsible for his or her budget except the capital part.

In the early 1980s several LEAs in Britain developed schemes which allowed schools to have more say in financial matters. In the 1988 Act, every LEA is required to have its own scheme within the rules laid down centrally. This provides the budget allocation to all primary and secondary schools, and delegates to the governors the power to spend those funds. Capital expenditures, expenditures supported by central government grants, other items prescribed by the secretary of state and items specified in the scheme approved for the particular LEA are not to be delegated to schools. The money arrives after applying a formula based on the numbers and age of pupils plus certain factors like the number of pupils entitled to free school meals and the number of children with special needs.

In both countries schools have received greater economic independence, strengthening the headteachers' position. But the latter are not educated in financial matters and have limited time to spend on these issues.

For Swedish compulsory schools, as well as upper secondary schools, there is a centrally compiled curriculum offering equivalent educational opportunities to all pupils, regardless of residential locality. In compulsory schools, these curricula have succeeded one another since 1962, when this type of school was established on a permanent basis. The curriculum now in force, Lgr 80, lays down goals and guidelines of a general nature including timetables specifying the number of periods per week at each three-year level for each subject. The implementation of Lgr 80 has advanced differently in the different local authorities. Dissimilarities between the areas within one municipality can also be found.

While wanting a variety of schools in Britain, the Conservative government argued for a strict uniformity in the curriculum, where they saw too much variety. The 1988 Act includes a National Curriculum for all pupils between the ages of 5 and 16, including tests at four different times, covering all subjects in the curriculum. With these tests it will be possible to make comparative assessments between different classes and between schools. Reports on the implementation of the National Curriculum will be required from the inspectorate.

The Education Act 1980 provides a right for British parents to express a preference for the school which they wish their child to attend, and for the preference to be met wherever feasible. The LEA and the governors must make arrangements to enable parents to appeal if not satisfied with the place offered. Local authorities used to have the power to fix a limit to each school's intake. But now schools have the right to admit as many pupils as parents wish to send to them, so there will be competition between schools.

What do headteachers think about the procedures? In both countries the headteacher has great possibilities to mould the school in terms of his or her own values. In recent years their options have become even greater. A reform which he or she dislikes will probably not be implemented, or will at least be moderated. It is not possible to be totally loyal to every suggestion from above. However, none of the headteachers surveyed used to the full their considerable freedom of action.

Proposals for less extensive direction and regulation have been met with enthusiasm by some of the headteachers in both countries. They see great possibilities to create their school as they want. The strong heads know exactly what they would do if they just received a 'bag full of money', while the weaker ones fear that the demands from below would increase.

Perhaps the headteachers need more education and encouragement if they are going to fulfil the expectations of central government. The earlier strong regulation of the Swedish school is still affecting the headteacher's line of thought, and parental choice obstructs headteachers' attempts to be more effective.

Structure

In this section we will consider both the structure given from the centre and the structure created within the schools. In the British 1988 Education Reform Act, two main areas are related to structure: financial delegation to schools; and opting out. Financial responsibility is almost completely devolved to the governors, and probably, in practice through delegation, to the headteacher. Warnings have been given that this implies too much work for the headteacher as a manager. Another question is whether parents will volunteer to be governors, given the very large responsibility involved.

Schools, where governing bodies and parents wish to, may apply to opt out from the local system of which they are a part, and receive funds directly from the Department of Education and Science instead of the local authority. In Sweden there are no school governors and no possibility to opt out from the municipal system.

In Sweden schools are divided into headteacher districts. Every such district includes several schools with either all three levels or junior and intermediate levels only. The headteacher is the head of such a district, assisted by one or more directors of studies, who are generally full-time administrators.

The role of these directors of studies is not quite clear. They are supposed to assist the headteacher mainly in pedagogic work, but their tasks vary from one area to another. The deputy headteachers, one in every school unit, also have a diffuse management role. In their daily work they function as a kind of local manager of the school unit. They supervise non-teaching staff and are responsible for localities and material. They have no managerial tasks directly connected to teaching activities, but in practice they are often involved in emergency situations.

The leaders of the working units have not been able to strengthen the management function in the way they were supposed to do. The reduction of their teaching obligation has often been too small, about one to three hours a week. Secondly, they find it stressful to be a member of both the management team and the teaching staff. Finally, they are often appointed for only one year at a time, which makes it difficult to develop a more long-term and carefully prepared management strategy.

In contrast to Sweden, each headteacher in Britain is responsible for only one school. This ought to make it easier to get an overview of the situation. The headteacher has one deputy teacher, who spends most of his or her time on ordinary teaching work. The precise nature of the deputy's work is left to the individuals to develop. What they do ranges from carrying out a few administrative chores at one extreme to a full association with policy making at the other. It is rare for the deputy to have a distinct area of authority separated from that of the head. In Sweden there are many recommendations about what a director of studies, as well as the managers at the first level, should do.

British schools have no directors of studies and no leaders of working units. Sometimes 'heads of the year' have special administrative tasks. This means that there cannot be a management team in the same sense as in Sweden. The headteacher can, of course, construct a team together with some or all of the governors, but the latter are seldom in school and cannot support in the same way.

There are different opinions among the headteachers about the value of such a team. Some of them want to decide everything on their own, as they are being held responsible; some see both advantages and disadvantages; and some think it is essential to build a management team.

If the team is strong, the middle manager's dilemma is easier to resolve. The Swedish head feels a dilemma when superiors want something implemented that subordinates dislike. The British head also has problems with the governors and the parents, but feels less pressure from the LEA. It is possible, however, that this situation will grow worse as the National Curriculum is implemented. Personality and relationships to superiors and subordinates seem to be of considerable importance in this aspect of implementation.

School-based management is founded on the belief that many important decisions must inevitably be made at school level (Boyd, 1989). It is here that the professionals close to pupils can decide what to do and how to implement goals set at a higher level. However, research has shown that hardly any headteacher has the skills or can find the time to execute an optimum management.

In Sweden we find the same ideas about the importance of involvement and responsibility, but staff and parents are not involved in management. No school councils are created, but it is the duty of the headteacher to give information about and discuss coming major events and decisions in school with representatives of staff, pupils and parents.

In the past, if a group of parents in a British school were known to favour a certain kind of curriculum emphasis, the effect was quite noticeable, especially if there was competition in the area concerning admission. The introduction of the National Curriculum may give the headteacher a reason to override such pressures.

Parental power in Britain is strengthened, however, in at least two ways: they have more say over the admission of their child to the school of their choice; and they have more influence on the running of the school through their appointment of parent governors, who are given a much wider power by the 1988 Act. Some of this power is delegated to the headteacher, who together with the governors will work out how extensive the involvement of governors is to be. The governors meet once every term, but more often if special questions emerge. This board of governors must include representatives of the LEA, parents and teaching staff, and in addition there are co-opted members.

Governors can, after hearing a parent's appeal against a decision of the headteacher, direct the head 'to take such action authorised by the regulations as they consider appropriate in the circumstances'. In other words, they can overrule the headteacher. The 1988 Act allows governors almost complete freedom to appoint and dismiss staff as they choose, even against the headteacher's will. Sometimes the governors do not look for professional qualities, and there is a risk that they may make political appointments. All this can, of course, make the work of the headteacher much more difficult.

It is therefore important for the headteacher to build up a good relationship with the governors. They must trust the headteacher and let him or her guide the work. While, strictly speaking, the headteacher is their employee, he or she will have the advantage of having more information, but needs a certain political skill to use it effectively.

The increasing power of the governors and the growth of special grants have weakened the power of the local education authorities. The LEA touches the schools and institutions in many ways, but it does not now directly manage them. They are self-managing institutions, as the enhanced importance of the governors emphasises. But LEAs still have planning functions because they still have some control over resources of cash and staffing levels. A school with problems, whether human, financial or related to buildings, will still have to rely on the LEA (Leonard, 1988).

It is now possible to get a local firm to sponsor a teacher, and schools are encouraged by central government to do so. Besides increasing the number of pupils, this is a way to get more money. However, this is a very controversial innovation.

The middle manager's dilemma is felt a little differently in the two countries. The Swedish headteacher is standing between strong subordinates, who dislike some parts of the National Curriculum, and the local education authority, which tries to force the headteacher to implement the curriculum. To get support a management team can be created. The British head, on the other hand, has to deal with the governors, who make different kinds of demand. He or she must be able to co-operate and negotiate with them in order to get a mandate for managing the school. To obtain support, the British headteacher often makes contacts outside the organisation, with other headteachers or someone at the LEA.

Personnel

Teachers are generally regarded as 'professionals', and regard themselves as such. This legitimates their claim to be consulted about reforms. The autonomy they are required to exercise in carrying out their tasks means that without their co-operation it is impossible to carry out large-scale reforms. Directional failure in schools is mainly concerned with the teachers' tasks (Sannerstedt, 1987). As these tasks imply special competence and independence, they cannot be governed from outside. Different kinds of negotiation and persuasion technique are often suggested for managing professionals.

In a professional organisation, the horizontal and collegial influence is of great importance. Translated to the school, teachers affect other teachers. Persuading a few teachers may result in gaining acceptance from the others as well. Information management and management by influence are stressed in much of the literature on ways of achieving change (Clarke in preface to Stewart, 1986).

A school is a horizontal organisation where the teachers are undertaking the same tasks independently of experience; the tasks are not demarcated. It is also an organisation with many personnel, very few of whom have a room of their own. These factors may give rise to conflicts. If school management is weak, an informal power structure is easily developed.

As street-level bureaucrats and professionals, teachers are hard to direct. Headteachers in both countries agree on that. They also offer other reasons for difficulties in directing their teaching staff. In recent years, for example, many reforms have been made in Swedish compulsory schools, and unfortunately some of them, like the new mathematics and English in year three, have turned out to be mistakes. This has made teaching staff sceptical about changes.

Swedish teachers are negative towards the new curriculum mostly because they do not want to have other tasks besides teaching; they just want to teach in their specialist subjects and do not want to change their teaching habits and routines. They are not used to working in a group and are not used to showing their weaknesses in front of others. Teachers at the senior level are much more negative than the others. It has been impossible to organise the working units without having some teachers work in more than one unit. The whole idea of units and teams seems like a meaningless construction to some of the teachers.

In the previous Swedish system, class teachers were trained for grades one to three or four to six and teachers of special subjects for grades seven to nine. This was reformed with effect from 1 July 1988. An integrated study programme qualifies teachers for service in grades one to seven or four to nine. Teachers serving in the senior grade take more subjects than hitherto. These changes are designed to facilitate co-operation within working units and also to make it possible for every unit to have an integrated teaching team.

The age structure among subordinates has been argued to be important when it comes to the propensity to accept new ideas (Bass, 1981; Katz and Kahn, 1978). Elderly staff who have been working together for a long time and who know each other well are much more difficult to affect than younger persons who have not been in the area for such a long time and who have not yet established their routines. If the headteacher is weak, one or more elderly, street-level bureaucrats can easily become informal leaders.

While the influence of the teaching unions is limited, the individual representatives can either be a support for the head or create much discomfort for him or her. This negative influence is often greatest in new large schools, where it sometimes adds to a headteacher's credibility problems.

Those Swedish headteachers who have been less successful in the implementation of the National Curriculum emphasize the attitudes of teachers as the main reason for failure. Those who have gone far in realising it, however, claim that they have been able to do so thanks to these very attitudes. The difference seems to be the capacity for inducing the street-level bureaucrats to work to the new rules. Perhaps some headteachers see the personnel as tiresome only because they are poor managers, trying to put the blame on the staff. And perhaps some personnel are good just because they have an excellent manager.

Teachers in British schools are not used to so many central rules as their Swedish counterparts. This probably means that they are more independent. They are, in any case, not used to a National Curriculum.

There are no particular differences between the two countries concerning the personnel variable. The headteacher has the same problems in trying to direct the professional street-level bureaucrats. Perhaps the British teachers are somewhat harder to direct, having a long tradition of working independently.

Culture

The culture of a school in Britain, or a district in Sweden, is influenced considerably by the headteacher, and there are certainly great cultural differences between schools. But it is not only the head who creates this; the teachers and the other staff are also influential. If the manager is weak, there can be an air of uncertainty if no one else takes command. If the management team is not accepted, rival groups may be developed.

Research has shown that different Swedish schools can have different cultures despite being within the same headteacher district (Yttergren, 1986). The structure of the local community affects the working conditions in a way that makes teachers at different schools develop various patterns of actions which produce the environment. New schools within new areas have been most amenable and positive towards changes. The culture here is not yet fixed (Arfwedson, 1983).

In Britain research has also shown that there is a close personal identification of the head with the school, and a close relationship between the personality of the head and the philosophy of the school (Whitaker, 1983). Some of the managers do steer their schools by creating a special kind of culture. Others have problems because the existing culture is strong and constitutes an obstacle to them.

On this topic no great differences between the two countries have been found. Perhaps the cultural aspect is more important in Britain, where each school has its own headteacher. It is probably harder for the Swedish head to affect the culture in several different schools.

Management in practice

Research on what headteachers actually do has shown that they spend little time on instructional programmes and entrepreneurship and much more time on disturbance handling. Headteachers usually try to maintain a smooth-running organisation with harmonious staff relationships and assume that teachers are competent to solve their own problems. Effective headteachers have been shown to be more task-oriented (Boyd and Hartman, 1988). Successful implementation often occurs at places where administrators exert strong and continuous pressure on teachers.

Headteachers are perhaps reluctant to push for more productive behaviour because the cost of working out such exchanges with subordinates is perceived to be greater than the benefits received. Moreover, heads are dependent on teachers largely because of the ambiguous nature of their own authority. Their autonomy depends on their ability to gain the trust of their superiors, but this relationship is fragile and can be threatened by unsatisfied teachers. Because of this many headteachers choose not to take risks with new programmes (Boyd and Hartman, 1988). When they cannot or will not direct their subordinates, it is easy to hide behind the management style earlier called 'consideration'. To create a good climate, to be popular, to solve conflicts and to make everybody feel well becomes the most important goal.

According to management theories (Handy, 1985), delegating is one way to make subordinates feel more responsible and participant, which in the long run will cause them to be more positive and work harder. The managers who are seen as delegating have good or quite good implementation results, which strengthens this hypothesis. But some of the others also have good results, which contradicts the hypothesis. Perhaps the reason to delegate is more important. A headteacher who feels uneasy about increasing the burden on fellow workers is more popular and gets more respect than one who delegates just because he or she cannot manage doing everything alone. It also seems very important to delegate to the right persons; not everybody is prepared to take on more responsibility, or suitable to do so.

Looking at the authoritarian–democratic scale, nearly all the headteachers studied were situated in the middle of the two poles. In some situations 'order steering' is more natural: for instance, when the issue is a mere trifle, when there is a shortage of time or when the manager is more well informed or has better knowledge. Otherwise the headteachers try to be more or less democratic. According to the theories (Nealey and Blood, 1968), subordinates accept 'order steering' better if they are less professional, but I have seen no proof of this in Sweden. Teachers, who have the same education as their manager, are so used to rules and regulations that they feel helpless without them. Somebody has always told them what to do. Perhaps historical organisational circumstances are as important as professionlism when it comes to the preferred management style.

Managers at this level are supposed to give concrete form to the goals. Most of the heads surveyed said that it is important to tell teachers how they want the work to be done and what they stand for. It is not enough, however, just to tell professional subordinates what to do. There are many other ways of steering them. The headteachers studied use different methods when handling different tasks. Some of them work resolutely with the third dimension of power, to shape subordinates' perceptions, cognitions and preferences (Lukes, 1974). However, this process needs a lot of time. To try to convince subordinates of the positive aspects of change, information management is another alternative. Interesting programmes at teachers' seminars and other kinds of further training are thus important tools.

Various forms of evaluation are used by some of the headteachers, but they complain about not having received any proper education for this. The subordinates are aware of these evaluations, which sometimes make them change their behaviour.

Some Swedish headteachers give project money to subordinates who want to develop new methods of work. By letting the other teachers see that this is interesting, that perhaps they should participate, the head can affect most of his or her staff. It has a kind of snowball effect which in the end creates a group pressure on those with a negative attitude. A British head has no extra money to give, receiving only a very small sum per teacher each year for further training. But this money can be brought together and spent on only a few teachers. If there are no rewards it is hard to negotiate with the teachers, even if this is something the headteacher often tries.

When dissatisfied with a teacher's performance, a British headteacher may talk to officials at the local authority. These may then investigate and arrange a conference with the teacher in question and the headteacher. The governors may then be able to dismiss the teacher. Although this is difficult in practice, and strong reasons are needed, it is a powerful weapon that does not exist in Sweden.

Organisational rewards and punishments are used by some Swedish heads. It is not possible for the British headteacher to give a teacher a bad timetable or to move him or her to another working place. As teachers are in school the whole day, it is not possible to punish them by manipulating the timetable. As in Sweden, it is possible to give loyal teachers better classrooms and better pupils, although in practice none of the British headteachers surveyed believed in trying this.

Having organisational skill can sometimes be a way of influencing subordinates. It is valuable to be able to find some money if the subordinates have an idea they want to try. The manager gets respect and trust, which make it easier for him or her to be successful in other matters.

Directing by consideration means that a good climate is created, which makes the subordinates so positive that they are willing to follow the directions. The headteachers varied greatly in the extent to which they believed in this approach: some did not try anything else, while some of them did not believe in it at all.

Conflicts between persons or different groups of the staff, and between pupils and personnel, can be found in many schools. Trying to solve these conflicts and also trying to prevent them from occurring is one way of creating a good climate and satisfying subordinates. Other ways are support, encouragement, praise and understanding.

From the British headteacher's point of view, the public relations aspect is of great importance. In a report from the Department of Education and Science in 1977, describing the elements of a good headteacher, 'a public relations officer' came as number one. Since the 1988 Act this role has become even more important because it is necessary to keep the number of pupils at a constant level. The Swedish headteacher, on the other hand, does not have to worry about this kind of problem.

There are different ways of marketing the school. The siting of the school is important: parents do not want their children to have a long distance to go to school and they do not want it to be situated in an area with heavy traffic. Parents like good discipline, and they want high-quality teachers. They want children to have homework to do, but not too much. Lots of sporting activities, computers and other technical facilities are other enticements for parents. It is important to establish a good communication with parents by arranging regular meetings and listening to them when they pick up their children after school.

Many local authorities in Britain offer courses for headteachers and deputies, but the national pattern of preparation and training for headship is still somewhat haphazard. The best training should be experience as a deputy, but not many deputies are fully involved in the management of their school. In Sweden, many headteachers have formerly been directors of studies, which implies nearly full-time management skills. This has given them good experience and an insight into the work. All Swedish headteachers have some kind of education for their task.

Conclusions

In both countries central government has placed great confidence in lower-level management in order to create better, more efficient schools. New management principles have been derived from the private sector. It is interesting to see the same ideas developing in Britain and Sweden, despite the fact that there are at least two important differences between British and Swedish schools.

The first difference is in organisational variables:

- In the task: the Swedish headteacher has new, difficult tasks in changing the method of working.
- In the structure: the strong position of the governors and the lack of a management team in British schools.
- In the procedure: different rules and regulations.

Controlling the teachers' work was not seen as such a big problem in Britain as in Sweden. This results partly from the fact that the British headteacher has only one school. The teachers make plans and reports and it is possible to see if these plans are being carried out. It also seemed to be more common for the British headteacher to visit the classrooms.

But in Sweden, with new administrative work, it is hard for headteachers to find time for this. One reason is that headteachers have other problems besides directing teachers. The competition between schools, to keep up the number of pupils and to get enough resources, is perhaps a more serious concern than self-indulgent and conservative teachers. British teachers are not supposed to change their behaviour to the same degree as in Sweden, which also makes it easier to co-operate with them.

The second difference is in the centralisation process taking place in Britain, at the same time as decentralisation is going on in Sweden. The Department of Education and Science has tried to increase its influence over the education system, through the introduction of special grants, by giving inspectors a more active role, by ministerial initiatives and by legislation, which has been designed partly to strengthen parental influence on schools. The increased power of governors and the growth of special grants have weakened the power of the Local Education Authority.

In Sweden the development has been in the opposite direction. Efforts have been made to decentralise decision-making power to local educational authorities, school management and school staff, acting in consultation with pupils and their parents. The roles of the local authority, the headteacher and the managers at the first level are emphasised.

Despite these differences, headteachers in both countries now seem to work much like managers in the private sector. Most of them appreciate their new freedom; they see advantages in the new system. Earlier, local authority regulation in Britain and central regulation in Sweden could be rather bureaucratic; now things can be handled in a more flexible way. Headteachers often see themselves as chief executives, and their hierarchal position has been strengthened. Theirs is much more a managerial job then before. Theoretically they have a considerable amount of power, but they do not use it to a large extent.

School management has not, however, been functioning in a satisfactory way in either country. The headteachers have received so many new or extended tasks of an organisational, economic and administrative nature that they are not able to fulfil pedagogical management in a desirable way. In recent years their job has become more of a bureaucratic service function, where economic and administrative duties dominate over pedagogic tasks. Extra resources in the form of more clerical support staff are not given in either country.

The managerial role has been stressed by central government in both countries, but nobody seems to have paid enough attention to the many organisational obstacles that still make the working conditions hard for the headteacher as a middle manager. Headteachers need education and changes in procedure and structure if they are going to be effective managers, created to copy a prototype in the private sector as suggested in some central documents. Whether this is desirable and appropriate is another question.

References

Arfwedson, Gerhard (1983) *Varfor ar skolor olika?*, Stockholm: Liber utbildningsforlag.

Barber, James D. (1972) 'Classifying and predicting presidential styles: two weak presidents', in Glenn D. Paige (ed.), *Political Leadership: Readings for an emerging field*, New York: Free Press.

Barrett, Susan, and Michael Hill (1984) 'Policy, bargaining and structure in implementation theory: towards an integrated perspective', *Policy and Politics*, 12(3), pp. 219–40.

Bass, B. M. (1981) *Stogdill's Handbook of Leadership*, New York: Free Press.

Billis, David (1984) *Welfare Bureaucracies: Their design and change in response to social problems*, London: Heinemann.

Boyd, William Lowe (1987) 'Public education's last hurrah? Schizophrenia, amnesia, and ignorance in school politics', *Educational Evaluation and Policy Analysis*, 9(2), pp. 85–100.

Boyd, William Lowe (1989) 'Balancing for competing values in school reform: the politics of perestroika', in Judith Chapman and Jeffrey Dunstan (eds), *Democracy and Bureaucracy: Tensions in Australian government schooling*, Australian College of Education.

Boyd, William Lowe, and William T. Hartman (1988) 'The politics of educational productivity', in David Monk and Julie Underwood (eds), *Microlevel School Finance*, Cambridge, Mass.: Ballinger.

Bryman, Alan (1986) *Leadership and Organisations*, London: Routledge and Kegan Paul.

Cole, G. A. (1986) *Management, Theory and Practice*, Hampshire: DP Publications.

Elmore, R. (1980) 'Backward mapping: implementation research and policy decisions', *Political Science Quarterly*, 94, pp. 601–16.

Glasman, N. S., and David Nevo (1988) *Evaluation in Decision Making*, Dordrecht: Kluwer.

Handy, Charles B. (1985) *Understanding Organisations*, Harmondsworth: Pelican.

Katz, D., and R. Kahn (1978) *The Social Psychology of Organisations*, New York: Wiley.

Kellerman, Barbara (1984) *Leadership: Multidisciplinary perspectives*, New York: Prentice Hall.

Leonard, Martin (1988) *The 1988 Educational Act: A tactical guide for schools*, Oxford: Blackwell Education.

Lipsky, Michael (1980) *Street-Level Bureaucracy: Dilemmas of the individual in the public sector,* New York: Russell Sage.

Lukes, Steven (1974) *Power: A radical view*, London: Macmillan.

Lundquist, Lennart (1987) *Implementation Steering: An actor–structure approach*, Lund: Studentlitteratur.

McGregor, Douglas (1960) *The Human Side of Enterprise*, New York: McGraw-Hill.

Nealey, S. M., and M. R. Blood (1968) 'Leadership performance of nursing supervisors at two organisational levels', *Journal of Applied Psychology*, 52 (5), pp. 414–23.

Olsen, Johan P. (1970) 'Local budgeting: decision-making or a ritual act?', *Scandinavian Political Studies*, 5, pp. 85–118.

Sannerstedt, Anders (1987) 'Politisk styrning av skolan svarigheter och mojligheter', *Forskning om utbilning*, 4, pp. 14–30.

Schartau, Mai-Brith (1993) *The Public Sector Middle Manager: The puppet who pulls the strings?* Lund: Department of Political Science, University of Lund.

Stewart, John (1986) 'In search of the management of education', unpublished paper.

Whitaker, Patrick (1983) *The Primary Head*, London: Heinemann Educational Books.

Yttergren, Magdalena (1986) *Arbetsorganisation och styrkallor, Arbetsrapport nr 115 fran Pedagogiska institutionen*, Uppsala: Uppsala universitet.

Index